HELL OF A VISION

Hell of a Vision

Regionalism and the Modern American West

ROBERT L. DORMAN

THE UNIVERSITY OF
ARIZONA PRESS

TUCSON

THE UNIVERSITY OF ARIZONA PRESS

© 2012 The Arizona Board of Regents

www.uapress.arizona.edu

Library of Congress Cataloging-in-Publication Data

Dorman, Robert L.
   Hell of a vision : regionalism and the modern American West / Robert L. Dorman.
      p. cm.
   Includes bibliographical references and index.
   ISBN 978-0-8165-2850-9 (cloth : alk. paper)   1. Regionalism—West (U.S.)   2. West
(U.S.)—Historical geography.   3. Human geography—West (U.S.)   4. West (U.S.)—
Civilization.   5. West (U.S.)—History.   I. Title.
   F591.D67   2012
   978—dc23   2011051823

Manufactured in the United States of America on acid-free, archival-quality paper
containing a minimum of 30% postconsumer waste and processed chlorine free.

17   16   15   14   13   12   6   5   4   3   2   1

In memory of
John L. "Jack" Thomas

Contents

Figures

Preface

Regionalism has been an important part of my mental landscape since I moved back East to attend graduate school over twenty-five years ago. I first discovered it as a concept at Brown University under the mentorship of the late John L. Thomas, to whom this book is dedicated. He is ultimately responsible for this book and many others that his students have written about the power of place and what he called the "adversary tradition" in American history.[1]

In an earlier book, *Revolt of the Provinces: The Regionalist Movement in America, 1920–1945*, I depicted western regionalism as one segment of a broader engagement with region that occurred in response to the profound economic and political crises of the interwar years. Southern, midwestern, and New England artists and intellectuals joined with their western counterparts to explore the possibilities of an ideology of regionalism that might restructure American society along more decentralized, pluralistic, and symbiotic lines. The present book is focused more fully on western regionalism, but with an eye to similar developments elsewhere in America and abroad. It has a larger temporal canvas than my previous work, covering the "modern West," which I define as the late 1800s to the early 2000s. Regionalism has waxed and waned in the West during this period, revealing a greater ideological variety than was apparent in the interwar years, both radical and conservative. This book is also more freewheeling in its definition of culture than *Revolt of the Provinces*, finding western regional identity and consciousness in evidence across a wide spectrum of expression, including popular magazine articles, government reports, letters, movies, pamphlets, novels, advertisements, paintings, maps, speeches, histories, scientific papers, and sculptures, among others.

This book makes no attempt to fix definite boundaries on the West, but tries to show the wide range of answers to that question that have arisen over the years. As students of regionalism have long realized, the region is too ambiguous a concept to provide any final answers about what places are and are not "western." It would be disingenuous of me, however, not to disclose that I have had a working definition of the West to guide the scope of my research. This is a legitimate use of the region concept, which if nothing else is a tool to organize thought. My definition coincides with one offered several years ago in a major government report, *Water in the West: Challenge for the Next Century* (1998): "the West is the 17 coterminous states located on and westward of the 100th meridian."[2] This definition differs from, say, the one guiding the coverage of *High Country News*, a contemporary western magazine that I admire, which excludes the central tier of Plains states from the Dakotas southward to Texas—despite the fact that there is plenty of "high country" in South Dakota's Black Hills and Texas's Guadalupe Mountains. But you see how these arguments can get started.

My seventeen-state definition roughly outlines in its entirety what I call the *nationalist* West, an amorphous region that has served as a kind of projection screen for American national identity, yearnings, and ideals. It also encompasses in the same space a much more diverse collection of subregions of every shape and size that I label the *localist* West. The localist West might be as large as the Columbia River basin or as small as a single pasture; some of its subregions might overlap into Iowa or Missouri, and some into Mexico or Canada. These places were all "the West" for someone. My own portion of the West lies in central Oklahoma, where my family has been farming and ranching for most of the period covered by this book. Indeed, my mother and brothers still operate the cattle ranch that my father established fifty years ago in metropolitan Oklahoma County, where Oklahoma City sprawls. Perhaps growing up on this rural-urban interface explains why regionalism has resonated with me for so long.

I gratefully acknowledge the advice and support of David Wrobel and Richard Etulain, two outstanding historians of the West and editors of the Modern American West series for the University of Arizona Press. Above all, I would like to thank my wife, Sarah, a fellow Brown-trained historian and Jack Thomas, student, who has always been my best critic.

HELL OF A VISION

Introduction: The Regionalist Gaze

Generalizations, therefore, upon the West as a whole are apt to be misleading.

FREDERICK JACKSON TURNER,
"THE WEST — 1876 AND 1926"

After two failed attempts, John Wesley Powell and his men at last reached the top of Longs Peak on the morning of August 23, 1868. "Glory to God!" Powell exulted as he took in the view, and the men of the expedition gave three cheers. For hours they wandered the summit, a flat six acres of rock mostly barren of snow and life. The barometer indicated 14,000 feet. To the east they could see the oceanic expanse of the Great Plains. To the south Denver lay, with the rest of the Front Range extending away into the clouds. Westward there were more ranks of mountains, the Williams Fork, the Gore, the Sawatch. Immediately below, in Middle Park, streams began flowing either toward the Pacific or the Gulf of Mexico. North of their latitude, except for Mt. Rainier a thousand miles away, there were no summits higher than where Powell and his men stood until one reached the Canadian Yukon.[1]

Half a century ago, such a scene might have opened an admiring account of Powell's explorations of the West, including his epic river descent through the Grand Canyon and his pioneering ethnographic work among Native Americans. The imperturbable Major Powell, who lost an arm in the Civil War, would have been lauded as a man of science who strove to overturn misconceptions about the West. He would have been singled out as one of the few among his contemporaries who valued and respected Native American cultures. But today we live in more skeptical and cynical times. Scholars have taken to calling experiences like Powell's atop Longs Peak the "magisterial gaze," a view from a great height overlooking a scene of future conquest, a panorama devoured with "imperial eyes." Ethnologi-

1

cal work such as Powell's is said to have exhibited "imperialist nostalgia," a perverse yearning to save and cherish the remnants of what he and others were guilty of destroying.[2]

I find this contemporary view of western history to be as problematic in its way as the older, rosier one. I believe that the modern tradition of western regionalism, of which Powell was the founding figure, still constitutes a usable past for the twenty-first century, that is, a past that embodies the values of democracy, pluralism, communitarianism, and environmental consciousness. At the same time, however, it is important to recognize how regionalism has been implicated in the dispossession of Native Americans, racial subordination, environmental exploitation, and other aspects of empire-building in the West, which this book also attempts to do. For this reason I have taken the book's title from the words of Captain Call at the closing of Larry McMurtry's novel *Lonesome Dove* (1985), which seems to capture well the ambiguity of western regionalism as seen today. On the one hand, regionalism could be a "hell of a vision" in the sense of "visionary," "breathtaking," or "inspiring," such as Powell's own basin commonwealth plans for the Arid Region, or more recent bioregionalist schemes for "reinhabiting" and "rewilding" the western landscape. Yet regionalists have also depicted the darker, hellish side of westward expansion and conquest, from Angie Debo's history of the systematic theft of Indian lands, *And Still the Waters Run* (1940), to Patricia Nelson Limerick's wholesale rewrite of western history as an epic of exploitation, *The Legacy of Conquest* (1987). And many expressions of western regionalism, like *Lonesome Dove*, have intentionally and unintentionally encapsulated the ambivalence of Captain Call's words. McMurtry's novel draws on trail-drive conventions reaching back to Emerson Hough's *North of 36* (1923), including heroic rangers, villainous Indians, and gold-hearted prostitutes, but the tone of the story is suffused with loss and regret. Hough himself, though he wrote some of the most valorizing, cliché-ridden westerns ever published, authored a series of popular articles in the early 1900s indicting environmental destruction in the West. One also thinks of Mari Sandoz's biography of her father, *Old Jules* (1935), the ferocious defender of small homesteaders in Nebraska who was shown to be a chronic abuser of women and children.[3]

John Wesley Powell is an appropriate starting point for a history of modern western regionalism because his ideas were similarly splayed between impulses to nurture and to conquer. His feats of exploration and ideas about the West have continued to resonate down to the present, carried forward especially through later classics written by Walter Prescott Webb

(1931) and Wallace Stegner (1954). Although he was born in New York State in 1834 and was never a permanent resident of the West, Powell always saw himself as one of the old-timers who had seen the region before civilization arrived. In his own era, Powell was widely regarded as the preeminent national expert on the West. But conceiving the West as a region or group of subregions hardly originated with him.

It's all a matter of choosing where to pick up the thread. Longs Peak, for example, was named for an earlier explorer, Stephen H. Long, who helped popularize the idea of the West as the "Great American Desert." William Gilpin, whom Powell met with in Colorado during his earlier expedition in 1867, is credited with promoting the term "Great Plains"—and with spreading unrealistic depictions of the West as a future agricultural paradise. Of course, maps of the West had existed for centuries before Powell and other surveying parties arrived after the Civil War, including maps created by Native Americans. These latter might incorporate personal events as well as geographical landmarks to demarcate western space, literally drawing oneself into the landscape.[4] Such maps embody the three dimensions of regionalism that guide my definition of it throughout this book: the spatial conceptualization of a region, which can be represented by a map but also by visual art and narrative description; the identity of a region, that is, its qualities and characteristics; and self-identification with a region, or the feeling that one is a native, inhabitant, or otherwise has special ties to a particular region. All of these dimensions of regionalism contribute to that amorphous yet concrete experience known as the *sense of place*.

Powell, too, exemplified all of three of these aspects of regionalism—spatial concept, regional identity, and self-identification. Certainly, with his classic adventure tale *Canyons of the Colorado* (1895), he did his part in defining what I call the *wilderness West*, the West's regional identity as a natural wonderland. But other artists and intellectuals, including John Muir, Ferdinand Hayden, Albert Bierstadt, Thomas Moran, and William Henry Jackson, were doing as much or more in the late nineteenth century to shape this identity, as were travel promoters like railroad companies. The many publications issued by the Bureau of Ethnology, which Powell founded and directed for two decades, also played a role in shaping a positive regional identity for what I refer to in coming chapters as the *Native American West*. Again, others played as prominent a part (if not more so) in creating this identity for the West during Powell's lifetime, including George Catlin, Helen Hunt Jackson, Adolph Bandelier, and Charles Lummis. Instead, Powell's signal contribution should be traced to what was arguably the urtext of modern western regionalism: his chapters in *Report on the Lands of the Arid Region of the United States* (1879).

Two things about the West immediately become clear in the *Report*: that aridity must be considered an important characteristic of the West's regional identity, and that, as our opening epigraph from a befuddled Frederick Jackson Turner indicates, there are few (if any) characteristics that are common to the West as a whole, including aridity. It is more accurate to think of the West as a collection of subregions than as a single unified region, and Powell made this point clear at the outset. "The eastern portion of the United States is supplied with abundant rainfall for agricultural purposes," the *Report* opens famously, "but westward the amount of aqueous precipitation diminishes in a general way until at last a region is reached where the climate is so arid that agriculture is not successful without irrigation." Powell's definition of aridity was essentially utilitarian; the Arid Region was delineated not by the ability to support plant life in general but by viable agriculture. Thus his larger regional scheme fell into place: the Humid Region to the east of the twenty-eight-inch rainfall line, the Arid Region roughly to the west of the twenty-inch rainfall line or the 100th meridian, with a volatile transition zone in between that he dubbed the "Sub-humid Region," encompassing much of the Great Plains. Then there were the subregional exceptions. A humid Lower Columbia Region ran inland from the Pacific to the Cascade Range in Washington, Oregon, and northwest California. Farther down the coast lay the San Francisco Region, where a rainy season made agriculture possible on a more than sporadic basis. Within the Arid Region itself, according to Powell, lands could be differentiated by altitude into three classes: the "small portion" of irrigable lands below, a mid-level region of "valleys, mesas, hills, and mountain slopes bearing grasses . . . for pasturage purposes," and an "upper region set apart by nature for the growth of timber necessary to the mining, manufacturing, and agricultural industries of the country."[5]

Like many later competing definitions of the West and its subregions, Powell's definition was very much a product of the needs and concerns of its time. In the case of *Arid Region*, it was a government report written at the behest of an expansion-minded Congress to determine the economic possibilities of western lands. What startled its contemporary readers—and inspired later generations—were Powell's recommendations for the most socially equitable and environmentally viable means of settling those lands. This was his "regionalist gaze" at the West, as it were, and with it he joined the expanding chorus of promoters who helped impose the *agrar-*

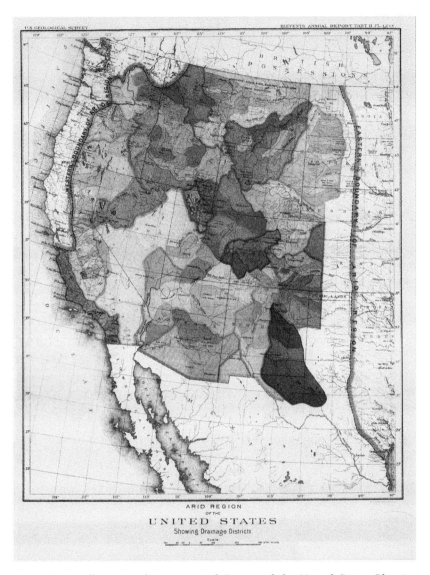

Figure 1 Powell's regionalist gaze. *Arid Region of the United States Showing Drainage Districts*, from *Eleventh Annual Report of the United States Geological Survey, 1889–90*, by John Wesley Powell, 1891. Courtesy of Regional and Historic Maps Collection, Archives & Special Collections, Mansfield Library, University of Montana.

ian West as one of the West's chief regional identities, an imprint lasting down to the present day.

Unlike Gilpin and similar fantasists arguing that "rain follows the plow," Powell had a much firmer grasp of what would be required for settlement to occur beyond the 100th meridian. To his mind, the Arid Region presented an opportunity to organize a "new phase" of society. If lands were to be opened to "poor men," the scarcity of water would require "cooperative labor or capital" to develop the necessary infrastructure of dams, canals, and ditches. The scanty grasses of the "pasturage lands" would need "communal regulations" to govern "herds roaming in common" on tracts of at least 2,560 acres. Powell could get more specific; if surveys abandoned the obsolete grid and conformed to topography instead, the total number of farms fronting on water could be maximized. Residences could then be grouped to "secure the benefits of local social organizations." Powell called this the "district or colony system," appropriating ideas from the Mormons, among whom he had spent time in the early 1870s, and indirectly from the Hispanic and Pueblo irrigators who had inspired the Mormons' techniques. Many commentators have asserted that his plan reflected Powell's understanding that settlers must adapt to the limits of the West's arid environment, which was true to a certain extent. Evolutionary concepts, particularly the notion that organisms must be adapted to their environments, guided regionalist thinking well into the twentieth century, often leading to a facile environmental determinism. But Powell himself distinguished between what he called "biotic evolution"—the Darwinian variety—and "anthropic evolution," or human cultural evolution. It was not merely that humankind must adapt to the limits set by nature in the West. As he declared in an 1883 essay on evolution, "[Man] adapts the natural environment to his wants, and thus creates an environment for himself."[6]

So regionalism might be a prescriptive as well as a descriptive intellectual enterprise: a region's identity, including its spatial conceptualization, might refer not only to what is presently in the region or what has been there in the past, but also to what could be in the future. At their most extreme, these plans or visions for the region might verge on utopianism. Powell's certainly met with that accusation; some called his plan "communism." In coming chapters we will see western regionalists frequently filling the role of cultural radical—that is, challenging and pushing the edge of the so-called mainstream—but Powell did so out of his devotion to the values of traditional agrarianism. In the context of the nation's shift to a corporate-industrial economy, his plan—extolling decentralization, small-scale production, and cooperation—became "radical," and it has remained so to the present, a touchstone for all manner of western social critics and environmentalists.

While upholding old-fashioned virtues, Powell's plan for the Arid Region was also quite modern in an important sense. It required science and engineering to create in the West this new artificial setting for the American yeomanry. It would be like the midwestern homesteads where Powell had grown up before the Civil War—only better. In the Arid Region, the isolated pioneer farm, which Powell knew all too well, could be a thing of the past. Laying the gridlines and constructing the waterworks to engineer a more concentrated pattern of settlement would secure the "benefits of local social organizations of civilization" for the settlers.[7] It was what was later known as a "quality of life" issue, and many regionalists were to be very much engaged with quality of life issues over the next century, particularly those involved with regional planning. Powell remained the West's most famous planner, and what he attempted to achieve for rural dwellers—a more cohesive, intimate, and sustainable place to live—his intellectual descendants strived to accomplish as well for the *urban* West. A high quality of life was a critical element of this regional identity for the modern West, where cities and suburbs were assumed to be places of comfort and luxury, yet also close to nature. Trying to make this urban idyll a reality was the primary challenge facing urban-regional planners in the West throughout the twentieth century, particularly as millions of Americans moved to western cities for their share of the dream.

The first western regionalist thinker to articulate the connection between regionalism and quality of life explicitly was philosopher Josiah Royce. The longtime Harvard professor might seem an unlikely regionalist, but he did sport a western-style hat around Cambridge and identified himself in many public utterances as a Californian. Royce's parents had barely survived the Overland Trail in 1848, saved literally when the US Cavalry rode to their rescue. Like many regionalists of the nineteenth-century generation, Royce spent part of his youth in a frontier context. His ne'er-do-well father had moved the family many times before and after Josiah's birth in 1855, until a period of relative stability at a farm near the gold-mining town of Grass Valley. These experiences inspired Royce's later California histories and other writings about regional culture along with his career-long interest in the problems of community life. As he put it in 1915, "My deepest motives . . . have centred about the Idea of the Community"—a preoccupation that he shared with many other regionalists.[8] Coming from a nation and a region that prized so-called rugged individualism, western regionalists sought ways to inject communitarianism into American culture, yet without stifling the individual freedoms that they themselves cherished, too. Royce in particular, for all of his protestations about communalism, was a renowned nonconformist. Regionalism, mediating between the individual, the local, and the national, was a means to find the elusive balance between freedom and obligation.

Royce believed that "the detached individual is an essentially lost being," which partly explains his fascination with the tumultuous Gold Rush period of California's history. Here he was able to explore "the forces of order and of disorder" acting on a "community of irresponsible strangers." For him, it was very much a struggle of good versus evil, the good being the moral claims of society on the individual, and the evil "the struggle of the individual man . . . to escape, like a fool, from his moral obligations to society."[9] Royce was responding to the larger problem of civic engagement that prevailed in the Progressive era of the early twentieth century: as individuals increasingly tended to live a highly mobile and anonymously urbanized life, how could they associate for their mutual and personal benefit? Society as a whole had pressing public issues that must be addressed, and individuals required commitment to something larger than themselves to live a fully human life, Royce concluded. As political participation and party loyalties declined from their nineteenth-century historic highs, one solution that Progressive-era Americans turned to was the interest group, the national single-issue organization (such as the National Anti-Saloon League, or the Immigration Restriction League). In his major contribution to both western and American regionalism, "Provincialism" (1902), Royce proposed an alternative to this more abstract form of engagement, one grounded in the multiple immediate ties of place.

First and foremost, "Provincialism" offered definitions of region and regionalism (or "province" and "provincialism") that were cited for decades afterward: "any one part of a national domain, which is, geographically and socially, sufficiently unified to have a true consciousness of its own unity, to feel pride in its own ideals and customs, and to possess a sense of its distinction from other parts of the country."[10] In contrast to Powell, who in *Arid Region* and in a later work, *Physiographic Regions of the United States* (1895), set natural parameters to regions (rainfall, altitude, relief, drainage), Royce seated regional identity more in culture— "consciousness," "ideals," and "customs." The region as a spatial concept could be any scale and any geography, from a neighborhood up to a state-sized area, as long as its inhabitants possessed the requisite self-conscious unity (or self-identification).

Social science has subsequently come up with a term for the civically engaged consciousness and unity Royce described: the "civil religion," or the term that I prefer, *civic religion*. A civic religion is a "religion" not with reference to the worship of supernatural entities but in the sense that it manifests a reverence for collective ideals and involves widely recognized public symbols, icons, and rituals. For example, America's national civic religion includes the Pledge of Allegiance (ritual), the Statue of Liberty (icon), and the principles of the Declaration of Independence (ideals). Regions may also have their civic religions—witness the many Confederate memorials built in the courthouse squares of southern towns.[11] Regions may contribute icons to the national civic religion as well; the cowboy and the cowboy hat are widely identified abroad as quintessentially "American."

But Royce's focus in 1902 was on the "small social group," the provincial as opposed to the national community. It was the ominously growing presence of national entities in daily life that led him to write his regionalist manifesto, what he called the "leveling tendency of recent civilization"—a widely shared concern among regionalists in the West and elsewhere in the country for decades to come. Royce was among the first to give voice to this cultural anxiety: "We tend all over the nation," he wrote, "to read the same daily news, to share the same general ideas, to submit to the same overmastering social forces, to live in the same external fashions, to discourage individuality, and to approach a dead level of harassed mediocrity." This mass-mindedness could lead to a still greater evil, the "mob-spirit," familiar to Royce from his study of early California vigilantism, but now given "new form and power" under modern conditions (such as during the then-recent Spanish-American War). Only the province, Royce argued, could school individuals properly in true national citizenship, providing a concrete and intimate basis for loyalty and commitment to communal ideals. Only the province, as the focus of local pride and devotion, could become a bulwark against the fast-forming tide of mass culture that threatened to efface all variety of life and independence of spirit. Only the province, as a separate and distinct locus of customs and values, could serve as a brake on the dangerous waves of mindless emotion that periodically hypnotized the nation and led it to evil. Americans, Royce urged, "must flee in the pursuit of the ideal to a new realm . . . a realm of real life. It is the realm of the province." There they would find "renewed strength . . . social inspiration," and above all, freedom, which "dwells now in the small social group, and has its securest home in the provincial life."[12]

Under Royce's regionalist gaze, quality of life could be enhanced only when a local space of *negative freedom* (absence of restraint by external power) created a setting in which a greater *positive freedom* was possible—a nurturing social context in which individuals might achieve self-realization (self-expression, personal growth, happiness). Powell, however, sensitive to the threat of corporate monopolies, recognized that federal authority was needed to protect such spaces where "local social organizations" might flourish unmolested. In decades to come, at least a minority of western regionalists, including Rose Wilder Lane on the right and Edward Abbey on the left, argued that the federal government was also a power to be feared and resisted if true negative freedom were to be achieved in the West. But most western regionalists, especially those with an interest in regional planning, were to share with Powell the faith that a high quality of life could not just happen on its own in the West but required the deliberate application of expertise, science, and technology. Yet despite his belief in the need for federal safeguards, Powell still held out hope that private enterprise, small-scale and local, could provide most of what was necessary for western development. Of course, as it turned out, the West became a major consumer of federal largesse, particularly in the form of large-scale water projects. Powell was a more accurate prophet of the important role that private developers had in region-forming the West. Railroads, hoteliers, chambers of commerce, agribusinesses, resorts, real estate companies, publishers, and movie studios, among other private entities, have all promoted quite evocative images of the West to potential investors, residents, tourists, and audiences both nationwide and worldwide.

If Royce primarily defined positive freedom in terms of the individual's public life, it is important to remember that self-realization could also unfold through private activity—or so twentieth-century Americans were led to believe. They embraced the pursuit (or consumption) of diverse, novel experience as the means to self-fulfillment and quality of life, principally in the form of tourism. Diversity and exoticism were the stock-in-trade of regionalism, and western regionalism became readily appropriable by commercial interests always on the lookout for new thrills and attractions: cowboys, pioneers, Indians, Spaniards, natural wonders. Perhaps more than in any other region of the country, western regionalism became implicated with consumerism, especially the tourist and entertainment industries. Experiences and other commodities held up as "authentic" and "natural" proved irresistible to consumers, regardless of the fact that what was offered might be highly mythologized, stereotypical, and mass-produced. Even the vaunted wilderness of the West was in many ways a managed and largely artificial construct. Consider Longs Peak: a dude ranch was operating in its vicinity less than a decade after Powell's ascent; fences, buildings, irrigation ditches, and post offices had to be removed to make the area seem more "natural" when Rocky Mountain National Park was created in 1915. New roads were also promptly constructed to make the park more accessible to automobiles. The summit that nearly vanquished Powell and his men is now routinely climbed by thousands of tourists each summer hoping to bag a "fourteener," following a well-worn and clearly marked trail.[13]

In short, although western regionalism certainly had its share of cultural radicals who challenged the public's assumptions about the past, present, and future of the West, invention and mythmaking have been endemic to the regionalist enterprise. Here we may make a further distinction: while so engaged, some regionalists concerned themselves primarily with the *localist West*, that is, a subregion that is differentiated in terms of its own unique cultural and natural landscapes. Mary Austin's Inyo country and Mari Sandoz's Niobrara Sand Hills are two examples of this localist West. The subregions of the localist West could be identified with particular racial or ethnic groups, including Hispanics, recent European or Asian immigrants, and Native Americans. But other regionalists tended to see the West or its subregions as the embodiment of certain *national* myths and ideals, as the most "American" or Anglo-Saxon of the nation's regions; this is the West I label the *nationalist West*. Rooted in the antebellum slogan of Manifest Destiny, which predestined the United States to occupy the continent out to the Pacific, the nationalist West took on renewed urgency at the turn of the century, as immigration rose to record levels and seemingly threatened the dominance of older-stock Americans. This West spatially symbolized the triumph and unity of the American people through its imperial endeavors. For example, an influential geography text of the period, Ellen Churchill Semple's *American History and Its Geographic Conditions* (1903), argued that the march from "the Mississippi to the Pacific was natural. And in this advance the large and simple structure of the continent kept the Americans one people." The nationalist West also emerged from the pens of Theodore Roosevelt and Owen Wister, among others, and it was usually made synonymous with the frontier period of western history. It became the prime commodity of the *Old West culture industry*—the pulp novel publishers, Hollywood movie producers, and television studios that in time exerted a powerful influence nationally over the West's regional identity.[14]

Part of the appeal and evocativeness of the Old West lay in the idea that it represented a lost world of greater freedom, virtue, and opportunity—those aspects of American society that made it an exception among nations. Americans liked to think of their country as a place of never-ending progress, but this notion of a decline from a past that was more free, moral, and prosperous runs as an anxious minor chord through much of American cultural history. The great dread was a future nation riven by class conflict, subject to violent revolution, and squelched under autocratic government, an America that had lost its *exceptionalism* and become more like Europe. Many western regionalists gave voice to this anxiety over exceptionalism, particularly in times of national crisis, such as the 1890s and 1930s. Above all, Frederick Jackson Turner masterfully linked together American nationalism, exceptionalism, and the western frontier in his grand and widely influential synthesis, "The Significance of the Frontier in American History" (1893). But what is often forgotten about Turner's long, anticlimactic career after 1893 is that he spent much of it struggling to understand the United States as a nation of regions, or, as he called them, "sections," and the nature of the West as one of these sections. As Turner himself later recalled, his interest in sections practically coincided with his focus on the frontier process. The "Significance" paper seemed to offer a compelling case for American region-formation as well as exceptionalism, avowing "a steady movement away from the influence of Europe" because of local environmental influences, "peculiarly *American* influences," as he wrote, the most important being "free land." As it swept westward over the centuries, "the frontier became more and more American," resulting ultimately in the most "typically American region," what Turner called the "Great West," and the construction that I have labeled the nationalist West.[15]

The problem with pinning American nationality—and region-formation— on a historical process, as Turner became acutely aware, is that at some point that process must play itself out. Turner's difficulty was with "social evolution," the concept that historical processes took place in a set pattern of distinct stages. As the frontier of civilization shifted ever westward, each region must go through the same set of changes, starting with the initial reversion to the primitive level—the frontier period proper—then upward through pastoralism, farming, and finally urban-industrialization. But the social stages model also tended to undermine Turner's contention that the frontier was responsible for the American character. Whither individualism, exuberance, inventiveness, and the democratic spirit as each region passed away from the frontier stage? As he acknowledged in "The Problem of the West" (1896), wherein he tried to conceive the West as a processive "form of society" rather than a delimited region, "Gradually this society loses its primitive conditions, and assimilates itself to the type of the older social conditions of the East." Instead of the comforting image of an expansive all-American West filling most of the map, Turner was left with the dreadful question, "Will the nation become all eastern in its quality?"[16] The industrialized East, seat of monopolies and labor strife, its cities filling with new immigrants, foretold the coming Europeanization of America.

To patch these holes in the frontier thesis—and rescue American exceptionalism—Turner resorted to the sectional thesis. Region-formation happened, according to Turner, when the frontier encountered "new geographic Provinces or Regions, founding new regional societies, reacting with the environment to produce sectional ideals and traits differing in each region." These acquired sectional traits, in his view, did not disappear because of social evolution, but lived on as cultural "survivals." As he wrote, "Long after the frontier period of a particular region of the United States has passed away, the conception of society, the ideals and aspirations that it produced, persist in the minds of the people." He had first raised the idea in "Significance of the Frontier," using an analogy to glacial moraines in his native Wisconsin landscape. Turner was now on the more typical ground of the cultural nationalist—defining and inventing "peoples"—as gradually, in his scattering of later articles on sectionalism, geographical determinism faded and such factors as the "differing stocks" and the "psychological tendencies" of the inhabitants emerged to become more prominent factors in regional differentiation.[17]

By the 1910s and 1920s, Turner pressed a larger and more urgent argument: that such differences were not only resilient but flourished over time. Here he was running counter to observers such as geographer Albert Perry Brigham, whose book *Geographic Influences in American History* (1903), after making an extended case for an America of "geographic provinces," foresaw the "decline of sectionalism" as part of a grand and unifying process of national assimilation. Turner, in contrast, began as early as 1907 to make what seemed like a curious claim for someone intent on saving American exceptionalism. In his tellingly titled paper, "Is Sectionalism in America Dying Away?" he observed that the United States was "comparable with Europe in the fact that it is made up of separate geographic provinces, each capable, in size, resources, and peculiarities of physical conditions, to be the abode of a European nation, or of several nations." It was a perilous analogy, this equation of European nationalism with American sectionalism, but Turner had his reasons. He had started to recognize, as did Royce, that—quite apart from the spread of class conflict, socialism, and other manifestations of Old World social relations—there were more insidious homegrown forms of national homogenization at work in America. He pointed to consolidation in industry, banking, and transportation. He noted the increasing dominance of cities "upon the thought as well as the economic life of the country." Moreover, he wrote, "Newspapers, telegraph, post office—all the agencies of intercourse and the formation of thought—tend towards national uniformity and national consciousness."[18] In the absence of the westering frontier, renewing American values and generating new regional societies out of the wilderness, Turner had no choice but to cast American regionalism as quasi-nationalism.

American regionalism is frequently compared to movements on behalf of cultural nationalism in other countries. These movements have sought to define distinct nationalities in terms of the unique cultural expression of a people or ethnic group, supposedly rooted in ancient traditions and homelands. Language, religion, literature, art, music, and architecture are said to embody the soul or spirit of the nation, and they may provide a rallying point for political independence movements, as was the case in early twentieth-century Ireland. Radical though proposals like Powell's might be, he and other American regionalists generally stopped short of calling for a fundamental restructuring of the American nation-state. Rarely have such demands arisen from American regionalists; some Southern Agrarians of the 1930s were a notable exception, as were western bioregionalists in the 1970s and 1980s. Most western regionalists would agree with Royce's definition that the region must always be "part of a national domain."

Yet regionalism in the West and elsewhere in the United States might still be considered a "soft" form of cultural nationalism. American regionalists would do much the same things that cultural nationalists did in other countries—create magazines, produce art, write poetry and prose, establish museums, build monuments, preserve historic sites and natural landscapes. But they would do all these things without going the final step of requiring an independent political entity to embody their "people's" newly defined culture.[19] They tended, instead, to try to proselytize through a regionalist civic religion. In the end, if one accepted as a given the American union and the basic federal system, as most American regionalists did, then that set an ultimate limit to one's radicalism. The searing national experience of the Civil War, which permanently delegitimized secession as a political option, no doubt helps to explain the American pattern. State loyalties, too, tended to mollify any tendencies toward separatism, providing an alternate site for loyalty all within constitutional bounds. Federalism may have been the true "safety valve" in American history, as Turner recognized by the time he wrote his sectionalism essays of the 1920s. It dampened possibilities for regionalism if only because of the sheer complexity of slotting a regional administrative unit like a river basin authority or a metropolitan planning district in among the many levels and silos of national, state, tribal, county, and municipal government.

There were moments in the history of western regionalism, troubled times, when a civic religion seemed an insufficient remedy, and regionalists pushed further in an ideological sense. As will be seen in chapter 1, the first such moment arose in the 1890s, spurred by an epic agricultural bust. The next moment happened during the interwar years, when the Depression threw open the bounds of political possibility, as shown in chapter 3. A third moment arrived in the 1970s with the advent of modern environmentalism, explored in chapter 5. Periodically, too, there were smaller skirmishes against politics-as-usual here and there across the West, most frequently upwelling when local people struggled to save the places they loved from runaway growth and to find a means of governance that embodied their ecological, cultural, and aesthetic concerns. For despite the ever-growing power of national government, the pervasiveness of mass culture, and the widening reach of global capitalism, belief in the West and its subregions as distinctive, special places has persisted. At the conclusion of his 1907 essay, "Is Sectionalism Dying?" Turner declared that he would "venture upon the role of prophet": "sectionalizing influences," he wrote, would "become more marked . . . in spite of all the countervailing tendencies towards national uniformity." With the Great West still in his regionalist gaze, he concluded in "Sections and Nation" (1922), "The sections serve as restraints upon a deadly uniformity. They are breakwaters against overwhelming surges of national emotion. They are fields for experiment in the growth of different types of society, political institutions, and ideals. . . . A national vision must take account of the existence of these varied sections."[20]

Like regions themselves, the history of regionalism is fuzzy around the edges. Because regionalism is by definition open-ended and multifaceted, its story in the American West is not linear or cleanly demarcated, either chronologically or geographically. Some of the following chapters overlap to an extent; while one trend might be gathering momentum in a specific part of the West, another elsewhere might be winding down, or taking an altogether different direction. Chapters 1 and 2 cover the period from the 1890s to the early 1930s, when much of the enduring artistic, intellectual, and institutional groundwork for the modern West's regional identities was first laid down. Chapter 1 focuses on the predominant agrarian West identity—the land of the pioneer and the cowboy—and chapter 2 examines an array of alternative identities that emerged in counterpoint to the agrarian West: wilderness, urban, Hispanic, Native American. Chapter 3 explores the Great Depression years, when the possibility of an ideology of regionalism flared briefly and left a potent legacy of western social criticism, along with piecemeal New Deal regionalist programs that promised substantial reform and development. In chapter 4, western observers are shown trying to comprehend the impact of World War II on the region, while western regionalism went into eclipse under the pall of Cold War ideology. Chapter 5 chronicles the renewed interest in regionalism that emerged out of the environmental movement and the identity politics of the 1960s and 1970s, highlighting the importance of regional consciousness to Native American activists, radical bioregionalists, and Sagebrush Rebels.

Chapter 6 brings the story of western regionalism from the 1980s to the present, looking at the phenomenon of the New West and the debate over whether regionalism will remain a valid way of understanding the West. A short conclusion assesses the current state of western regionalism in the age of globalization.

CHAPTER ONE

Back-Trailing

What did the Great Plains do to our "insides?"
WALTER PRESCOTT WEBB,
THE GREAT PLAINS (1931)

In 1878, John Wesley Powell had noted that farming on the Great Plains was an iffy proposition at best, but heedless of his data, home-seekers by the hundreds of thousands poured into the Plains states and territories during the next two decades. This Plains land boom prompted the Census Office to announce the disappearance of the frontier line in 1890. The homesteaders were lured by railroads eager to sell land grants to future shippers, investors happy to bankroll mortgages, and government officials looking to fill territories recently cleared of bison and Indians. The newspaper ads and fliers depicted a kind of infinite Iowa prairie that was cheap or free for the taking—not that the settlers needed much convincing.

Among the takers were the parents of twelve-year-old Laura Ingalls, who arrived in DeSmet, Dakota Territory, in 1879, the place where Laura's own daughter, Rose Wilder Lane, was born seven years later. Hamlin Garland's parents came to Ordway, ninety miles to the northwest, in 1881, bringing their reluctant high schooler in tow. Two years after this, Theodore Roosevelt purchased some ranchland around Medora, 300 miles to the northwest, and Frederic Remington, who had recently sold his first magazine illustration, bought a sheep ranch down near Peabody, Kansas. Ten-year-old Willa Cather's family moved to a new farm on the Nebraska Divide near Red Cloud in 1883, though her father—in the spirit of the times—soon found an easier way of making a living as a land agent and lender in town. Meanwhile, Jules Sandoz, the father of Mari Sandoz, was fighting ranchers for his piece of the Niobrara Sand Hills 200 miles to the northwest, and 600 miles southeast the Casner Webb family, late of Mississippi, was settling onto an east Texas farm.

In 1889, the year after the Webbs' son Walter was born, Powell renewed his warning that the Plains could not support so many farmers ("disaster will come upon thousands of people"). Not finding east Texas much of an improvement over Mississippi, the Webbs moved again when Walter was four years old, farther west to the edge of the Plains. Soon afterward, on a single day in 1893, more than 100,000 additional home-seekers formed up at the starting line for another in the series of Oklahoma land runs, and two months later, Frederick Jackson Turner pronounced the frontier closed. O. E. Rölvaag caught the tail end of the excitement in 1896, moving to North Dakota all the way from Norway, joining the settlers that he later imagined stretching "neighbour to neighbour, clear out to the Rocky Mountains!" A total of 673,460 new farms were established in the Plains states and territories between 1880 and 1900.[1]

No sooner had this Plains boom swelled than the bust began. In the northern reaches, the legendary winter of 1886–87 killed livestock by the thousands and virtually ended the range cattle industry in many areas. A bigger disaster quickly followed: drought. Some unusually wet years earlier had emboldened promoters and lulled settlers into misplaced optimism. By the late 1880s Plains rainfall was reverting to its usual unpredictability, causing widespread crop losses. When their fields began to wither, farmers had difficulty "proving up" their homesteads or making their loan and mortgage payments. Things were made worse by monetary policies that favored banks over borrowers, making debts more onerous over time; a general economic depression, starting in 1893, did not help matters. By 1888-89, a massive retreat was under way, continuing into the next decade. Counties and towns that had seen their populations double and triple during the good years now emptied out; the population of Greeley County, Kansas, for example, fell from 4,646 to 502 between 1887 and 1898. Rose Wilder Lane recalled that "it took seven successive years of complete crop failure . . . and interest rates of 36 per cent on money borrowed to buy food, to dislodge us from that land." Struggling to stay on their farms, some thought of chasing the mirage deeper into the arid West to an irrigated spread somewhere else. Others pulled up stakes and returned to the rainier states from which they had come. As Lane remembered, "The whole Middle West was shaken loose and moving. We joined long wagon trains moving south; we met hundreds of wagons going north; the roads east and west were crawling lines of families traveling under canvas, looking for work, for another foothold somewhere on the land."[2] But many Plains farmers fought to hold on where they were, and they began to look around for someone to blame for their predicament. They took their politics seriously in the nineteenth century, and feeling that their plight was being ignored by the two major parties, the result was a vast grassroots uprising known as the Populist movement, which for most of a decade sent shockwaves through the national political scene.

The Plains land boom and Populism set the stage for the emergence of modern western regionalism, particularly those major dimensions of it concerned with the values of agrarian republicanism and the frontier myth. Most immediately, the census report that the boom had filled the frontier inspired Frederick Jackson Turner's epochal "Significance of the Frontier" paper, which codified the myth. The scramble for land and increased demands for irrigation also drew the contrarian Powell into the fray, leading him to dust off that most evocative of all regional plans for the West. The Populist outbreak sounded a powerful note of sectional animosity and antimonopolism that fostered regional consciousness, especially when, in the heat of the moment, those grievances were shifted from crops to culture by Hamlin Garland and others. The defeat of the Democratic-Populist ticket in the presidential election of 1896, moreover, heralded three decades of probusiness administrations in Washington, under which urban and corporate concentration proceeded apace. Thus was sealed the victory of the Industrial Revolution over agrarian republicanism, which petered out in the rural socialism of the southern Plains and the Nonpartisan League of the northern Plains and Northwest. Thereafter, besides the homage to independent farmers and their way of life that might be heard in farm bureau speeches (long after government subsidies had made such rhetoric absurd), agrarian republicanism lived on primarily as memory, regional history, literature, and art—those things that contributed powerfully to regional identity. Perhaps most important to the long-term development of the West's regional identity, the Plains boom brought regionalists like Cather, Sandoz, Webb, and others to their places of formative experience, shaping their consciousness and depictions of the West well into the twentieth century.

If Cather and the others perpetuated agrarian republicanism as memory, Hamlin Garland and John Wesley Powell, it may be said, saw it to its end as a real (if unlikely) political possibility. Although it belies his reputation as a sedate, minor literary figure, Garland was for a time among the most politicized regionalists in the history of the West, virtually a Populist firebrand who campaigned for the party in 1892 and fervently believed in Henry George's utopian single tax (a 100 percent tax on land rents that would effectively make land ownership communal). His activism coincided with the period when he wrote a number of the essays of his regionalist manifesto, *Crumbling Idols* (1894), themes of which comprised his own presentation at the World's Columbian Exposition, scheduled two days after Turner delivered "The Significance of the Frontier." Garland is often quoted in histories of the Chicago fair, urging his parents to "sell the cookstove if necessary and come. You *must* see this fair."[3] But this moment was actually part of a larger regionalist parable that he recounted in the final poignant chapters of his 1917 memoir, *A Son of the Middle Border*— the backstory to his fervor, and an episode that exemplified the regionalist response to the Plains bust. Garland's career actually typified many of the major themes of pre–World War II western regionalism: the stab at cultural radicalism, the calls for local cultural production, the tendency toward political utopianism, and the seduction of mythologization.

For some time prior to the fair, Garland had been in agony over the thought of his infirm mother, a stroke victim, stranded with his aging father on their failing thousand-acre farm in South Dakota. Its emptiness and loneliness repulsed him. He became determined to rescue his mother from her exile. He laid plans to purchase a quaint cottage on four acres back East at his birthplace, West Salem, Wisconsin, a village of tree-lined streets nestled in a rich valley with relatives close by—one of several locations where his peripatetic father had moved the family during his youth. But Garland was appalled when his father, the personification of the westering pioneer spirit, suggested that rather than returning to Wisconsin, he would "sell out here and try irrigation in Montana." Of this frontier attitude he had imbibed all his life, Garland reflected bitterly, "Now suddenly I perceived the futility of our quest. I felt the value, I acknowledged the peace of the old, the settled."[4]

As part of his campaign to convince his parents to return to what he called the "Homestead" in West Salem, Garland brought them to the Chicago fair. On their last evening, he rolled his mother in her wheelchair out to the vast Court of Honor. The twilight off Lake Michigan illuminated the immense ornate buildings outlined in electric lights. "Stunned by the majesty of the vision, my mother sat in her chair, visioning it all yet comprehending little of its meaning," Garland recalled. "Her life had been spent among homely small things, and these gorgeous scenes dazzled her, overwhelmed her, letting in upon her in one mighty flood a thousand stupefying suggestions of the art and history and poetry of the world. . . . At last utterly overcome she leaned her head against my arm, closed her eyes and said, 'Take me home. I can't stand any more of it.'" Garland noted with chagrin, "We had oppressed her with the exotic, the magnificent . . . the color and music and thronging streets of The Magic City." Whether this reaction had been Garland's intention, the prospect of West Salem, which when they arrived there "seemed the perfection of restful security," now rose greatly in his parents' estimation, and his father at last agreed that he "*must take the back trail*" eastward. As Garland realized, "To accept this as his home meant a surrender of his faith in the Golden West, a tacit admission that all his explorations of the open lands . . . had ended in a sense of failure on a barren soil."[5]

Garland's intended regionalist parable, it appears, portrayed a spectrum of cultural development that ran from the cultureless frontier rural to the hypercivilized urban, from West to East, with an idyllic balance between these extremes struck in what he called the "ideal New England homestead," a facsimile of which he believed he had found at West Salem. Until the cultural awakening that he envisioned in *Crumbling Idols* occurred, a satisfying life could not be lived in places like South Dakota. The good life was to be found through cultivation rather than the mere expansion that his father's pioneer generation had so doggedly pursued. The supersaturated environment of the modern big city, full of empty spectacle, was also not a fit home, as it failed to be humanly scaled and close to nature. What fueled Garland's anger and his politics was that the economic forces that made New York and other big cities so dominant were undermining society-building not only in wind-blown hinterlands like South Dakota but also closer in on the Middle Border, in Iowa, Minnesota, and Wisconsin. There nature was more generous but humanity couldn't make the numbers work, at least not as long as monopoly capitalism held sway. So Garland clung to the single tax just as fervently as he did the idyll of West Salem—in fact, it was the key to creating more places like West Salem. "Land being held for use, not for sale," he reasoned, would result in a "closer society" for rural areas, and with this would come "the higher education, art, music, the drama, and the leisure to enjoy all these"—much the same enriching cultural life that Powell had designed into his Arid Lands colonies. With the single tax enacted, Garland believed, "The reign of justice will have begun"—and also, the reign of regional culture.[6]

When viewed in this light, the broadsides on behalf of cultural nationalism coming from the pen of Garland and other regionalists seem less silly than at first glance. They had no explicit concept of cultural hegemony such as we do today, but they knew a monopoly when they saw one. Before the skeptical audience at the Chicago fair and at other venues, Garland promoted what he called "veritism," calling on would-be authors to put aside "all models, even living writers," especially English literature and the classics. "Write of those things of which you know most, and for which you care most," he asserted. "By so doing you will be true to yourself, true to your locality, and true to your time." He deplored "dependence on a mother country for models of art production." Once this colonial relationship had been with England; now Eastern cities, especially New York, acted as a "central academy" that would "threaten and overawe the interior of America." Cultural "decentralization" was essential to prevent "original genius from being silenced or distorted" and to overthrow the "enslavement of our readers and writers" to the cultural hegemony of the East. In short, America must become "democratic in art," particularly an art to embody the "infinite drama . . . going on in those wide spaces of the West."[7]

That cultural power followed in the wake of economic power seemed a truism to Garland and other regionalists. Bankers in New York pulled strings, and thousands of farmers in Kansas, Nebraska, or Iowa found themselves foreclosed on, homeless. Was it not the same case with the New York literary establishment and aspiring writers in the West? It is true, as literary scholars have come to appreciate in recent years, that local color fiction offered an avenue to publication in national magazines like *Scribner's* and *Century* for women as well as farm boys like Garland. But as Garland perceived, local color was not deemed serious literature by establishment critics and was relegated to "women's work." He along with writers such as California's Frank Norris sought to prove otherwise, as did, indeed, Mary Austin and Willa Cather. Garland in his way felt just as aggrieved as women and minorities did in later decades, demanding that their experiences and values, as embodied in literature, be given voice and respect. "Everything has really tended to repress or distort the art-feeling of the young man or woman," he wrote in *Crumbling Idols*. In what seemed like the final crisis of Jeffersonianism, farmers suddenly mattered less. Now even a literature chronicling their despair had to fight for recognition. As "a farmer by birth and a novelist by occupation," Garland felt obligated to defend it.[8]

The single tax, in Garland's estimation, promised to break the cultural hegemony of the East by enriching local communities and providing them with the means of self-expression. The logic of such a radical scenario could be compelling, with monopolies, speculators, and other predatory forces stalking the western landscape—these were not imaginary, as John Wesley Powell also discovered. Given that "cooperative" was one of the watchwords of the Populist revolt, the cultural moment seemed to have arrived for a reconsideration of his 1878 plan for the Arid Region. Powell's own brother-in-law, John Davis, was a People's Party congressman elected from Kansas, who had long stoked his relative's already strong agrarian leanings and continued to bring the movement's issues to his attention. The Plains land boom first swept up Powell beginning in 1888, when settlers who had crowded into the high plains of Colorado and similar areas of the West discovered how sporadic the rainfall could be. On his authority as head of the US Geological Survey, Powell launched a separate Irrigation Survey, seeing an opportunity to begin laying down the lines of development scientifically. Unknown to him, however, the Interior Department's General Land Office, responding to concerns about a questionable water company in Idaho, decided to invoke a blanket suspension from entry (the filing of land claims) on all potentially irrigable lands in the West in 1889—a somewhat draconian response but also a measure of how chaotic the land-grabbing had become.

A political firestorm was consequently unleashed by frustrated claimants and their congressmen, with the Irrigation Survey as its focus. Rather than lying low, in the spring of 1890 Powell went on a public relations offensive, issuing a series of articles explaining his original vision in the popular *Century* magazine. It seemed to offer the chance to introduce rationality and equitability into the settlement process, because what Powell had warned of in 1878 seemed to be coming true. The "farming industries of the West are falling into the hands of a wealthy few," he wrote. He admitted frankly, "The plan is to establish local self-government by hydrographic basins." Farmers irrigating crops in the lowlands had a vested interest in governing the source of their scarce and precious water in the forested uplands. Nature itself dictated that power and authority be drastically decentralized in the West. "The people in such a district have common interests, common rights, and common duties, and must necessarily work together for common purposes," Powell declared. They would be left to tend to their own affairs within the hydrographic basin, "segregated by well-defined boundary lines from the rest of the world," with legislative safeguards to prohibit the accumulation of water monopolies, and with the federal government retaining title to all the different classes of lands except the irrigable. Depending on one's viewpoint, the proposal was either ominously centralizing or disturbingly democratizing. Coupled with the meddling of the Land Office in current land claims, it was sufficient to provoke the backlash that led to Powell leaving the directorship of the Geological Survey by 1894.[9]

The phrasing here—"segregated . . . from the rest of the world"—is revealing, especially given Powell's role as a special commissioner of Indian affairs in the 1870s, involved in efforts to establish reservations for the Utes, Paiutes, and other tribes. He saw them as necessary to prevent violent conflict (the Indian wars did not end until 1891) and to give tribespeoples room to adapt and assimilate to the rapidly expanding industrial society that was engulfing them. From this perspective, Powell's proposed hydrographic commonwealths seem like nothing less than reservations for white people, telling and curious inversions of those on which the Indians lived. Settlers, too, were to be "segregated" from rampant capitalist exploitation, albeit on the choicest rather than the more marginal lands. Instead of inculcating individual initiative—as the friends of the Indian hoped for the reservations and the allotment process—the basin commonwealths were to nurture communalism among a footloose and competitive people. Anyway, the landmark Newlands Act of 1902 ultimately found a different means to shield irrigators from market forces, the federal subsidy, which would foster not Powell's symbiotic cooperative vision but rather the illusory quasi-individualism that in years to come prevailed through much of the rural West. About all that was left officially of agrarian republicanism in the Newlands Act was the 160-acre homestead limit, which proved to be more of an inconvenience than a true limit to corporate agribusiness.

This is not to say that Powell lacked heirs; his ideas were still being quoted in the year 2000 and beyond (which perhaps was indicative of the problem). Most immediately, William E. Smythe kept cooperatism in the public eye with his book *The Conquest of Arid America* (1900), featuring a chapter on such "Real Utopias of the Arid West" as Greeley, Colorado, which Powell himself had judged an "eminently successful" example of irrigation through "cooperative labor." But Smythe also happened to mention that Greeley's planners had greatly underestimated the cost of the colony's irrigation works, which turned out to be some twenty times more expensive than originally assumed, inadvertently bolstering the case for the Newlands approach. On balance, Smythe's state-by-state account of the promise of "Undeveloped America" ("The New Day in Colorado," "The Potential Greatness of Nevada," etc.) probably did more to boost irrigation fever in general than to build a constituency for more "real utopias." The main obstacle to future utopias, Smythe pointed out, was a lack not of land or labor but of "surplus capital." Powell's actual descendant, nephew Arthur Powell Davis, who served as head of the Reclamation Service from 1914 to 1923, helped solve this problem with his own "vision" of the giant multipurpose dam (specifically, Boulder/Hoover Dam), which would finance itself through the sale of hydroelectricity. Such projects were put over the top politically when big irrigators were joined by urban municipalities looking for water and power supplies. But to reorient the rural West into a hinterland of the urban West (as opposed to the urban East) was hardly what Powell or Garland had in mind. As Powell's recent biographer Donald Worster has noted, the major's plans entailed a plenitude of smallish, localized water projects rather than massive constructions on the Hoover Dam scale.[10]

For a time, engineer Elwood Mead seemed to have assumed Powell's mantle (including, by very strange coincidence, a missing right arm). He first learned about the promise and pitfalls of western irrigation in 1882 after moving with his new bride to take a teaching position at Fort Collins, Colorado, on the heels of a years-long water dispute with its downstream rival colony, Greeley. Mead's revision of Wyoming's water laws in the late 1880s was widely seen as a model; among other innovations, ultimate ownership of all water was retained by the state and rights of use were tied to land ownership. He opposed the Newlands Act, as Powell would have. Though less focused on the river basin ecosystem than Powell, Mead in truth far surpassed Powell in his real-world experience with planned agricultural communities, spending years abroad in Australia and Palestine to help establish systems of what he called "closer settlement"—communities where irrigation, farming, and marketing were all done cooperatively, and farm sites and towns were laid out in intimate configurations to encourage social life. Describing an effort to transplant his Australian ideas to California, he put forward in *Helping Men Own Farms* (1920) his guiding vision of the rural good life: "A new social fabric had to be created. Recreation and social enjoyment had to have a place." The end was a "high rural civilization" much like Garland dreamed of. But after he was appointed commissioner of the Bureau of Reclamation in 1924, Mead, too, was seduced by the imperial grandeur of Hoover Dam. He oversaw its completion as well as the start-up of the Grand Coulee Dam and additional giant multipurpose dams. Like Powell, an immense artificial lake in the desert was later named in his honor, though with less irony.[11]

Garland's single tax faith relied less on direct social planning than Powell's or Mead's vision to restore the republican agrarian idyll, but of course it suffered much the same fate politically, going nowhere. Some other means must be found to redeem and uplift Western rural life, an issue that went national with the Country Life movement after 1900. Garland quickly abandoned both the single tax and Populism after 1893, and the reasons why he retreated from politics, and where to, throw light on the larger direction of western regionalism as it entered the twentieth century.

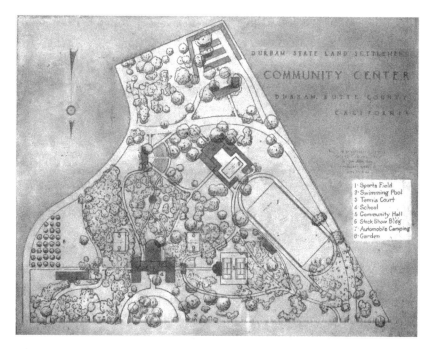

Figure 2 Mead's closer settlement plan, featuring a community center with swimming pool and tennis court. *Durham State Land Settlement Community Center, Durham, Butte County, California, John William Gregg, Landscape Architect,* from *Helping Men Own Farms,* by Elwood Mead, © 1920, The Macmillan Company.

Some of Garland's fire simply went out once he had his parents safely relocated and Populism was no longer personal. He also learned the hard way that veritism, writing of what he knew firsthand, the suffering and hardship that he saw on the farm, did not sell many books, and more than anything he wanted to be a professional writer. As he put it in *Crumbling Idols,* "The question forced on the young writer, even when he is well disposed toward dealing with indigenous material, is, Will it pay? Is there a market for me?" He found to his dismay that some of his harshest critics, who saw his early fiction as disloyal, filthy, or worse, resided in the Middle Border. The last straw was the outraged reception to *Rose of Dutcher's Coolly* (1895), which featured some rather mild depictions of a woman's sexual yearnings. In the aftermath of the critical fallout over *Crumbling Idols,* Garland went on an extended tour through Colorado, New Mexico Territory, and Arizona Territory, including several Indian reservations, a trip that piqued his interest in possibly changing the setting of his fiction.

After the *Rose* debacle, he joined the Klondike gold rush, spending many months in the wilderness of British Columbia and earning credentials as a "Western man."[12]

Thus began Garland's transition from regionalist enfant terrible to the safe figure known to posterity. The self-proclaimed son of the Middle Border, for whom local color had once required that a novel could not have been written "by any one else than a native," went on to write six novels set in Colorado, all romances or variations on the standard Western, and all forgotten while *Main-Travelled Roads* (1891) remains in print. In the second volume of his memoirs, Garland was honest about what had happened: "All my emotional relationships with the 'High Country' were pleasant, my sense of responsibility was less keen, hence the notes of resentment, of opposition to unjust social conditions which had made my other books an offense to my readers were almost entirely absent in my studies of the mountaineers," he wrote. "The cattle rancher . . . appealed to me with ever-increasing power."[13] In other words, unable to sustain the cultural radicalism that brought forth *Main-Travelled Roads* either psychologically or financially, Garland resolved his ambivalence toward the frontier myth by finally embracing it. In the end, he was as enthralled by it as his father had been. He abandoned the localist orientation in which he had been so emotionally invested for the psychological and professional security of the more generic, nationalist West of popular taste.

Such a temptation was always there for many western regionalists, who after all were very much about mythologizing and sacralizing history. Garland had learned what many promoting western tourism and entertainment would learn — that regional myth could be commodified; it could be bought and sold, just as Garland himself had purchased a "New England homestead" for his mother in Wisconsin. It need have no relation to reality. Local colorists helped pave the way for tourism in many regions of the country, the West included. Lamenting the passing of the quaint or the exotic at the hands of modernity, they effectively invited modernity in. The temptation to revert to the frontier myth or the cowboy archetype remained potent for western regionalists throughout the twentieth century, especially as they came to be embodied in hugely popular mass cultural forms such as pulp novels, country and western music, and Hollywood movies. To slot one's creations into the formulaic, rather than challenging the preconceptions and expectations of the audience — who could resist? Garland was among the first to succumb, but others, some more tough-minded than he, also found it difficult to maintain their ambivalence about frontier life on the Plains.

There remained the issues that Powell and Garland confronted: what if there are problems that are larger than states, and what if national policies and precedents cannot be applied to those problems? What if one or two cities dominate the cultural life of a nation, foisting their tastes and values on faraway places where they are irrelevant? In resolving issues such as these, regionalists in the West sought to define a place for region in American life and for their region in particular. They succeeded phenomenally well: by 1930, no other region of the country enjoyed such positive opinion and identification nationally as the West. The West and its agrarian archetypes, the cowboy and the pioneer, came to be seen as quintessentially American, part of the pantheon of the national civic religion. The tourism, film, and publishing industries were critical to disseminating them to the broader public. Yet the more widely shared these western archetypes became, the more generic and abstract—and disconnected to a specific place—they necessarily were. It was communalism of a sort, perhaps, but not the rich, intimate local life that Royce, Powell, Garland, and other regionalists originally envisioned.

Theodore Roosevelt and the circle of western writers and artists that revolved around him were some of the principal architects of the nationalization of the cowboy icon and, more broadly, the notion of the "Old West"—that imaginary place to which Garland retreated. Although the roots of the cowboy as a cultural figure preceded them, Roosevelt, Frederic Remington, Owen Wister, and Emerson Hough were instrumental in monumentalizing him for a modern audience, defining those characteristics of heroic masculinity that transmuted the workaday cowboy (whom all of them knew firsthand) into mythic symbol and genre type. Turner may be widely credited with first explicating the end of the frontier, but Roosevelt and his circle began to make the American people truly *feel* the implications of it. In doing so, they put a powerful stamp on larger perceptions of the West as a distinctive region for decades to come.

What Roosevelt and his talented friends sought to accomplish was a kind of instant archaicizing of the recent western past, rendering it as something lost in time, rooted in the past, precious—and ripe for monuments. In part, this rhetoric stemmed from their own deeply personal sense of nostalgia over their youthful experiences out West. Recalling the period in 1883 when he went to Dakota Territory and "took hold of two cattle ranches," Roosevelt wrote in his autobiography (1913): "It was still the Wild West in those days, the Far West, the West of Owen Wister's stories and Frederic Remington's drawings, the West of the Indian and the buffalo-hunter, the soldier and the cow-puncher. That land of the West has gone now, 'gone, gone with lost Atlantis,' gone to the isle of ghosts and of strange dead memories." Roosevelt's *Hunting Trips of a Ranchman* (1885) had been among the earliest popular accounts of authentic ranch life, published when TR was still actively engaged with his operations in Dakota. Noting how the Plains land boom had "risen over the West like a flood," the resulting competition for land with homesteaders made open-range ranching "from its very nature ephemeral," Roosevelt wrote. "I doubt if it lasts out the present century."[14]

Owen Wister, another transplanted Easterner who had his own inter-lude among the cowboys of Wyoming in the mid-1880s, wrote in much the same vein by 1895. In a landmark article with input from his erstwhile collaborator Remington, "The Evolution of the Cow-Puncher," Wister in fact posited no "evolution" but conceived the cowboy as a static, anachro-nistic racial type comparable to a medieval knight, "who for thirty years flourished upon our part of the earth, and, because he was not compatible with Progress, is now departed, never to return." Five years later, Hough, an Iowa farm boy who had gone to New Mexico Territory in 1881 looking for adventure, put it most bluntly, "The West of the good old days is gone forever. . . . There is no West."[15]

Hough, less artful than his counterparts, was more explicit about his motives in using such rhetoric. *The Story of the Cowboy* (1897), the work that established his reputation as a western writer, opens with an extraordi-nary scene in which a sculptor of Hough's acquaintance (not Remington) entertained guests at a party by shining a light on some of his productions placed one at a time on a pedestal—a buffalo, a grizzly bear—throwing their shadows onto the wall as if to create the ideal types of Plato's cave. Finally, to much applause, he set the small figure of a mounted cowboy on the pedestal, then took it away, and as it vanished a pensive silence fell on the room. Hough reflected on the moment, again in a classicist vein, "The story of the West is the story of the time of heroes." The cowboy, he wrote, "would scoff at monument or record, therefore perhaps he deserves them." Remington, for his part, took up sculpture after closely observing another artist working on a piece of public art. An admiring Roosevelt asserted pointedly that the cowboy and other western types would "live in his pic-tures and bronzes, I verily believe, for all time," constituting a "permanent record of certain of the most interesting features of our national life." In a 1907 interview, Remington himself joined in the refrain that "the typical figures of the plains are as much gone as the Civil War or the Paleozoic period"—though significantly, the former was still being monumentalized at a steady pace North and South by Remington's contemporaries.[16]

If the "Old South" myth offered a vision of harmonious racial subordination at a time when race relations were in turmoil, and the corollary "Lost Cause" myth an image of valor in defense of the Old South, the "Old West" that Roosevelt and his circle were seeking so rapidly to enshrine offered its own tribute to Anglo-Saxon racial mastery. Certainly having a self-identified cowboy in the White House did not hurt their effort, particularly one who was calling on Americans to continue their empire-building overseas now that the home frontier was gone. But Wister's nameless *Virginian* (1902) most fully embedded the archetype in the public consciousness at the outset. As huge best sellers often do, *The Virginian* appealed across a broad spectrum of readers, and its independent, virile, outdoorsy, incorruptible hero resonated with a middle class leading an increasingly urbanized and bureaucratized existence, turning away from party politics and toward sports, parks, and other forms of active leisure. The deeply conservative Wister, whose next novel was set in the Old South, proffered the Virginian as a natural aristocratic ideal to counter what the more moderate Roosevelt derided as the "demagogy" and "mob rule" represented by western Populists. Wister's own feelings were made clear enough in "The Evolution of the Cow-Puncher," in which he (and co-writer/illustrator Remington) lionized the knightly "Saxon" in contrast to the "debased and mongrel . . . hordes of encroaching alien vermin, that turn our cities to Babels and our citizenship into a hybrid farce."[17]

The cowboy and other archetypes of the Old West were in this way used to anchor a particular definition of American nationality; monumentalized, they comprised a civic education in Anglo-Saxon values and superiority in a period when wave after wave of immigrants were challenging that definition. Of the original circle, Hough most explicitly carried this agenda forward after 1910, first in *The Passing of the Frontier: A Chronicle of the Old West* (1918). He wrote the book fresh from his work for the American Protective League during World War I smoking out dangerous disloyal aliens. At the beginning of his narrative, Hough immediately rejected the notion of a "melting-pot" as an "odious appellation" for the nation, and, ostensibly borrowing from Turner, he depicted a "new people . . . America and the American . . . conceiving" on the frontier. References to the *Iliad* and the Elizabethans set the proper mythopoeic context. With the frontier passed away by the end of the book, Hough held to his faith that the "blood of the American West, diluted though it has been by far less worthy strains," might retain some of the "iron of the old home-bred frontiersman." He closed by reminding his readers once again of the frontier's "strong lessons, its great hopes, its splendid human dreams."[18]

Inspiring himself if no one else, Hough proceeded to write one of his most popular novels, *The Covered Wagon* (1922), joining the crop of imitators that had quickly distilled the modern Western genre from Wister's prototype (the hero's name in *The Covered Wagon*, Will Banion, even sounds like "Vir-ginian"). More important for the future dissemination of Old West archetypes, *The Covered Wagon* was made into a blockbuster silent movie by director James Cruze in 1923, one of the most widely viewed since *The Birth of a Nation*. Filmed on location in Nevada, it featured panoramic shots of the rolling wagon train as well as scenes of the circled wagons repelling Indian attacks, later replicated in countless movies and television series. During the next half-century many of these productions played through the public awareness like mythic Muzak, reiterating over and over again—along with the tourism industry—the Old West as the West's regional identity. Wister's *Virginian* was issued in no fewer than five film or TV versions between 1912 and 2000. The irony is that while they were helping invent the Old West that would be thus appropriated, Hough and the rest of Roosevelt's circle had decried the pulp or dime novels ("weirdly illustrated Apocrypha of the West," Hough called it) that to their minds distorted the "authentic" picture of the West that they claimed to have personally experienced. But as was the case with Garland, the siren song of "stereotyped characters" was difficult to resist for those who made a living from their pens. Hough cranked out one more Western, the trail drive romance *North of 36*, shortly before his death in 1923, in seeming anticipation that it, too, would be adapted to the screen.[19] It was.

The problem with the national genericization of the West as Old West was that all too quickly it began to resemble a cultural hegemony all its own, a culture industry emanating from Hollywood studios and New York pulp publishers. Novelist Zane Grey, virtually a one-man culture industry, was made a millionaire by it, launching his own film production company; at last count, in his lifetime and beyond, more than 100 movies were made of his novels (40 million copies sold). Underneath this outpouring, the myriad subregions that comprised the West were obscured in their diversity. In such a context, serious artists and intellectuals from these subregions with something unique to say might have difficulty receiving acceptance by the critical establishment or finding an audience. They continued to confront not only the genteel, Anglophilic, and Eurocentric orthodoxies that Garland had complained of but also the burgeoning Old West culture industry that seemed to threaten to drown out their voices. If history were to penetrate the miasma of myth, and art to break through the schlock, the subregions of the West—the West in all its diversity—must begin to be heard from. As H. G. Merriam, editor of the Missoula, Montana–based magazine *The Frontier* put it in 1928, he was seeking "the true expression of Northwest life, as opposed to the usual 'western.'"[20]

There was an upsurge in localist cultural activity across the West from the 1890s to the 1920s that ran both as an accompaniment and counterpoint to the emerging nationalist Old West culture industry. The greatest congruence occurred in tourist promotion. The flavor of the Old West was offered at places famous and obscure, from the Grand Canyon to the plethora of resorts and dude ranches that began by catering to railroad travelers (often built by the railroads themselves) and then automobiles. The advertisements for these locations appeared in national magazines and offered a set of emblematic landscapes that shaped public perceptions of what the West was like: canyonlands, saguaro cacti, alpine mountains. These images drew from nineteenth-century landscape paintings by Bierstadt, Moran, and others; in fact, as early as the 1870s, Moran himself was hired by the Union Pacific Railroad to supply landscapes to the company. It should be no surprise that it was rarely possible to disentangle the booster impulse entirely from cultural development in the West.[21] For example, the art colonies that sprang up in these years—most famously in Santa Fe, Taos, and Carmel as well as in Denver, Colorado Springs, Portland, and Salt Lake City—usually had commercial galleries and other businesses that drew in the tourists. It was their response to the crucial question that Hamlin Garland had posed for the aspiring regional artist: "Will it pay? Is there a market for me?"

Yet it was also true that many western artists and intellectuals were driven by the need to express deeply personal ties to particular places. As these depictions were appropriated and marketed to a growing audience, they necessarily complicated, diversified, and fragmented the regional identity of the West. One measure of the localist impact could be seen in the revised 1933 edition of Ellen Churchill Semple's *American History and Its Geographic Conditions*. The main body of the text still included her original nationalist assertion that "the large and simple structure of the continent kept the Americans one people," but the book now ended with a new appendix dividing the continent into no fewer than nine broad regions, each with a representative sampling of regionalist literature. The West had become the "Trans-Mississippi Prairie Plains and the High Plains," the "Arid and Semi-Arid Basins of the Western Highlands," the "Trans-Continental Trails," and the "Pacific Coast Region."[22]

Institutionally, the localist cultural impulse flourished most strongly at the state level. Almost every western state after 1900 had a state historical society with a museum and quarterly magazine. Many states had old settlers associations, which promoted the frontier experience as a common statewide heritage. State fairs became essential sites for states to define and represent themselves and for their citizens to self-identify with the state and often, a larger subregion or greater region (the Southwest, the West). Some states touted themselves in effect as their own region, most notably the "Lone Star state" of Texas, which in 1936 threw a huge centennial celebration not of statehood but of Texas independence. State parks were established in many states to preserve natural and historical sites of local pride and interest (and to bring in tourist dollars). In addition, state universities, as the preeminent educational institutions in most western states, provided support for scientific investigation of local conditions and, of particular importance, for university publications. By 1930, university presses especially in California (founded in 1893), Washington (1920), Oklahoma (1928), and New Mexico (1929) were already becoming substantial players in fostering regional knowledge and consciousness in the West. State and regional periodicals also emerged in many states during this period, most notably the *Land of Sunshine/Out West* in California (1894), the *Southwest Review* in Texas (1915), the *Frontier* in Montana (1920), the *Prairie Schooner* in Nebraska (1926), *Folk-Say* in Oklahoma (1929), and the *New Mexico Quarterly* (1931).

These presses and magazines, though state-supported, positioned themselves as more broadly regional publishing venues with the goal of authentically expressing the life of the local. By appropriating locally indigenous folk cultures, writers and artists could communally integrate themselves and their modern audiences with the experience of the traditional, becoming rooted to place. Otherwise, audiences would be left adrift as consumers of the mass-cultural "world without a country," to use regional planner Benton MacKaye's words, or, just as alienating, the whole gamut of East Coast literary production with no relation to life in the West. As Merriam noted in a 1930 letter to journalist Carey McWilliams, "Culture to me is not and can never be an importation. . . . Culture is a 'growing out' process." He posited regionalism as an alternative to the "tea party poetry and skylark verelets" of genteel literature as well as the "crazy sophistication" of modernist, avant-garde writing. Neither fulfilled the culturally democratizing outreach and civic religiosity promised by regionalism. Nor did rejection of eastern standards automatically imply small-mindedness or parochialism. Merriam, for one, declared himself "in sympathy with labor, feminist, anti-imperialist, and anti-militarist movements."[23] Yet not all fronts in this culture war were toward the East; some had to be fought against collaborators at home, as James Stevens and H. L. Davis pointed out in their 1927 manifesto "Upon the Present Condition of Northwestern Literature," *Status Rerum*. They attacked the "avalanche of tripe" that was being produced by all of the "posers, parasites, and pismires" in the region, naming names at the universities of Oregon and Washington.[24]

Stevens and Davis set their standards high, demanding a northwestern literature on a par with the works of Dreiser, Lewis, and Frost, and Davis soon enough fulfilled his own prophecy with his Pulitzer Prize–winning novel set in rural Oregon, *Honey in the Horn* (1935). But not every struggle to define region ended with such a clear-cut localist victory. There were defeats as well, nowhere more visibly so than at Mount Rushmore. Doane Robinson, who is credited with originating the idea of carving a monumental sculpture on the granite of the Black Hills, in many ways personified the growth of state-level cultural institutions in the West. After arriving in Dakota Territory during the Plains boom, he discovered a talent for poetry and published in the *Century* and other major magazines. He went on to found and edit a magazine of local history and culture, the *Monthly South Dakotan*, beginning in 1898. In 1901, he helped establish the South Dakota State Historical Society and served as the state historian for the next quarter of a century. He wrote several histories of South Dakota, including one on the Sioux Indians (Lakota).

So there was no individual more steeped in South Dakota localism than Robinson, and when he learned of the project to sculpt Confederate leaders on Stone Mountain in Georgia, his initial concept for South Dakota's granite appears to have centered on "some notable Sioux, as Redcloud, who lived and died in the shadow of these peaks," with others unnamed to follow on a series of giant rock needles. The purpose was frankly to promote tourism, as Robinson later told one of South Dakota's senators: "It will 'sell' the Black Hills . . . as nothing else could. . . . Money could not buy the good advertising this thing will give us." By now Robinson's vision had expanded beyond the local and indigenous to something he saw as grander: "I can see all the old heroes of the west. . . . Lewis and Clark, Fremont, Jed Smith, Bridger, Sa-kaka-wea, Redcloud, and in an equestrian statue, Cody and the overland mail." As had happened with Garland, the compulsion to appeal to generic western frontier hero worship proved irresistible. Significantly, despite the inclusion of two Native American figures, Robinson neglected to consult with any local Lakotas about the project, and the actual monument in time came to be bitterly resented by many of them (it was twice seized by the American Indian Movement in later years) as a blatant occupation of sacred ground.[25] Robinson need not consult; he was in a position of cultural authority in South Dakota and able to set the agenda.

Or so he thought. As it turned out, Robinson and his mildly generic western agenda were no match for the man he recruited for the Black Hills project, sculptor Gutzon Borglum, the Teddy Roosevelt of the art world. Borglum, born in Idaho and raised in Nebraska, had begun his career in the 1890s as a "western artist." But after creating a long succession of monuments and memorials spread from Connecticut to Arizona, his perspective had become decidedly more deracinated by the 1920s. His abortive work on Stone Mountain in Georgia, which was ending badly just as Robinson came calling, inspired him to aim higher in the pantheon than the white South's regional deities, Lee, Davis, and Jackson. If the monument were to culminate and justify his career, he must think bigger.

Borglum, in short, arrived on the scene predisposed to a grandiose nationalist statement, and he rejected Robinson's proposed list of western heroes out of hand. His initial design perfectly encapsulated the notion of the West embodying national ideals. Tourism promotion was the furthest thing from his mind, but Mount Rushmore was to be a classic case of the sometimes vanishingly thin line separating boosterism from civic religion. To Borglum, the grouping of Washington, Jefferson, TR, and Lincoln would be "a nation's memorial" representing "a serenity, a nobility, a power that reflects the gods who inspired them and suggests the gods they have become." The central figure for him was Jefferson, by virtue of the Louisiana Purchase—"in the center of which, on a spur of the Rocky Mountains, this memorial is located." As he wrote at an early stage, "I am literally converting a spur of the Rockies into a memorial and monument to the great Western Republic." Borglum's original, nationalist-western design was also to include a panel in the shape of the Louisiana Purchase, wherein giant letters would be carved spelling out the greatest events of the nation's history, seven of which (as critics have noted) involved territorial acquisition. But soon enough his own interpretive spin on the monument evolved in still more generically national directions. His stated intention was simply to represent the whole history of the national republic—its establishment, expansion, and preservation as symbolized in four powerful white "Empire Builders." And so, shortly after his death in 1919, TR himself became the subject of the very monumentalization that he and his circle had helped promote about the West. After all, he was "preeminently an all-American president" who represented the "restless Anglo-Saxon spirit," wrote Borglum.[26] (Despite resemblances, down to the pince-nez, the two were mutual admirers and acquaintances only.)

From a regionalist perspective, Mount Rushmore's violation of context was twofold: its bald if bland assertion of national power spurned not only local indigenous culture but also the loosely relevant icons of the Old West. Yet the ways of culture are complex and mysterious, especially with regard to issues of authenticity. A case in point again involved the immediate legacy of the TR circle, but in this instance nationalism did not necessarily win the day. The Emerson Hough controversy erupted soon after the author's death in 1923, and it concerned a review of his book *North of 36* written by Stuart Henry in the New York–based magazine *Literary Digest International Book Review*. The title of the review was "Faults of Our Wild West Stories," and Henry took Hough to task for his "rapid romantic writing," questioning the accuracy of numerous plot elements in his depiction of cattle drives, particularly at the terminus in Abilene, Kansas. Henry also seemed to cast aspersions on frontier womanhood, noting (as had Garland in his early realist phase) how "weazened, weary" and "forlorn" they were, leading lives that were "hard, even to sordidness."[27] There was a furious reaction to these statements among western editors, authors, and other defenders of Old West mythology, including members of the Old Time Trail Drivers Association and the Texas and Southwestern Cattle Raisers Association.

Prominent amid the uproar was Texas historian Walter Prescott Webb, who wrote an article asking "Can the West Be Heard?" and sent Henry a questionnaire to test his knowledge of things western. While sharing in the widespread regionalist critique of the eastern literary hegemony voiced by Merriam and others, there was often a nastier, nativist, anti-intellectual edge to the attacks on Henry. Webb, along with novelist Eugene Manlove Rhodes and their allies among Texas boosters, variously demonized him as one of the decadent East Coast "Mencken crowd," "Euramerican critics," or as Henry himself later bemusedly noted, a "kind of Frenchman" who was making un-American slurs against their ancestors. It seems that Henry had written a number of books about Paris and its cultural scene in years past, after having lived there and attended the Sorbonne. But if the Hough defenders had checked their facts more carefully, they would have learned that Henry had grown up in Abilene during the trail drive days and had graduated from the University of Kansas. As Henry pointed out, it was Hough who was the "outsider" lacking local knowledge.[28]

At some point the absurdity of his fulminations against "university intellectuals" must have struck Webb, whose address (as Henry observed in a long, sardonic reply to his critics) was "History Department, University of Texas." The controversy died down quickly enough, but it was not entirely in Webb's imagination that there was an academic bias against western history. Regardless of Turner's seat at Harvard, academic history remained largely dominated by the European or American political and diplomatic fields, along with ancient (classical) history. When the Hough controversy erupted, Webb was still licking his wounds from having failed his doctoral examinations at the University of Chicago, which he defensively ascribed to his professors' disciplinary narrow-mindedness. What Henry called the "wild-west fictionists and moving picture folk" did the few serious scholars of the West no favors in academic circles. As early as 1901, California's Frank Norris—in his own manifesto against the eastern literary establishment—had also noted the stultifying effect of "dime novels" on serious writing about the West, and the Old West culture industry had grown far more ubiquitous by the 1920s.[29]

At bottom, however, Webb's defense of the pulpy *North of 36* was rooted in his regard for another of Hough's works, *The Way to the West* (1903), which had inspired the epic vision of Plains historical development that had first come to him in 1922, only to be squelched at Chicago. The Hough controversy, rousing his sectional and professional ire, redoubled Webb's determination to fulfill his vision in a book, *The Great Plains* (1931). It became personal for him, as his biographers have pointed out; the farm boy with a toehold in academia must prove his worth and that of his family history, which were being ridiculed. "This book is a part of all that I have been and known," Webb wrote.[30]

The Great Plains arguably did more than any other work since Turner's "Significance of the Frontier" to establish the scholarly legitimacy of western history. Along with Herbert Bolton's *The Spanish Borderlands* (1922), it was also a major and influential assertion of the localist, subregional conceptualization of the West. *The Great Plains* was an explication of Powell's contention that settlement beyond the 100th meridian (Webb put it at the 98th) had summoned a "new phase in Aryan civilization." Webb acknowledged his debt to Turner much less explicitly, but in effect his work was a case study in Turner's sectional thesis—dispensing with the nationalist framework. Webb did not vest American exceptionalism in the collective regionalization of America, as had Turner. Rather, he saw it adhering singularly to the distinctive Plains culture that arose beyond the "institutional fault" of the farmable rainfall line. Entering the unique physiographic province of the Plains, a "gigantic human experiment with an environment" had occurred, according to Webb. Influenced by the environmental determinism of Friedrich Ratzel, which reigned for decades among American geographers thanks to Semple and others, Webb showed how the Anglo-American Plainsmen had to innovate and adapt their "weapons, tools, laws, and literature" to the new conditions, so that their culture could no longer be understood as a "mere extension of things Eastern."[31]

For much of *The Great Plains*, Webb's emphasis was less on the failure and breakdown of the old than on the novelty and distinctiveness of the new, the six-shooters, the barbed wire, the windmills, the attempts to change water laws. His allusions to the Plains bust are relatively few, as it would spoil the triumphalism. He must above all prove (as he wrote privately many years later) that "the Great Plains is not only a separate region historically and culturally, but it is something apart in practically all its aspects." Webb strove to make a compelling case of the sort that Turner did not live long enough to accomplish: the emergence and persistence of an American region, from its geology to its literature. To complete this portrait, Webb did his share of mythologizing, to be sure—all those years of reading Hough and the like had worn off on him—but he more successfully clothed it all in social scientific categories than Turner had. The Plains "cattle kingdom" became in this guise one of various "cultural complexes" that had undergone "natural selection" to become "adapted to its environment," yet it was also a place of "men in boots and big hats, with . . . jingling spurs and frisky horses," where "men were all equal," and each was "his own defender." Rhetorically, Webb often juxtaposed or qualified the use of "West" with "the Great Plains," bringing the larger myths to bear on the less familiar subregional context. His mental map of a broadly defined "Plains environment" encompassed much of Powell's Arid Region and reached back as far east as Illinois.[32]

So while it was one of the first widely successful western subregional case studies, *The Great Plains* also grounded generic Old West myth in what appeared to be concrete historical proof. It rendered this service as well to the cause of Anglo-Saxon predominance, narrating how the Anglo-Americans had finally triumphed over the "untamed savagery" of the Plains tribes, while the Spanish had failed. Just to show that logical consistency should never stand in the way of racial valorization, Webb resorted—in a final, unfortunate chapter passage—to Turner's solution to the problem of regional persistence and historical change: survivals. Apparently, only some eastern antecedents were liable to break down at the institutional fault line. The Plains remained home to "a survival of the early American stock, the so-called typical American of English or Scotch and

Scotch-Irish descent." True, there were German descendants in the Prairie Plains and Scandinavians in the Dakotas and elsewhere. But if you still wanted to find your "pure American stock," look to the southern Plains—Webb's own country. For as everyone knew, the "Negroes did not move west of the ninety-eighth meridian, the Europeans were not attracted by the arid lands, the Chinese remained on the Pacific coast, and the Mexican element stayed close to the southern border." This was largely nonsensical as history, but as regional myth-making it advanced the notion of the Plains as an Anglo-Saxon *heartland* untainted by the demographic and cultural shifts that were transforming America into an increasingly diverse and polyglot nation. In this way, *The Great Plains* strained to become perhaps the culminating document of the Anglo-American male's view of the West. "It is a little tough on those of us who are bowing out the old life," Webb once confided to a friend.[33]

Published in 1931 on the cusp of the Dust Bowl and the deepening Depression, many assumptions of *The Great Plains* soon came to be challenged. As the next two chapters show, much of the truculence that first inspired Webb to hunker down and write the book stemmed from his realization that the intellectual climate (if not the popular) had already shifted against uncritical avowals of white Anglo-American supremacy and the frontier myth, updated or not. And one of the most powerful revisions, if not repudiations, had come more than a decade earlier from a former Plains-dweller, Willa Cather.

Although her agrarian works were imbued with a powerful sense of nostalgia like those of the TR circle and Webb, Cather avoided the kind of male posturing that was implicated in theirs. Implicitly, the assertions of Hough, Wister, TR, and the rest that they had personally experienced the now vanished, genuine frontier were meant to privilege their accounts and enhance their masculine status. That they were part of the events that were to be monumentalized made them, in effect, somewhat monumental themselves. Cather, in contrast, took a step back and turned memory and nostalgia into thematic elements of her plots, especially in her masterpiece, *My Ántonia* (1918). Her intent was less to monumentalize than to universalize her settings and characters. To achieve this required an intensely localist focus, much more so than the half continent-sized subregion of Webb's Great Plains. Cather looked neither to Powell's nor to Turner's regional maps for the proper scale, but to Sarah Orne Jewett, Mary Austin, and other local colorists who explored place through the rural neighborhood.

Garland had found ways to connect these local places to larger sectional-national political themes, but Cather's agrarian works were studiously apolitical. Her scale was peasant rather than epic, extending only so far as her folkish characters and their web of communal ties to the landscape. She *began* at the place where the chastened and depoliticized Garland arrived at the end of his regionalist parable, bringing his mother home to a snug village life. Discontent with such a life for himself and heeding the siren song of the frontier myth, he thereafter struck off for the Klondike and the Old West. The later Garland and the Old West mythologizers looked to violence, grand scope, physical courage, and other manly virtues to enchant the West. Cather chose otherwise for her art. Like her character Neighbour Rosicky, she believed in the wisdom—and power—of the humble. Certainly Cather quite self-consciously played to her audience's agrarian preconceptions to enchant her farm folk with pastoral and other mythic attributes, but without losing sight of the fact that they were grounded in the particular: an obscure yet specific place (the south central Nebraska prairie), an individual ordinary character (a farmwife). Compare the scene from Hough's *Story of the Cowboy*, wherein western figurines are projected reverently as giant-size shadows on the sculptor's wall, to this famous passage from *My Ántonia* in which the characters have caught sight of a plow illuminated from behind by the setting sun, "heroic in size": "Even as we whispered about it, our vision disappeared; the ball dropped and dropped until the red tip went beneath the earth. The fields below us were dark . . . and the forgotten plough had sunk back to its own littleness somewhere on the prairie."[34]

Cather's subregional West was enlarged through its owned littleness. It was to be understood through the stories of plain people in small rural communities. At this resolution, the West looked much different than that pictured by the Old West mythologizers: one could begin to see its ethnic diversity. The French, Norwegians, Swedes, and especially the Bohemians who peopled her agrarian novels and stories were a critique of the racialist nativism posited by Webb and TR's circle—indeed, struck at its core. Cather was explicitly celebratory of the immigrants' contribution to frontier progress, albeit progress of a qualified sort: the landscapes left in its wake featured country churches, orchards, and hedgerows; they were decidedly folkish and Europeanized. In *My Ántonia*, when Jim Burden returns home after a long absence, he notes how "the whole face of the country was changing," but the "changes seemed beautiful and harmonious" to him.[35]

The reason behind this apparent symbiosis could be perceived at a still closer resolution. There one saw that the West was not comprised of independent heroic men, each his own defender. Instead, such ethnic communities were made up of families, and at the hub of each family, in Cather's estimation, there was a woman, a woman like Ántonia, Mary Rosicky of "Neighbour Rosicky" (1930), or Alexandra Bergson of *O Pioneers!* (1913). Here again, Cather's perspective was in sharp contradiction to that of Garland or Webb, who both emphasized (with some justification) how hard life could be for frontier farmwives. The corollary, of course, was that the West was primarily a man's world. It was more than just a difference over historical fact. Cather was reenvisioning life on the Plains, and in the West generally, in feminized, domestic terms. In the right hands the rural landscape could become a garden-like extension of the home. As she wrote in *O Pioneers!* describing Alexandra's farm, "When you go out of the house and into the flower garden, there you feel again the order and fine arrangement manifest all over the great farm. . . . You feel that, properly, Alexandra's house is the great out-of-doors, and that it is in the soil that she expresses herself best." Any man lucky enough to be a part of such a household, like Neighbour Rosicky, could lead a "complete and beautiful" life.[36]

Cather was arguably the most gifted novelist the West has produced, yet her feminized view of the region has remained a minority one thanks to the relentlessly masculine depictions of the Old West culture industry and the long-entrenched academic defenders of Turner. Cather did not deconstruct Old West agrarian myths so much as she provided an alternative set of her own, a multiethnic (at least among Europeans), feminine, symbiotic, communitarian alternative. The eulogizers of the Old West pronounced it dead once the schoolmarm arrived, as in Wister's *Virginian*. For Cather, this moment was precisely when the West began to fulfill its promise, when communities such as hers flourished at a poise between a past of nomadic emptiness and a future of banal modernity.

Whoever engages in it, mythologizing by its very nature involves selection and exclusion, and Cather's vision had its share of limitations as well. She was hardly the first to write of the immigrant settler experience on the Plains. By the 1920s, for example, there was already a substantial shelf of Norwegian-language realist novels set in the Dakotas, culminating in the widely regarded *Giants in the Earth* (1927) by O. E. Rölvaag. Certainly Rölvaag fully embraced the notion of the Plains as a small freeholders' empire, but he focused more intently on the hardships of the harsh natural environment and the psychic costs of assimilation for immigrants, both themes largely sidestepped by Cather. Native Americans were also scarcely mentioned in her Nebraska novels and bit characters or ancient absences in her southwestern works. By comparison, Laura Ingalls Wilder, another strong proponent of a domesticated West, depicted Native Americans as a constant and often intrusive presence for the settlers in her phenomenally popular children's book *Little House on the Prairie* (1935), climaxing in the stunning scene of a day-long procession of dispossessed Indian families. Pa Ingalls at least was frank about the contest for land, that there were winners and losers: "When white settlers come into a country, the Indians have to move on. . . . That's why we're here, Laura. White people are going to settle all this country, and we get the best land because we get here first and take our pick."[37] Rather than living happily ever after, the Ingalls family were soon themselves evicted as squatters by the government.

As a historian, Cather suffered still more seriously when compared to her sister Nebraskan Mari Sandoz. In works such as *Old Jules*, which took her more than a decade to write, Sandoz made the reader much more aware of the blood price that had to be paid so that Ántonia and Alexandra could have their fine farms on the prairie. Perhaps no individual among the generations touched by the Plains land boom more fully problematized the myths that were erected around the frontier experience than Sandoz did. Her reality check was her brutal father, Jules, an egomaniacal force of nature who abused his wife and children as he was carving his fiefdom from the Nebraska Sand Hills. His daughter began her fictionalized biography of him in the early 1920s, and after a long and difficult writing process (including numerous rejections from eastern publishers), she finally published the book, her first, in 1935.

As Sandoz depicts him, Jules was the very type of frontiersman admired by TR, Hough, Wister, and Webb (if they could get beyond his foreign birth)—resourceful, wily, fearless, a crack shot. While he was surely the independent man of action, Jules also shared much the same communal vision that Powell and Cather had, according to Sandoz: "There, close enough to the river for game and wood . . . where corn and fruit trees would surely grow, Jules saw his home and around him a community of his countrymen and other home seekers, refugees from oppression and poverty, intermingled in peace and contentment." But as Sandoz also reveals, this frontier paragon routinely beat, belittled, and coerced those closest to him, including those most vulnerable, like his "cringing" daughter, Mari, as she described herself. Tough-minded—or scarred—though she was, Sandoz admitted freely that there was "no affection" between them and that she "feared" her father—not the sort of hero worship one would expect to read in a Book of the Month Club selection.[38]

What redeemed Jules from being simply a monster was the communal vision, in Sandoz's eyes; the hellishness was what was required to settle up the country. "This country will develop—in time," a neighbor told Jules. "But not until the ground is soaked in misery and in blood." Sandoz's West, as exemplified in the Plains Niobrara subregion, thus took on the aspect of a war zone; the reader is plunged into the thick of the land boom when the scramble was most desperate. The violence was not valorized, Old West–style, ending in individual glory. It was a long, grinding conflict between the land-hungry—cattlemen versus settlers, settlers versus each other, while the conquered Lakotas looked on, bereft. As Jules retorted at one point in the fighting, "Like hell—it's the country of the poor man with a gun"—and, what he would never have added, of the poor women who lived under his roof.[39] In time, they had a fine farm with orchards, where he engaged in horticultural experiments.

CHAPTER TWO

Walking

Their identity seemed as lost as though they had never been; and when their resurrection came it was not to be remembered but recreated—not rediscovered but invented.

CHARLES F. LUMMIS, THE LAND OF POCO TIEMPO (1893)

Charles Lummis had to walk 3,507 miles to begin to see beyond the frontier myth. The distance between his starting point in Ohio and his destination in California was actually much shorter, but the route he took during that fall of 1884 was, appropriately, far from linear. It is true that Lummis was traveling west for a very conventional reason—a new job was awaiting him at the *Los Angeles Times*. His narrative of the trip, *A Tramp Across the Continent* (1892), was also full of dubious dime-novel episodes of macho action and peril, including a hand-to-paw altercation with a wounded mountain lion in Colorado. He gave a further tip of his hat to the frontier myth with some mention of being "outside the sorry fences of society." Nevertheless, there were aspects of Lummis's escapade that seem distinctly new and modern. The walk was an unabashed publicity stunt by a man who was on his way to becoming a tireless regional booster and self-promoter; the dispatches he sent to the *Times* along the way, later collected in *A Tramp*, were read nationwide. He could easily have made the journey by rail and written the usual travelogue. Instead, Lummis chose to walk for 143 days across mountains and deserts "purely 'for fun,'" he wrote. The West, especially the Southwest, became in his depiction a place to know such "physical joy" and "to have the mental awakening of new sights and experiences."[1]

What seems most genuine about *A Tramp* was this sense of Lummis's awakening to the region before him. White and Harvard-educated, he presented himself as a world-wise Yankee who was also a virile outdoorsman, an exemplar of the "strenuous life" well before TR coined the phrase. Lum-

44

mis was speaking to an increasing number of middle- and upper-class Americans who were embracing an emerging consumerist ethic of play and leisure, quite at odds with the producerist toil and sacrifice implicit in the agrarian frontier myth. Lummis reveled in the West and Southwest as a physical challenge, a temporary one taken on for sport (his enthusiasm wore a little thin in the Mojave Desert). Whether for tourism or more active recreation like hunting and fishing, the West was no longer to be seen simply as an expanse of free land for homesteaders but as a wonderland for visitors. Thomas Moran, Albert Bierstadt, and William Henry Jackson had been conveying the message in paint and photograph since the late 1860s, and railroads like the Atchison, Topeka, & Santa Fe (AT&SF) had begun touting attractions like the Grand Canyon at about the same time Lummis walked by. Honing his skills as Southwest booster par excellence, he did his part as well: "I shall not attempt to describe the Grand Cañon of the Colorado, for language cannot touch that utmost wonder of creation. There is but one thing to say: 'There it is; go see it for yourself.'"[2]

There was more to Lummis's awakening than his personal exploration of the dramatic natural landscapes of the Southwest. What predominated in his narrative were his encounters with the region's exotic *cultural* landscapes. "My eyes were beginning to open now to real insight of the things about me," he recalled, "and everything suddenly became invested with a wondrous interest." His first such encounter happened while walking south out of Colorado into New Mexico Territory—as he put it, "We stepped into a civilization that was then new to me": a Hispanic village. He admitted to then being "very suspicious of the people," but by the time he wrote *A Tramp*, several years of living among them in New Mexico had overthrown these notions. Even though his depiction of poor "simple" Hispanics retained a tinge of elitism, Lummis also offered a remarkable commentary for the early 1890s, a decade that nationally saw racism and nativism rise to a feverish and often violent pitch: "Why is it that the last and most difficult education seems to be the ridding ourselves of the silly inborn race prejudice? . . . The clearest thing in the world to him who has eyes and chance to use them, is that men everywhere—white men, brown men, yellow men, black men—are all just about the same thing. The difference is little deeper than the skin." Directly challenging the Anglo-centrism of the frontier myth, he noted of Hispanics in particular that "it would be a thorn to our conceit, if we could realize how very many important lessons we could profitably learn from them."[3]

This sentiment was redoubled with regard to the Pueblos, with whom Lummis—like many Anglo artists and intellectuals after him—fairly fell in love at his next cultural encounter. "It filled me with astonishment to find Indians who dwelt in such excellent houses. . . . Indians who were as industrious as any class in the country, and tilled pretty farms, and had churches of their own building, and who learned none of these things from us," he wrote.[4] The depth of Lummis's admiration was shown by the fact that he lived at Isleta Pueblo, recuperating from health problems, from 1888 to 1891, just prior to publishing *A Tramp*.

The egoistic Lummis always liked to claim precedence in the discovery and promotion of western and southwestern culture. There is no doubt that *A Tramp* and other works of his, including his editorship of the California-based magazine *Out West*, placed him at the nexus of a wide array of cultural activity whereby alternatives to the agrarian frontier myth and the Old West were being invented during the first decades of the twentieth century. For the Plains subregion, Willa Cather and Mari Sandoz were carrying this work forward from within the terms of frontier agrarianism. But in other major subregions of the West, particularly the Southwest and Mountain states, those terms became less and less relevant, though the generic Old West identity still hovered rootlessly over all. Lummis pointed the way to four alternative cultural fronts that emerged in the definition of the West and its subregions: the wilderness West, the urban West, the Hispanic West, and the Native American West. The first of these was quite nationalist in orientation and the most encompassing in geographical extent, spread across interconnected subregions from the Pacific Northwest and intermountain region down to the Mexican border, albeit perceptually centered on discrete famous places like the Grand Canyon, Yellowstone, and Yosemite. Similarly, the urban West was still confined in the public eye to two or three cities—Denver, San Francisco, and just emerging from its shadow, Lummis's destination of Los Angeles. But increasingly after the turn of the century, the urban West was perceived as the new national realm of opportunity and mobility, just as it had beckoned Lummis: no frontier farm for him—instead, a desk job downtown. The Hispanic and Native American Wests were localistic both spatially and ideologically, with their heartland in the Southwest—which dominated regionalist cultural production outside California—and extending into the scattered patches of land throughout the West later known as "Indian country." Their hold on mainstream American culture was, for the first three decades of the century, still largely limited to what Anglo devotees and promoters made of them.

Lummis's close ties with the tourist industry (*Out West* was originally a chamber of commerce magazine) emblematized the reciprocal relationship between many western regionalists and commercial interests. The connection was often less direct than in Lummis's case, comprising more the milieu in which regionalists worked. There is no question that railroad companies, hoteliers, and other corporate players had a very significant impact in forming the West's regional identities. On the other hand, these corporate entities were often appropriating and commercializing ideas and motifs originally created by explorers, artists, scientists, illustrators, travel writers, and other individuals seeking to make sense of their experiences in the West. That they were usually doing so at the behest of commercial magazine and book publishers made it less than a stretch for their creations to become regional advertisements, since they were already framed to appeal to a mass audience.

At least one major player in western tourism, the AT&SF Railroad, decided in the 1890s to eliminate the middle man, so to speak, and began hiring artists and intellectuals to create a marketable image of the Southwest for its passenger trade, including the famous Thomas Moran and Native American expert George Dorsey of the Field Museum of Natural History. Working in tandem with the AT&SF, the Fred Harvey Company, owner of the ubiquitous Harvey House restaurant chain, began selling Native American arts and crafts at such locations as Albuquerque and the Grand Canyon as early as 1902, well before the idea had occurred to the mavens of Santa Fe and Taos. Native American arts and crafts by then had already become a middle-class collectible, available for purchase at large eastern department stores. Even the notorious Snake Dance of the Hopis was packaged by the AT&SF as a regional tourist attraction.[5]

Yet it is worth noting that western regionalists like Lummis were institution builders as well, and at places like Santa Fe their museums, galleries, art colonies, restored historic sites, and other attractions frequently made them destinations for the tourists riding the railroads and staying in the hotels. As Lummis indicated with his frank disavowal of racial prejudice, regionalist artists and intellectuals could also go places culturally that commercial interests dared not. In this role as cultural radicals, they made some of their most important contributions to forming the regional identities of the West. The difference between corporate tourist promotion and regionalist cultural radicalism was the difference between Lummis' 3,507-mile publicity stunt and Mary Austin's "Walking Woman," as will be seen.

On April 24, 1903, Theodore Roosevelt presided at the cornerstone laying of a new gateway into Yellowstone National Park. In a brief speech he elaborated what were to be the main directions of conservation policy over the next two decades, of particular relevance to the westerners and tourists gathered there. "In this region of the Rocky Mountains and the great plains the problem of the water supply is the most important . . . and nothing is more essential to the preservation of the water supply than the preservation of the forests," he said. "Therefore this Park . . . is of the utmost advantage to the country around from the merely utilitarian side." But TR also hastened to point out that Yellowstone's primary purpose was "to be preserved as a beautiful natural playground." He himself was going camping with John Burroughs while at the park; later, on this same western trip, he was to camp with John Muir at Yosemite. "Here all the wild creatures of the old days are being preserved," TR vowed, so that the general public "will be able to insure to themselves and to their children and to their children's children much of the old-time pleasure of the hardy life of the wilderness . . . for all who have the love of adventure and the hardihood to take advantage of it." This future would only happen, he warned, by the people "assuming ownership in the name of the nation" and "jealously safeguarding and preserving the scenery, the forests, and the wild creatures." Roosevelt went on to praise the "essential democracy" of Yellowstone, and he declared that the government must continue "completing and perfecting an excellent system of driveways" within the park, like the new carriage road where he and his audience stood. Once these roads were finished, TR said, "we shall have a region as easy and accessible to travel . . . as any similar territory of the Alps or the Italian Riviera."[6]

Of the many ironies and contradictions that time later revealed in Roosevelt's words, one of the most glaring was his implicit critique of frontier individualism on behalf of saving some vestige of the frontier experience. When he spoke of the public "assuming ownership" and "jealously safeguarding" the natural wonders of Yellowstone, these were actions to be taken over and above the claims of private appropriation of western land. TR was treading lightly here for his local audience, but in an earlier fight to secure Yellowstone's boundaries, citizen Roosevelt had lambasted the "greed of a little group of speculators, careless of everything save their own selfish interests." Others in TR's circle were less restrained. His conservation lieutenant Gifford Pinchot, the chief forester of the United States, wrote frequently of the waste and short-sightedness of the "pioneer pillage of natural resources" and the moral imperative of the "fight for public rights." Surprisingly though, among the fiercest critics of rampant frontier individualism to emerge in this period was TR's fellow Old West monumentalist Emerson Hough. "Continually we make war upon the wilderness, its people, its creatures," Hough wrote in an article titled "The Wasteful West" (1905); "yet, having done so, we covet again the wilderness, yearn for it." In his most famous conservation essay, "The Slaughter of the Trees" (1908), Hough edged toward true cultural radicalism: "With our fatuous adulation of success, have we not encouraged these men in stealing the public domain?" he wondered. "We can continue to respect nothing but 'success,' no matter how unscrupulous it may be. Perhaps, after all, we do not care for any remedy. Perhaps, after all, we prefer to show the world that the American republic is a failure."[7]

Hough later retreated, as his 1920s novels show, but in his history *The Passing of the Frontier,* he found a way to reconcile his monumentalized frontier with the one where "our resources were grabbed and filched and sneaked and burglarized." Frontier freedom, it seemed, could produce not only upright, independent, incorruptible men, but also men who were "rough, course, brutal, murderous"—the individual "reverted to worse than savagery."[8] The government, unfortunately, had been sadly lax in reining in such men, which had led to much bloodshed as well as the squandering of the public domain. TR's conservation policies fell along these same moral lines. Just as there were "good trusts" and "bad trusts" in the corporate economy, there were good claimants and bad claimants to the West's public lands. TR sought more efficient exploitation of western resources, with a greater recognition (as he noted in his 1903 speech) of regional environmental interdependency; denuding hillsides in one area may affect water supplies elsewhere. For the legitimate claimant (including ranchers, farmers, loggers, miners, and others willing to pay some minimal fees, obtain leases, and otherwise submit to a modicum of rules), there was still plenty of public largesse to be had, including government-built irrigation works. The bad claimants were anyone who refused or evaded the new regime through theft, squatting, legal action, or lobbying their congressman.

While the Progressive reform window was open in the early 1900s, TR and Pinchot implemented these beginnings of a conservation land-use policy in the West, much compromised in practice, but at least a start. Their now underappreciated legacy included 90 million acres added to the forest reserves system, bringing the total to 150 million acres, virtually all of it in the West. Roosevelt also created several dozen federal bird sanctuaries nationwide (he was an expert and passionate birdwatcher), two preserves specifically for bison in Montana and Oklahoma, five new national parks (all in western states), and numerous national monuments, interpreting the Antiquities Act broadly to protect such natural sites as Muir Woods, Devil's Tower, and Mt. Olympus. The Grand Canyon, one of the jewels of the emerging system, went through a series of incarnations—forest reserve, national monument, game preserve—to increase its protected area before finally being designated a national park by TR's successor in 1910.[9]

Some have credited John Muir with stoking TR's interest in wilderness preservation, citing their 1903 campout together at Yosemite. But it is difficult to say who impressed whom more on that trip, and in any case TR already agreed with Muir that wild nature was a place for individual renewal. Muir showed in works such as *The Mountains of California* (1894) and *Our National Parks* (1901), which anchored the nascent literary canon of the wilderness West, that the frontier myth had no hold over him. He believed nature to be aglow with divine spirituality, and so could never quite countenance TR's enthusiasm for hunting. To TR, the parks and monuments existed essentially to provide a bracing simulation of frontier wilderness experience. They would become a "beautiful natural playground" for the masses, in the words of his 1903 speech, just as the frontier had once been the "great playground of young men" like himself, as Owen Wister wrote in *The Virginian*, published a few months earlier.[10]

There can be no doubt of the importance of national parks to the West's regional identity. The West—in actuality, a highly urbanized region—was to become "branded" as a natural wonderland by a particular set of emblematic landscapes, most of which were enclosed within parks, including Yellowstone's Old Faithful geyser, Yosemite Valley, the Grand Canyon, and somewhat later (thanks to filmmaker John Ford), Monument Valley. These park landscapes were among the most potent symbols of the nationalist West, projected to the rest of the country and the world as must-see embodiments of America's heritage. The railroads had begun this process of branding with Yellowstone, hoping to stir up some passenger trade, and their advertisements were important to forming the region's all-natural image in the public mind. Individual artists also played a role in this process over the years, most notably photographer Ansel Adams. Compelled by an explicitly preservationist agenda (he sat on the board of directors of Muir's Sierra Club for decades), Adams made his first attempt at iconizing Yosemite in the late 1920s. The whole thrust of his photographs, which updated the romantic sublime for a more modern sensibility, reinforced the wilderness West identity with a black-and-white, documentary concreteness.

Yet ironically, and despite TR's hopes for the parks as frontier simulacra, they were in fact quite artificial constructs. Congress ensured that most of the early parks and other protected areas were as small as needed to encompass their particular attractions, lest economically productive land might be precluded from development. Pinchot jealously guarded the turf of the USDA's Forest Service against the expansion of the Interior Department's high-profile parklands. Within these politically and bureaucratically determined boundaries, steps were often taken to remove certain blights on the "wild" scenery, such as grazing sheep and local Indians. From the point of view of Hispanic shepherds whose traditional commons were enclosed in forest reserves (as in New Mexico), or of Lakotas who saw sacred areas such as the Black Hills suffer the same fate, the heroic age of federal land conservation seemed like just another white Anglo land grab. It differed little whether the land was harvested of trees, leased to ranchers, or developed for tourists; *their* access to such places was dramatically altered or ended. It interfered with landscapes that were being composed for display as unspoiled nature.[11]

Especially in the case of the national parks, the display of wilderness could require extensive development. "Playground" was, after all, a good analogy. TR had inadvertently captured the contradiction in his 1903 address: some visitors might want to have their "hardihood" tested "just for fun" like Lummis, but most wanted to enjoy nature appreciation and outdoor recreation with the standard tourist conveniences, like in the Alps or the Riviera. After 1910, tourist convenience meant roads in the parks, lots of roads, particularly around the main attractions. Even in the pre-interstate era, the parks very quickly became *the* destinations for the public to try out their new automobiles. Muir had been famously sanguine about the prospect of traffic in the parks (he just wanted a happy parks constituency), but his chief intellectual heir to biocentric preservation, Aldo Leopold, perceived the basic disjunction between roads and true wilderness experience.

During the 1910s and early 1920s, Leopold was working in the Southwest for the Forest Service, primarily in New Mexico. In a landmark 1921 article for the *Journal of Forestry*, "The Wilderness and Its Place in Forest Recreational Policy," he proposed a new land-use unit, the "wilderness area." Leopold noted that "the Parks are being networked with roads and trails as rapidly as possible." In the popular sporting magazines, "lamentations over this or that favorite vacation ground being 'spoiled by tourists' are becoming more and more frequent." The pressing issue was to find some "reconciliation between getting back to nature and preserving a little nature to get back to," he asserted. For his readers (and indirectly, his superiors at the Forest Service) Leopold envisioned an "actual example" of what he called the "highest use" of forest system land. The Southwest, he observed, was a "distinct region," its wilderness important historically and possessing a "high and varied recreational value." In his opinion, "a big sample of it should be preserved" as a wilderness area: the half million acres comprising "the headwaters of the Gila River on the Gila National Forest" in southwestern New Mexico. This "semi-virgin" subregion had not been "penetrated by railroads," he wrote, "and to only a very limited extent by roads." The area included cattle ranches, but Leopold saw them as an "asset from the recreational standpoint because of the interest which attaches to cattle grazing operations under frontier conditions." A roadless protected wilderness area would prevent both "new settlers" as well as the "hordes of motorists." Here, in other words, was as close to a facsimile of Roosevelt and Wister's Old West as was likely to be found anywhere. Always on the lookout for opportunities to steal the Park Service's thunder, Leopold's superiors at the Forest Service approved his plan in 1924, and 755,000 acres of the Gila National Forest became the first officially designated wilderness area in the United States.[12]

In 1931, the Forest Service built a road across it.

Such a compulsion emanated ultimately from the urban West, whether as an expression of the consumer culture of convenience or as infrastructure of the resource stream feeding city growth. In any case, frontier and wilderness must recede from view. For several decades up to the 1920s, the West had urbanized at a faster rate than the rest of the nation, a trend fueled by oil and mining booms, railroads, agricultural expansion, and real estate speculation. Riding on a train across rustic Indian Territory in 1904, German sociologist Max Weber—in the United States to deliver a paper on contemporary rural society—could see with his own eyes the consequences of urban growth for the hinterlands. His conclusion? Rural society, in the sense of an ancient, inherited, local entity "separate from the urban social community, does not exist at the present time in a great part of the modern civilized world." Outside his train window, it became obvious to Weber that "the virgin forest's hour has struck even here," as he wrote home in a letter. Everywhere he looked, he saw "old Indian romanticism blend with the most modern capitalistic culture." Some "genuine old log cabins" of Native Americans passed by, as did some "quite modern wooden houses from the factory." Rolling onward through mile after mile of "veritable virgin forest" in an "utterly wild state," his train approached a town, "and suddenly," Weber noted, "one begins to smell petroleum." The boomtowns of Indian Territory, with their "fabulous bustle," were something new to him, each "really a crazy thing" hewn out of the raw countryside,

"Eiffel Tower-like" derricks towering over the shacks of oilfield workers, but each already featuring "a power plant, a telephone network . . . electrical railways under construction," and all of it spreading into the "unbounded distance." This disequilibrium of boomtowns, virgin forest, and folk culture was a curious historical spectacle, Weber reflected, though one that could not last: "With almost lightning speed everything that stands in the way of capitalistic culture is being crushed."[13]

Apparently, things looked different from the behind the wheel of an automobile, especially if the driver were a correspondent for *Sunset*, the "magazine of western living." In a 1915 article titled "Motorizing the Frontier," Randall R. Howard declared: "The automobile must answer the charge of destroying our old-time picture of the frontier—but nobody save the fiction writers will ever waste a breath of regret." (The same issue featured a photograph of James Earl Fraser's sculpture of an exhausted Indian and his mount, "The End of the Trail.") The very transformation that Weber deplored and Leopold had sought to mitigate through land-use planning—the ubiquity of urban influence in the West—had "verily given a new life outlook" to the people of the "railroadless" rural hinterlands, according to Howard, a whole set of urban expectations regarding quality of life. Surveying the previous half century, a 1933 government report on recent social trends called this one "metropolitanization," which recognized that the city should be understood "not only as an agglomeration of people but as a way of living." The automobile, which country folk purchased at a higher rate than city dwellers, was one of the principal agents of the metropolitan pattern by which the "large city . . . brought under its sway much territory that was formerly rural." As a consequence, the report noted, "Smaller communities within a wide radius of every urban center have lost much of their former isolation, provincialism and independence."[14]

Yet if the tropes of the vanishing Indian or the closing frontier might make good copy for an article or a letter home, the urban West was no new-fangled novelty invading the countryside, but an integral part of the region's historical development. A key factor was the "trade area," defined as the "surrounding geographical territory economically tributary to a city and for which such city provides the chief market and financial center," as a federal official put it in 1931. Urban boosters in the West had long touted their towns and cities as seats of these subregional trade areas with identities all their own, like the "Inland Empire" centered on Spokane, Washington. By marketing the rich homesteading opportunities in their subregion, they simultaneously improved the prospects for their city. Greeley, Colorado, settled initially as a utopian colony, was a literal manifestation of this supposed town-and-country integration, requiring its original residents to own town lots with adjoining farm acreages. The more conventional trade area, which could extend across state boundaries and encompass thousands of square miles, remained an enduring means of subregion formation in the West, with larger cities like Denver or Dallas pulling smaller towns and rural populations into their orbits. Along with tourism and advertising, it was another way capitalist economic activity—and not just art or folk culture—could generate varieties of regionalism.[15]

But as many forms of employment and leisure became more urban-oriented by the turn of the century, the city itself and the lifestyle it offered came to be more and more the focus of boosterism, especially for the larger urban centers. Magazines like *Sunset* were devoted to disseminating images of this mode of "western living," defined not in terms of the homestead but of the suburb or vacation home of the American "good life" as it might be lived in places like California, which was good indeed. Utopian hyperbole was hardly limited to outright experiments like the community of Greeley. The technological mastery over nature embodied in the urban West's emerging water infrastructure seemed to herald Powell's new phase of civilization, but delivered to affluent urban households rather than the farms of "little men."

Expressions of this "California dream" could be found, for example, in "The Home in the West," a regular *Sunset* department usually written by women contributors. A typical column featured topics such as "Beauty in Garden Pools." California was a land where "the rain forgets to fall," Elizabeth Elkins noted, but "I have heard a traveler say that nowhere else has he heard and seen so much water as in California where it is up to man to show Nature that he is really no sufferer by this whim of hers."[16] Many other early twentieth-century articles and advertisements offered similar paeans to the West's wonderful climate, depicting the possibility of a truly singular and rarefied existence there—Josiah Royce's works among them. Before he delivered his "Provincialism" address, Royce had spoken to the National Geographic Society in 1898 on what he called the "psychology" of the Pacific Coast, but which was virtually an ontology of the California lifestyle. There the "union of the man and the visible universe is free, is entirely unchecked by any hostility on the part of nature," he wrote. There one could expect "a regularity of existence, a definite reward for a definitely planned deed," Royce argued. "All this is encouraging to a kind of harmonious individuality that already tends in the best instances toward a somewhat Hellenic type."[17]

Lesser minds bent on mere promotion easily followed Royce's lead (which, after all, was mostly rhetorical; Royce himself did not see fit to live in his home state). A 1915 *Sunset* account of a grand modern-style house, for example, rhapsodized over the way the interior walls reflected the "many hues of a California evening sky. At no two hours of the day are these walls alike in color, nor to the eyes of any two people. It is like living in the heart of a shell." This comfortable, effortless, aestheticized lifestyle, close to benign nature, could be yours for a price. Though relatively few could afford the custom version, cheaper copies were within reach of the masses, or so social critic Herbert Croly observed in a 1906 *Sunset* article analyzing California's suburban architecture—following page after page of real estate advertisements. He praised the "ranch houses" and the "little bungalows" because they were "admirably adapted to the Californian climate; they are within means of all but actually poor and over-worked people"; and they could be sited on an "inexhaustible number of charming spots both on the sea-coast and in the hills and mountains." Three decades later, John Steinbeck brilliantly invoked this California idyll in *The Grapes of Wrath* (1939) to lure farm folk like the unsuspecting Joads from the hardscrabble Plains, where the weather was not so nice.[18]

Croly predicted that "during the next few decades," suburban ranch houses and bungalows near Los Angeles and San Francisco would "undoubtedly increase prodigiously in number." The timeframe for prodigious urbanization was actually much shorter than he realized. In the year that Croly published his article, the population of Los Angeles County was an estimated 350,000. A decade and a half later, in 1922, the figure stood at 1.2 million and counting; by 1930 the population had grown by another million—into the "unbounded distance," as Weber had put it. The idyll posited an "inexhaustible" amount of land, but by 1920, as cities in the West and throughout America sought to cope with the growth and disorder that spiked with World War I, the idyll was found wanting, including in vast jurisdictions like the 4,000 square miles of Los Angeles County. Between 1919 and 1921, a number of states in the West, including Texas, Kansas, and Nebraska, authorized cities to adopt zoning ordinances for the first time, and zoning remained the principal (albeit inadequate) means of regulating urban growth in most cities for decades thereafter. Several large cities around the country, including Boston, San Francisco, and Los Angeles itself, already possessed city planning agencies in some form by the early 1920s. But in Los Angeles, as local planning advocate G. Gordon Whitnall noted, "The city planning commission soon found that its plans would be inadequate to meet the needs of the future, because the city of Los Angeles would be but a small part of the metropolis of the future." The special case of Los Angeles County needed something more. Already in the early 1920s the metropolitan portion of the county encompassed 1,200 square miles, including forty-one cities and more than fifty unincorporated towns. In 1922, Whitnall presented the board of supervisors with a "Declaration of Inter-dependence" issued by a recent conference of the county's cities, and thus was born the Los Angeles County Regional Planning Commission, the nation's first.[19]

At a 1924 national meeting of planners, Whitnall's hand-picked choice as first director of the commission, Hugh R. Pomeroy, described the ethos behind their efforts. His words evoked the civic dimension of Royce's provincialism while anticipating many of the concerns that animated a more famous initiative in metropolitan planning at Portland, Oregon, half a century later. "Regional planning is based upon the conception of inter-community interest, or metropolitan unity," Pomeroy wrote. "In its larger conception Regional Planning is a function of citizenship as well as of governmental authority." His commission recognized early on that "the ultimate secure foundation for the work is in an enlightened and forward-looking public consciousness." The "work" must involve, literally, "the County as a whole": "The hillside residence areas . . . the commercial centers, metropolitan subnuclei, as it were, with supporting residential development; the industrial districts . . . the retreating frontier of agriculture, with the County still first in the nation in the value of agricultural products." Pomeroy declared, "The highest development of each is the purpose of regional zoning," along with the "provision of transportation and of open spaces."[20]

Clues as to why Pomeroy's words were more visionary than predictive were to be found in the same address. From the outset, the commission was faced with "rapid turn-over of real estate under the present market conditions." On assuming "the work," the commissioners were immediately overwhelmed, trying to lay out highways and sewer lines through a tangle of hundreds of proposed subdivisions and otherwise keep up with "subdividers" who were in the habit of selling lots before filing plats. As a later history of city planning noted, despite the county regional planning commission, more than 250,000 random vacant lots were left behind at the end of the 1920s as testimony of the chaotic growth of greater Los Angeles. What seemed a pleasant surprise to Pomeroy was the level of cooperation he received from the subdividers, perhaps because "whatever evils may be charged to the high rate of subdivision, it has done much in carrying forward the Regional highway plan." If regional planning concerned itself with "problems that are greater in extent than the mere man-made boundary lines of a political entity," as Whitnall said in his own presentation to the 1924 conference, there was also this thin line between *regulating* and *regularizing* growth.[21] "Subdivider" should have been an antonym for "regionalist," but in places like Los Angeles, all too often it was not.

Whitnall and Pomeroy were quite content with regionalism as a tool of liberal-capitalist expansion. Flying over the county in a plane at 12,000 feet to visualize the region's "inherent unity," all that Whitnall saw was growth and prospects for growth. "We know where the reservoirs of population are," he noted, and where the "topographical restrictions" were that would determine "where the great flow of population must occur." He could see where communities were "encroaching on each other," and where, in time, they would "continue to merge, so that finally they would be one." Just as the commission's regional highway plan smoothed the way for more subdivisions, so the commission was intended to bring about an "amalgamation of political units that heretofore had been at each other's throats," Whitnall hoped. In the end, the commission was about as successful at achieving this "inherent unity" as it was in abating the "evils" of the "high rate of subdivision." In Whitnall's words, "This is our regional ambition for Southern California."[22]

Others had more radical aspirations for regionalism, seeking to ground it in two of the West's minority cultures. As regional identities, the Hispanic West and the Native American West proved to be a tougher sell than the West as wilderness wonderland and the glamorized urban West. The wilderness West played to already widely accepted nationalist myths about the region's exceptional freedom and epic scale. The urban West fed off of fantasies of mobility and consumer abundance. The Hispanic as well as the Native American West, in contrast, required white Americans to begin to yield their deeply ingrained racism and ethnocentrism, and the extent to which these attitudes budged during this period is debatable. The decades before World War II were some of the most virulently nativist and racist in the country's history, featuring immigration restriction, widespread lynchings, horrific race riots (such as at Tulsa in 1921), and the rise of the modern Ku Klux Klan, which had active chapters across the West, from Oklahoma to Oregon.

Among those who condemned these expressions of racial violence and hatred, and who were sympathetic to the plight of racial and ethnic minorities, tacit assumptions of racial inferiority often persisted. The so-called friends of the Indian, for example, took it as a given that Native Americans must give up their ways of life to join the white mainstream.

This prescription was legitimized by the cultural evolution theories of Lewis Henry Morgan, which were adhered to by many western regionalists of this earlier generation, including Powell and Turner. In this view, Anglo-Saxon civilization represented the apex of human progress, but less advanced races might move up the scale by abandoning their backward ways—languages, religions, economies.[23] Those regionalists who admired and empathized with minority cultures convinced themselves that acculturation (voluntary or involuntary) meant survival. They lamented the "inevitable" disappearance of what they deemed to be the defining characteristics of "folk" cultures: preindustrial, handcraft-based, oral, communal, pious.

While Morgan's anthropology held sway, another, more modern view of cultural difference and diversity began to challenge it. This intellectual revolution is most readily traced to the influential Columbia University anthropologist Franz Boas. After living many months with the Inuit of Baffin Island during a field trip in the mid-1880s, Boas had concluded that the more he saw of their way of life, the more he realized that "we have no right to look down upon them." As he later put it, "Anthropology teaches better than any other science the relativity of the values of civilization." Cultures were not to be considered superior or inferior to one another, only different. As compelling as this nascent multiculturalism was, scholars in recent years have realized that as it came to be practiced by scientists, artists, and other intellectuals, it was still permeated by an implicit ethnocentrism: whites in positions of cultural power and authority treating other cultures as objects of study, determining how they would be interpreted to the dominant society, and expropriating their values and products to do so. It made cultures into collectibles. Of course, this form of cultural domination had been true as well of Morgan's anthropology, but under Boasian relativism, its presence was obscured.[24]

Many western regionalists who appointed themselves as interpreters of Hispanic and Native American cultures fell on a continuum between the evolutionary and relativist viewpoints. In accord with the former, they depicted Hispanics and Native Americans as simple, primitive folk living by traditional and ancient ways. But they also found much to admire in those cultures, much that they considered to be superior to "advanced" society. Even John Wesley Powell, thoroughly schooled in Morgan's theories, could get carried away in his enthusiasm. There is no reason to doubt his sincerity when he said of the "red man" at a public forum in 1882, "I love him as one of my own kind."[25]

Like Powell, Lummis had long periods of intimate contact with Native

Americans and Hispanics during his years living at Isleta Pueblo, and the experience may have affected him personally in ways similar to Boas among the Inuit. He became a collaborator with another Morgan disciple, archaeologist Adolph Bandelier, who instructed Lummis in the antiquity and diversity of Hispanic and Native American cultures not only in the American Southwest but abroad on an 1892 expedition to South America. Consciousness raised, Lummis decried against "race prejudice" at a time when it was hardly fashionable, certainly among the white middle-brow readers in his audience. It is also true that Lummis was a notoriously obsessive collector of southwestern artifacts (founding his own personal museum) and posed as the chief spokesperson on the region and its cultures. For all of these shortcomings, there still remains the positive side to what Lummis and others like him accomplished in seeking to legitimize Hispanics and Native Americans to whites as distinctive, cultured peoples rather than peons and savages. Lummis once told Bandelier of his plans to popularize his friend's discoveries quite deliberately as part of a civic religion: "With your leave, I am going to make it my part in this, to say to the World: Lookee! Don't be scared! . . . All these Ologies are only the Story of Man—the story of you and me. . . . A million Americans will understand where one understands now. . . . It will become part of the consciousness of America."[26]

The cultural radicalism of Lummis and other modern western regionalists becomes apparent in contrast to more stereotypical accounts of the Hispanic West, such as *California Pastoral* (1888) by H. H. Bancroft, the grand old man of western history. Bancroft's point of departure was a withering (and often racist) indictment of the Spanish conquest in Latin America, before taking up the story of pre–Gold Rush California. There nature had created a "Lotos-land" where people were "ignorant" and "lazy," the ruling class "foolish, improvident" and "incapable." The Native American's status was "practically that of a slave," and near the missions there was a "mortality among the Indians . . . perhaps unequalled in any country." Nevertheless, almost in spite of themselves, Bancroft wrote, "it would be difficult to find in any age or place, a community that got more out of life, and with less trouble, with less wear and wickedness, than the people of Pastoral California." In fact, a surprising ambivalence pervades Bancroft's book, as if he could not quite bring himself to depict California as anything but the most exceptional part of exceptionalistic America, where the very horrors of Spanish colonialism could be modulated to mellowness. "Golden Age" or not, however, cultural evolution decreed that the Californios' regime must pass: "As the savages faded before the superior

Mexicans," Bancroft concluded, "so faded the Mexicans before the superior Americans."[27]

Lummis, in comparison, dispensed with ambivalence and racial determinism altogether, adopting an aggressively revisionist tone in his 1893 work, *The Spanish Pioneers*. "That we have not given justice to the Spanish Pioneers is simply because we have been misled" and, at bottom, because of "race prejudice," he asserted. Far from being lazy and improvident, the Spanish "had already discovered, conquered, and partly colonized inland America from Kansas to Buenos Aires, and from ocean to ocean," by the time the English founded Jamestown. "Hundreds of Spanish towns had been built; Spanish schools, universities, printing-presses, books, and churches were beginning their work of enlightenment in the dark continents of America." As for their treatment of Native Americans, Lummis considered the case of New Mexico, and he rejected the depiction that the Spanish had "enslaved the Pueblos, or any other Indians of New Mexico; that they forced them to choose between Christianity and death; that they made them work in the mines, and the like,—all are entirely untrue." Spanish legislation with regard to Native Americans was "incomparably . . . more humane than that of Great Britain, the Colonies, and the present United States all combined." The entire Spanish colonial enterprise was marked by a "humane and progressive spirit," according to Lummis.[28]

Statements such as these were more propaganda than history ("No, Cortez was not cruel to the Indians"). By framing the story hemispherically, Lummis was able to obscure the role of Mexicans and foreground the more ethnically acceptable Spanish for his white Anglo readers—what became common rhetorical strategy during the first several decades of the Hispanic colonial revival. At best one can say that in overinflating Spanish achievements, Lummis challenged the Anglo-centric tenets of cultural evolution, which pointed progress always in the direction of the American successors. But as history, what he was describing had no more relation to reality than such clearly utopian constructions as "El Pueblo de Las Uvas," the paean to Hispanic symbiotic communalism written by Mary Austin, his principal rival as chief interpreter of the Southwest: "Where it lies, how to come at it, you will not get from me."[29]

The Hispanic West, in short, like the agrarian West and the wilderness West, was an unself-conscious creation of myth and idealization, though no less compelling and evocative for being so. The burgeoning appeal of this romanticized Hispanic heritage was most clearly shown by the phenomenal popularity of Helen Hunt Jackson's novel *Ramona* (1884), which generated a cult following, if not its own culture industry. At last count, the book was in its 200th printing. Its romantic subplot involving Alessandro and Ramona—doomed under literary clichés, as with everything Spanish—seized readers' imaginations nationwide. They came in droves to California to seek out locations and people mentioned in the novel, remnants of the "half barbaric, half elegant, wholly generous and free-handed life" that Jackson depicted.[30] Most important for California and southwestern regionalism, *Ramona* laid the popular groundwork for efforts to preserve California's Spanish colonial mission buildings (Jackson's intention had actually been to save California's Mission *Indians*, but her audience had their own ideas).

The mission preservation campaign was initially brought to fruition by Lummis. The Landmarks Club, founded by Lummis at Los Angeles in 1895 and publicized in *Out West*, raised funds to preserve or restore several of the twenty-one missions, including San Juan Capistrano and San Diego. By 1903, Lummis and the Landmarks Club were also advocating for El Camino Real, a signature highway to link all of the missions running several hundred miles between northern and southern California, complete with iconic mission bell signs at almost every mile. Further ramifying across the built landscape, the Mission style of architecture also caught hold regionally during these years, first representing California at the 1893 World's Columbian Exposition in Chicago and later displayed on a grander scale with Bertram Grosvenor Goodhue's monumental towers and pavilions at the California-Panama Exposition in 1915. Goodhue's quaint buildings housed extensive Native American anthropological displays alongside the usual industrial wonders (not to mention the fact that the fair marked the opening of the Panama Canal), so the explicit message was once again of evolutionary progress: a benevolent and very modern American empire succeeding the long-lost splendor of imperial Spain (this amorphous identity again carefully obfuscating the place of Mexicans and Mexican Americans in California, past and present).[31] Eventually the sheer ubiquity of Mission and "Spanish" style architecture—not to mention the demographics of the Southwest—called into question how complete the "succession" had been, and whether all things Anglo-American necessarily signified progress.

The Anglo enthusiasm for the Hispanic West spread further still beyond California by the early 1910s, particularly at its other principal axis, Santa Fe. Coinciding with the civic self-awareness of statehood (1912), a cluster of region-building institutions was established in the capital city in the surrounding decade, including the School of American Archeology, the Museum of Fine Arts, and, most significant, the Museum of New Mexico under Edgar L. Hewett, a cultural entrepreneur and organizer of a similar stripe to Lummis. Museum staff were instrumental in first defining a distinctive Santa Fe or New Mexico Mission style of adobe architecture, consciously differentiating it from the California variety to convey northern New Mexico's unique sense of place. Ironically, though, the first major application of the style—to the renowned Palace of the Governors during its "restoration"—was largely a matter of invention; there were no images of the centuries-old palace in its "original" condition before late-nineteenth-century Anglo additions. In the same vein, folklorist Aurelio Espinosa at this time strove to construct an exclusively Spanish colonial (as opposed to a Mexican or *mestizo*) folk tradition for northern New Mexico, arguing in works such as *Studies in New Mexican Spanish* (1909) that the "sources of New Mexican Spanish are to be found in the Spanish of the XVth and XVIth centuries," especially the Castilian dialect.[32]

By the 1920s, Mary Austin and other Anglo artists and intellectuals in residence made it their business to preserve and promote what they delimited as New Mexico's Spanish colonial aesthetic, founding the Spanish Colonial Arts Society in 1924. Alarmed by unscrupulous antiquities dealers who scoured nearby villages for lucrative marks, the society raised funds to restore a number of historic churches and missions across the state, including $5,000 by member Willa Cather for the cloister at Acoma, a location featured in her novel *Death Comes for the Archbishop* (1927). Some scholars have criticized the Anglo-dominated society for imposing its romanticized aesthetic standards on the larger community, but in one instance at least, local Hispanic parishioners in the town of Cordoba were happy to have the society weigh in to prevent their priest from modernizing the adobe architecture of their church. In hopes of not merely preserving but perpetuating the Hispanic colonial aesthetic tradition, the society also established classes and studios for local aspiring artists, as well as a "Shop of Spanish Arts" where Santa Fe's ever-growing stream of tourists could buy wares marketed for their authenticity.[33]

In parallel with the greater popular acceptance of a Hispanic-themed West (at least if non-Mexican and consigned to a mythic golden past), the legitimacy of Hispanic culture as academic subject matter also grew during the 1910s and 1920s. Colorado-born Aurelio Espinosa, with positions at Stanford University and the *Journal of American Folk Lore*, was one of the leaders of this effort. But the work of Berkeley historian Herbert Bolton during this period had perhaps the greatest long-term impact on how the Hispanic West was conceived as a region. Like his former teacher Frederick Jackson Turner, Bolton challenged what he saw as the parochial version of US history written by New Englanders "almost solely from the standpoint of the East and of the English colonies." As early as 1902, he discovered a treasure trove of documents in the national archives of Mexico related to "territory just on the other side of the border and closely associated with the United States frontier," as he wrote in a 1908 article. In "The Mission as a Frontier Institution in the Spanish American Colonies" (1915), Bolton not so subtly began reorienting the map of American frontier history from a strictly westward to a more complex south–north orientation. Readers should think of the Southwest as part of the "northern provinces, from Sinaloa to Texas, from Florida to California." Ultimately, in *The Spanish Borderlands* (1921), this subregion—and a whole new field of study—got its name. Here he made his argument still more daring: we should reconceive an arc of present states from Florida to California as "Hispanic regions now in Anglo-American hands." The Southwest, he wrote, was to be considered "as Spanish in color and historical background as New England is Puritan."[34]

The borderlands subregion concept was not only a localist but also a transnationalist corrective to the faux national history that traced the country's origins to Plymouth Rock. This was a central contention of Bolton's sweeping and controversial hemispheric manifesto, "The Epic of Greater America," his 1932 presidential address to the American Historical Association (convened in Toronto) that was still being debated thirty years later. At the time of his AHA address, Bolton was teaching a course on the subject twice weekly to a thousand Berkeley undergraduates. "Western North America was . . . largely a matter of frontiersmen and international politics," he declared. "The spoils to be divided were the Spanish borderlands and the open spaces of the Great West and Northwest." The process created two "border zones" relative to British America and Spanish America, zones that were not only the "crux of international relations" but also areas of cultural influence, quite as significant as that of the isolated frontier." This insight—that "borderland zones are vital not only in the determination of international relations, but also in the development of culture"—retained its resonance over the next several decades and arguably became the heart of so-called borderland studies, an ongoing if modest academic franchise that blossomed into a hot topic by the 1980s.[35]

It was very much to Bolton's credit that he used the platform of the AHA presidency to publicize these ideas, above all that the Southwest borderlands revealed "Saxon and Hispanic America . . . inextricably linked together." The great failure of his major writings, true also of Turner and

Webb, was to ignore the contribution—and plight—of the many other "nations" present in the imperial borderlands—Native Americans. Filtered through Bolton's narratives of Hispanic frontiers, these were reduced to the "Indian problem," requiring policies, presidios, and missionaries, such things as left traces in the archives. As Bolton himself might say, "Here again the story has been distorted through a provincial view of history."[36]

There remained, then, still other vantage points from which to conceive the West, further outside the bounds of the frontier myth. Here it is worth pausing to consider that in seeking to walk beyond the frontier myth, western regionalists were entering a wilderness of another sort, an intellectual wilderness where there were few landmarks or signposts. The many regionalist expressions of the wilderness West and the Hispanic West, like Hough's frontier critique or Bolton's borderlands concept, had broken in on and questioned the racially hallowed nationalist West otherwise known as the "white man's country," along with the various orthodoxies it entailed: a providential god; a beneficent, limitless nature; historical progress; white Anglo-Saxon supremacy; boundless freedom and opportunity; patriarchy. The Old West culture industry still set its adventures there, to be sure, and continued to replay them for appreciative audiences. Politicians down to Ronald Reagan's time could spend an entire career there. But like the settlers who pulled up stakes during the Plains bust, western regionalists from the 1890s onward had to reckon with a more disturbing and less certain world even as they tried their luck elsewhere than the white man's country. Darwinism, Boasianism, philosophical pragmatism, the theory of relativity, Freudian psychology, the epic carnage of World War I—these and other intellectual bombshells undermined the old verities and also threw into doubt whether there could be any new permanent basis for certainty. Was the world truly knowable by the self? Without moral absolutes, how could individuals relate to one another? Where could the individual find meaning and direction in a universe ruled by chance? The specter that was dreaded, as Royce and others had envisioned, was a society of atomized, isolated individuals with no higher purpose, driven by mindless appetites and instincts, susceptible to mass conformity and hysteria.

Thus when Walter Prescott Webb railed against the iconoclastic "Mencken crowd" and the "Nietzschean" viewpoint, for example, or when Cather famously said that the "world broke in two" somewhere around 1922, they were giving voice to a general sense of cultural crisis.[37] This very sense of crisis and uncertainty, engulfing artists and intellectuals not merely in the American West but the western world as a whole, drove some, like Webb or Theodore Roosevelt, to try to monumentalize the white man's country and save some scraps of the frontier, and it brought more and more Americans to visit these touchstones of national memory. But other regionalists were seeking alternatives, new grounds of value and belief, in wild nature and in traditional Hispanic and Native American cultures, although it was feared that these were in danger of disappearing as the rate of change accelerated. Among these alternatives, Native American cultures seemed to offer the most radical departure from the white man's country, as well as (to their admirers) the greatest promise for reconstructing mainstream culture on wholly new terms. The most ancient cultures of the West, as construed by an array of artists and intellectuals from the 1900s to the 1930s, became the most avant-garde. Rather than the "Indian problem," they were the "Indian solution."

Perhaps no other western regionalist of this earlier generation more clearly articulated the cultural crisis—and its promise—than Mary Austin. In the late 1880s she had been a frontierswoman in the literal sense, leaving her Illinois birthplace and skipping over the Plains land boom to have a try at another one going on in the California outback. While riding a horse out to her family's claim in the Tejon area of the San Joaquin Valley, Austin first felt the full force of California's "indescribably awesome" landscape. This encounter began a profound attachment to place that survived many personal vicissitudes, including a developmentally disabled daughter, farm failures, and an unhappy marriage to a luckless land promoter, who went bust in the infamous Owens Valley water grab.[38] Much like what happened to Hamlin Garland, this particular personal experience left Austin disenchanted with the frontier myth, but unlike him, she did not double back to it after testing the cultural radicalism that lay beyond.

Instead, Austin embraced what she called the country of "Lost Borders," in actuality the Inyo subregion encompassing Death Valley and in metaphor the modernist void that was both "terribly disconcerting" and liberating at the same time: "Out there, then, where the law and the landmarks fail together, the souls of little men fade out at the edge," she wrote in *Lost Borders* (1909). "Out there where the borders of conscience break down, where there is no convention, and behavior is of little account . . . almost anything might happen; does happen, in fact." To convey this modern state of being, Austin personified and genderized the quest for meaning in the form of her greatest fictional creation, the Walking Woman, nameless like Wister's Virginian, and to Austin just as heroic. The Walking Woman lived outside the "frame of behavior called ladylike" according to her own rules, wandering randomly and endlessly through the desert, "in and about the haunts of rude and solitary men" as she desired. Though she appeared eccentric to the outside world ("a twist all through her"), the Walking Woman could only be understood within her own frame of reference; there was no fixed standard from which she could be judged. The Walking Woman was fully content, at home in the desert, symbiotic with it—as Austin concluded, "the track of her two feet bore evenly and white" in the sand.[39] Oneness between the self and the world was possible, in other words, but it required a free self-creative quest without end.

Like the Walking Woman, Austin "began to find herself, after the period of worry and loss in which her wandering began," in the course of writing her acclaimed first book, *The Land of Little Rain* (1903), while her husband was away hatching doomed irrigation schemes. The forbidding Inyo landscape where she then resided, situated spectacularly between the Sierra Nevada and Death Valley, as well as her own stressful family situation, put some distance between her life as lived and the reigning myth of California as a "new Eden." *Little Rain* not only presented a series of refutations of such myths, it also offered a way out of the cultural crisis. "Desert is a loose term to indicate land that supports no man," she noted in contrast to Powell's utilitarian definition of aridity, but "void of life it never is, however dry the air and villainous the soil." She seemed to revel in the idea that there might be land that could not be "bitted and broken," a biocentrism that must have been cold comfort for her family's economic situation.[40] Yet there was more at play in this vantage point: Austin was trying to imagine the western environment outside the folly of the white androcentric imperative of domination.

Appropriately, rather than drawing maps—one of the visual props of imperialism—Austin in this book narrowed the scale of region to a viewshed, a neighborhood, a place familiar to the perceptions of daily life. At this scale, the range and depth of regional meanings and associations multiplied, like Thoreau's at Walden Pond. In "My Neighbor's Field," Austin explored an attachment to place that transcended actual ownership, so dear to agrarian republican manhood. A succession of owners had contended for the field, now untended and weedy, but to Austin's mind, "all this human occupancy of greed and mischief had left no mark"—what was significant for her were the Indian and animal trails, and the redemptive "retaking of old ground by the wild plants." Erasing the sad history of Anglo occupation, Austin arrived in the borderlands metaphorically long before Bolton found a name for them. She offered an alternative, utopian vision of small-scale communal life in symbiotic harmony with its environment in "The Little Town of the Grape Vines," a place rooted in the "good customs brought out of Old Mexico or bred in a lotus-eating land." Even though El Pueblo de Las Uvas employed "headgates that dam up the creek for the village weirs," its agriculture melds with nature—"Wild vines that begin among the willows lap over to the orchard rows." In town, "every house is a piece of earth," Austin remarked, and the people there were "earth-born."[41] She had a faith, which grew over the following three decades, that from such remote western enclaves of folk values (real or imaginary), a rejuvenation of modern American culture might flow.

First and foremost, Austin looked to Native Americans to provide this wellspring. As she later wrote in *The American Rhythm* (1930): "All this time there was an American race singing in tune with the beloved environment." Austin had sought out the medicine men and women among the Paiutes and Shoshones who lived in her vicinity during her years in the Inyo country (which incidentally was adjacent to the home of Wovoka, prophet of the Ghost Dance movement, subsiding just as she arrived in the area). In time Austin came to believe that she herself possessed shamanistic powers, a special insight into Native American cultures and spirituality. The bridge she sought to forge between cultures was essentially aesthetic. She had come to California in 1888 already looking on the world as literary material, an attitude that no doubt made her ordeal more bearable. As she posited famously in *Land of Little Rain*, to aestheticize one's existence was a survival strategy, a way to endure. "Seyavi made baskets for love and sold them for money," she wrote. "Every Indian woman is an artist."[42]

This notion that Native Americans lived their lives as if they were works of art gained increasing resonance among western regionalists, especially those who, like Austin, moved to Santa Fe or Taos and took the Pueblos' culture as their standard. Self-expression within a set of shared aesthetic traditions seemed a way to achieve the elusive balance between individualism and community. An aesthetic engagement with the world—emotive, creative, spiritual—promised to bind the isolated self to external reality. Work, play, religion, place, and all other aspects of Native American life were integrated, it was believed, all inextricably bound to ancient traditions miraculously and tenuously held over into the twentieth century. These assumptions about Native American cultures reflected as much on the cultural and psychological needs of Austin and other white Anglo admirers as they did on Native Americans themselves. Life as art seemed a way to sustain the constant self-creation (modeled by the Walking Woman) for flourishing in a world of chance and change.

Some critics have depicted Austin, her friend Mabel Dodge Luhan, and other Anglo artists and intellectuals as "wannabes" and poseurs for their pretentions to Indianness, but others have taken their projects more seriously as genuine attempts at *transculturation*, the cross-fertilization of cultures through informed intermediaries. Frank Cushing, who lived for years among the Hopis in Arizona during the 1880s, probably took the role to its greatest extreme. During his time living at Isleta Pueblo, Lummis produced volumes of Pueblo folktales. Austin's later works included a Native American play, and *American Rhythm* was billed as a "re-expression" of traditional Indian songs. Such transculturative efforts were not limited to southwestern transplants, nor to white Anglo intellectuals. Zitkala-Ša, a Yankton Sioux from South Dakota, was published in *Harper's* and the *Atlantic* during the early 1900s and brought out a collection of Sioux legends in English as well as her own harrowing autobiography of navigating between Indian and white worlds, later collected in *American Indian Stories* (1921). Collaborating with a Utah composer, she wrote the libretto for *The Sun Dance Opera* (1913), based on Ute and Uinta motifs, showing her own willingness to appropriate across Native cultures. Similarly, many of Zitkala-Ša's nationally published books had covers and illustrations by Angel DeCora, a Winnebago artist who was meticulous about distinguishing the designs of different tribes as she adapted them for mass-market reproduction.[43] Nor was Native transculturation limited to the arts. William Jones, a Mesquakie (Fox) born and raised on the Sac and Fox reservation in Indian Territory, earned his Ph.D. in anthropology under Franz Boas at Columbia in 1904, focusing on the preservation of Algonquian languages as part of Boas's "Vanishing Tribes of North America" project. Besides publishing analyses of various aspects of Algonquian culture, Jones also wrote *Fox Texts* (1907), featuring folktales he had collected in Oklahoma and Iowa, written in the Mesquakie language and printed in parallel with their English translation on facing pages, thereby affording the Mesquakie coequal status. John G. Neihardt's *Black Elk Speaks* (1932), drawn from interviews with the Oglala holy man about his experiences with the Ghost Dance and Wounded Knee, has probably been the most widely read (and controversial) transcultural text of the century.[44]

If transculturation might run both ways between white European and Native cultures, Native Americans were also transfixed by the stereotype that they were living fossils of ancient societies, rather than fellow moderns in the twentieth century. The West in its vastness still provided a temporary refuge for these societies, according to this widely shared viewpoint among western regionalists, but time was running out. Pressing his colleagues on behalf of the "Vanishing Tribes" project, Boas himself in 1905 declared, "The most intensive work of a great number of students is immediately required, because the information is rapidly disappearing, and probably almost all of it will be lost inside fifty years."[45] This sense of urgency drove Jones and other of Boas's former students, who fanned out across the West in the early 1900s. It is true that such rhetoric, especially when it came from white Anglo anthropologists, had the air of wish fulfillment; much the same language was used by diehard assimilationists demanding that Native peoples conform to the mainstream or perish. But it was also true that nationally the Native American population reached its historic nadir in the 1890s. Many of the anthropological investigators hailed from natural history museums, which was itself degrading to Native cultures, and they were looking to collect artifacts as well as information, a potentially exploitive relationship that fostered many decades of bad blood. On the other hand, the very existence of Boas's project and others like it demonstrated the value and importance that Native American cultures possessed for their admirers, who hoped to communicate this to a broader audience through their writings and public museum displays: the Indians' world in the West, reconstructed.

Clark Wissler of the American Museum of Natural History, for example, after years of studying the Blackfeet in Montana and other Plains tribes, became a leading promoter of the "culture area" concept along with another Boas student, A. L. Kroeber. Particularly in works such as the *North American Indians of the Plains* (1912) and *The American Indian* (1917), Wissler redrew the national map minus the lines of the American empire, dividing it among vast subregions, each defined by a "culture center" from which "culture influences seem to radiate" as a set of shared "trait-complexes." In this light the West became the Plains area, the Southwest area (extending into northern Mexico), the Californian area, the Plateau area, and the North Pacific Coast area (extending into Canada). As was true of many other regional conceptualizations, Wissler's was open to the charge of "over-hasty and invalid generalization," but it was nonetheless a sincere attempt to begin classifying how diverse Native American cultures were, belying the monolithic stereotype. Kroeber, in *Cultural and Natural Areas of Native North America* (completed in 1931, not published until 1939), refined Wissler into a larger number of more complexly related regions and subregions based on "culture wholes"; the Southwest area, for example, was now divided into Lower Colorado, Sonora (Pima-Opata), Northeast Arizona, Inter-Pueblo (Navaho), Pueblo, and Circum-Pueblo (Apache).[46]

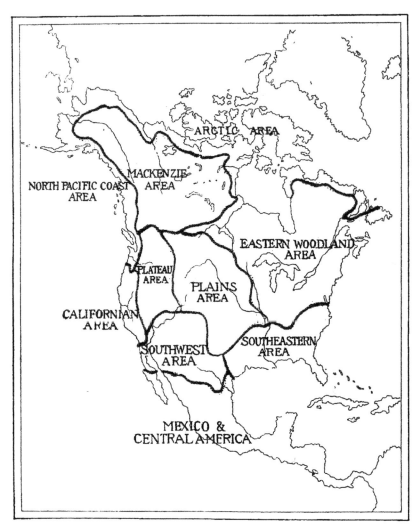

Figure 3 Native American subregional diversity. *Culture Areas in North America*, from *North American Indians of the Plains*, by Clark Wissler, American Museum of Natural History, 1912.

This project of subregional differentiation of the Native American West was taken still further by Ruth Benedict, another former Boas student. In her classic text *Patterns of Culture* (1934), Benedict compared the Plains tribes, the Pueblos of the Southwest, and the Kwakiutl of the Northwest. Perhaps no other book to date so strikingly conveyed the diversity of Native peoples or the complexity of their cultures (shocking several generations of introductory anthropology students, for example, with the revelation that Native American societies might include homosexuality). The book was therefore an especially effective broadside on behalf of subregional pluralism as well as cultural relativism. So too were these ideas conveyed more subtly by two encyclopedic projects of the period, their very scope indicative of the concern over Native acculturation. Photographer Edward S. Curtis's epic portfolio *The North American Indian* (1907–1930), despite its title, actually focused exclusively on western tribes including Alaska; his narrative retained references to US states, but the tribal areas he described minutely resolved the West into still more localistic subregions than Kroeber's, such as the "Qahatika [who] live in five villages in the heart of the desert south of the Gila" in Arizona. The University of Oklahoma Press, for its part, launched the tellingly open-ended Civilization of the American Indian monograph series in 1930, with over 250 volumes published up to the present day. Praising some of its early volumes in a preface, university president W. B. Bizzell marveled that "a society, the equal in richness of New England, flourished in Oklahoma as early as 1830"—the Cherokee.[47]

In 1929, the director of the university press, Joseph Brandt, had actually done Bizzell one better in avowals of cultural pluralism, proposing that the Civilization book series be but one element of a larger American Institute of Indian Civilization to be established at the university, which would "offer courses in the Indian languages, in Indian history, in Indian civilization, in Indian art," all of it to be housed symbolically in a "building to depart from the conventional collegiate gothic and to represent . . . features of Indian architecture." Brandt was not only suggesting the archiving of cultural remnants, or instructing acculturated Native Americans in their own fading traditions, but also actively incorporating Native American cultures into the university curriculum for the edification of the mainstream. Brandt's colleague at Oklahoma, folklorist B. A. Botkin, called such pluralist transculturation "folk-say," defined as the living, continually evolving cultural expression of Native Americans along with "as many folk cultures as there are regional, racial, and industrial groups." Botkin's view in this way diverged from the unexamined catastrophism of many of his regionalist counterparts, for whom Native Americans and other folk were perpetually on the verge of disappearance. His own series of *Folk-Say* anthologies, published under Brandt's broader regionalist civic educational program, were intended as evidence that the folk "lies not only in the past but also in the present and so forms a link to the future." Far from despairing over the vanishing Indian, Botkin felt excitement at the "privilege of 'helping to make a civilization,'" as he told *Southwest Review* editor Henry Nash Smith in 1930.[48]

Not all artists and intellectuals engaged with western Native American cultures were as convinced of the possibilities of transculturation. Skepticism seemed to run most strongly among professionally trained anthropologists like Wissler and Benedict. Although "primitive cultures" might serve as a "laboratory of social forms," Benedict wrote, it was "romantic Utopianism" to believe that "our society will heal itself of its maladies" through "a return to ideals preserved for us by primitive peoples."[49] To be sure, there was no shortage of utopianism among western regionalists in the 1920s and 1930s, especially at the cultural nexus of the Southwest region, Santa Fe and Taos. But what Brandt pointed to with his grandiose scheme (most of which went unfulfilled, except his publishing program) was that regionalist transcultural aspirations could have concrete institutional and political consequences.

In Santa Fe, for example, Edgar Hewett was one of the most prominent institution builders, and he remained among the most soaring in his beliefs regarding the transformational promise of Native American cultures, particularly in the aftermath of World War I. As he told a 1920 meeting of the American Association for the Advancement of Science in a speech titled "The Southwest: Yesterday and Tomorrow," the region's physical environment proffered a "state of freedom that is unknown in crowded centers of population," engendering the "mental and spiritual tranquility" to be found among the Pueblos and other peoples, who were "content without rapid movement, instantaneous communication, the division of time into fractions of seconds, the incessant shock of machinery; political campaigns, class hatreds, industrial revolutions and world wars." Ten years later, as the Great Depression and the upheavals of 1930s loomed, Hewett made the argument still more directly in his book *Ancient Life in the American Southwest* (1930): "Races called by us inferior have qualities that are priceless to human society, and . . . in the discovery, recognition and cultivation of the special abilities in the less powerful races lies our soundest insurance against spiritual decline and extinction by way of our own violence."[50]

There was no shortage of such high-flown rhetoric at Santa Fe and Taos during the 1920s, nor of people like Hewett who were seasoned at turning it into real-world organizations. Yet the question first posed by Powell and Garland in the 1890s remained unanswered: could regionalism be something more than an aesthetic genre, a tourist brand, a social scientific tool, a pluralist value, or a preservationist ethic? Could it be something greater in the public realm than a civic religion—a new ideology? Could regionalism be the basis on which American society might be organized? This was the critical question across regional America during the interwar years, one that was being asked in New England, the South, the Midwest, and the multiplying regionalist centers of the West. In northern New Mexico, the question had one of its first major tests. As in the economic and political crises of the 1890s, utopia was in the air, and issues of land, dispossession, and redistribution were involved, further complicated in the current case by racial tensions. It seemed that an ambiguity in the law had led Anglos and Hispanics to claim and squat on Pueblo lands, amounting to over 60,000 acres since the late nineteenth century. But a 1913 court ruling had left those holdings in doubt, a problem that was redressed by Congress in favor of the non-Indian settlers through the Bursum Bill of 1922.

That the Bursum Bill motivated the Pueblos from Taos and elsewhere to convene the first pan-tribal council since their 1680 revolt was one indication of the stakes involved. To activist John Collier, who shared the general belief that the Pueblos lived the model of an aesthetically and spiritually integrated existence, the stakes were larger still. Writing of the Taos Pueblo specifically in his landmark article "The Red Atlantis" (1922), he declared in no uncertain terms, "The white man, tacitly and also officially, has condemned it to die; to die not by sudden execution but through proscription and slow killing." Taos Pueblo was "potentially an inheritor of the future and a giver to the future of gifts without price, which future white man will know how to use," Collier wrote, ending portentously: "This is the drama and the huge social significance of Taos."[51]

With feelings running so high, the Bursum fight offered a preview of the broader politicization of western regionalists that occurred during the New Deal and Great Depression years. Collier, a native-born southerner who had earned his wings as a community organizer in the New York settlement houses, formed the American Indian Defense Association as part of the intensive mobilization against the bill, which included Mary Austin, poet Witter Bynner, and most of the Anglo artists and intellectuals resident in Santa Fe and Taos. They turned the controversy into a national cause, writing articles, publishing pamphlets, and enlisting the Boy Scouts and other prominent organizations. Above all, Mabel Dodge Luhan, with her Pueblo husband, Tony, acting as a tribal liaison, proved instrumental. Luhan had originally invited Collier to come to Taos, and she had money and connections that reached into the national media and the US Senate. She had moved to Taos to "save the Indians," as she indicated in her memoirs, after having lived a rarefied and aestheticized salon life in Florence and Greenwich Village (literally so: she was a character in several novels).[52] To arrive in Taos to live among a people who were, in the common view, anciently spiritual and innately artistic, seemed like predestination. Her money, her personality, and her reputation all made Luhan a catalyst for the kind of creativity and activism necessary for the consciousness-raising that finally stopped the Bursum Bill in 1923.

On the eve of the bill's defeat, Luhan wrote to Mary Austin in an almost oracular tone. "The country almost has seemed to *go Indian*," she believed. There had been a "*Universal* response." Their goal now was clear: "We want *interest & appreciation* of the indian life and culture to become a part of our *conscious* racial mind." To that end, "This publicity is invaluable," she wrote. "That it began in politics does not prevent its being channeled into aesthetics." As Luhan well knew, the reverse was also true; it was how they did things in Taos. At bottom, what she envisioned was nothing less than a "new world plan," Luhan told Collier: a world in which Native Americans could feel at home once again, able to live in communal harmony with nature because all Americans lived that way.[53] Transculturation, indeed.

Yet much more would be required to spread and legitimize an Indian-inspired regionalism as the new national ideology. Collier said as much to Luhan in response to her "new world plan": "We shall have to establish the right to dictate Indian policy, and build up a truly national movement, and get ourselves strongly 'on top' politically before we can demand for the pueblos the kind of thing you write of." As devoted as he was to the ideal of grassroots activism, Collier, like John Wesley Powell, understood that no fundamental restructuring of economic and power relations could occur in the West without the "express endorsement of, just one agency—the United States government," as he concluded in "The Red Atlantis." During the interwar years, such things still seemed possible. "Controlled social change is a very modern hope," Collier wrote.[54]

Utopian cultural and political aspirations like these could be seen as the culmination of the western regionalist avant-garde in the decades before the Great Depression, what had been wrought by the critical mass of mavens, organizations, museums, presses, magazines, and art colonies— all the things and more that sought collectively to redefine regional meaning beyond the frontier myth. But one could argue equally that culmination was to be found not in these various manifestations of a regionalist "movement," but in the lone figure of a walking woman circa 1917, striding across the Texas plains at sunset because she enjoyed the light and space.

Legendary cattleman Charles Goodnight still lived in the area when Georgia O'Keeffe first arrived in Canyon, Texas, to teach art. Across the flat surrounding countryside and down in nearby Palo Duro Canyon, she began to school herself in the shapes and colors of the West. She was seeking something elemental, and the cowboys and their cows had nothing to offer her—except their bones. Later, in 1929, O'Keeffe was drawn to Taos by Mabel Luhan but had no interest in becoming a collectible herself. Though she partook of some of the same subjects and motifs as the local artists colony—the pueblo, the mission church—she chose to live apart at a dude ranch twenty miles to the north, where she walked around absorbing the rocks and the sky. Cowboys rounded up skulls for her. By 1940, after she had actually achieved what Austin and Luhan always fancied themselves, when she had become the most famous woman artist in America and the preeminent modern painter of the West, O'Keeffe bought a house and a few acres at her beloved Ghost Ranch, where she could have a view of southwestern nature close up.[55] Her very life there became a kind of art installation. From this place off a dirt road in northern New Mexico, her persona and her art radiated into American culture with the force of a Mark Twain. Especially after it went into mass reproduction, O'Keeffe's West—simple, pure, organic, austere—became among the most potent challenges that regionalist cultural radicalism offered to the frontier myth and its culture industry.

CHAPTER THREE

Roll On, Columbia
(Valley Authority)

Any nation first avails itself of its geography, then at last casts its geography aside; after that, politics.

EMERSON HOUGH, "THE SETTLEMENT
OF THE WEST" (1901)

Caroline Henderson's farmhouse in Texas County, Oklahoma, sat close to ground zero of the Dust Bowl. From there she surveyed the American Dream in a series of nationally published letters during the mid-1930s. Henderson was the very type of the hardy pioneer stock rhapsodized over by frontier apologists. A native Iowan and Mount Holyoke graduate, she had arrived alone in 1907 out at the far end of No Man's Land to take up her homestead, and there she remained until her death in 1966. Thus she was believable when she wrote of her deep ties to the land in a 1935 letter addressed to Secretary of Agriculture Henry Wallace. "For twenty-seven years this little spot on the vast expanse of the great plains has been the center of all our thought and hope and effort," she began. "And marvelous are the changes that we have seen and in which we have participated." Fields stretched where formerly buffalo grass grew, modern homes had replaced dugouts, highways had been laid over trails, and tractors did the work of horse teams. But now as she sat in the midst of the worst environmental catastrophe in US history, "when for hours at a time we cannot see the windmill fifty feet from the kitchen door" because of the swirling dust, Henderson wrote of "our daily physical torture, confusion of mind, gradual wearing down of courage," such that all the region's former progress seemed "like a vanishing dream."[1]

If the nationalist West of previous decades had embodied the myths of American expansionism, egalitarianism, and individualism, the West of the "Dirty Thirties" became a territory of national anxiety and remorse, with the Great Plains the most visible disaster zone. A map correlating the

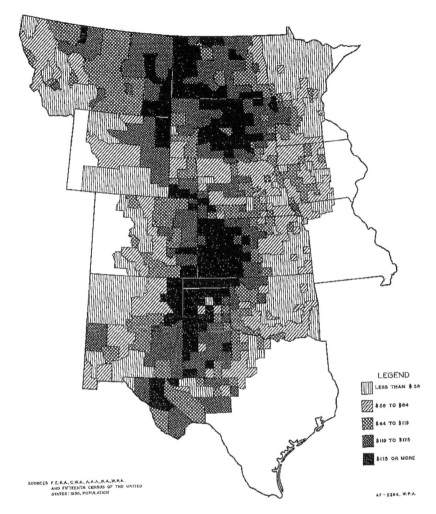

LEGEND

LESS THAN $ 58

$58 TO $84

$84 TO $119

$119 TO $175

$175 OR MORE

SOURCES F.E.R.A., C.W.A., A.A.A., R.A., W.P.A.
AND FIFTEENTH CENSUS OF THE UNITED
STATES : 1930, POPULATION

AF - 2284, W.P.A.

Figure 4 The West as America's disaster zone. *Federal Aid per Capita in the Drought Area 1933–1936*, from *Areas of Intense Drought Distress, 1930–1936*, by Francis D. Cronin and Howard W. Beers, Division of Social Research, Works Progress Administration, 1937.

counties receiving the most federal relief payments with those experiencing "intense drought distress" showed two dark subregional lobes in the northern and southern Plains. During the worst storms, dust from the region blew over the Eastern Seaboard, making the Dust Bowl much more than a faraway event seen on newsreels. As measures for relief and rehabilitation were undertaken by the federal government, the West also became a stage on which a profound ideological drama played itself out, as overlapping political and economic crises deepened the cultural crisis already manifested in the 1920s: "new" or New Deal liberalism arising to challenge the orthodoxies of nineteenth-century laissez-faire liberalism (or "conservatism," as it was to be known).

Amid this "confusion of mind" in which different political possibilities came and went, regionalism emerged as a tantalizing alternative to both the centralized welfare state and unfettered capitalism — not to mention the once unthinkable ideologies now lurking at the extremes, communism and fascism. The dominant strain of western regionalism exposed social inequalities and environmental degradation in the West and sought more radical forms of New Deal programs, such as tribal governments, rural resettlement, soil conservation, and river basin planning authorities. Many western regionalists literally went to work for the New Deal, and regionalist ideas could be found in many New Deal publications, if not always in actual regulations or legislation. Franklin Roosevelt himself (while governor of New York State) spoke at a national conference on regionalism convened at the University of Virginia in 1931, where he discussed his strong agrarian inclinations and support for planning. This synergy with the New Deal was not reciprocated by all western regionalists, some of whom became virulently anti–New Deal and attempted to revivify frontier-inspired localism and individualism as the best solution to the Depression. Overall, Caroline Henderson, who "did not vote for the New Deal and certainly not for the old one," captured well the unsettling sense of ferment and yearning for direction that marked the 1930s. As she acknowledged, there were fears of "regimentation" and "loss of liberty" with the advent of government relief programs, but she declared, "No regimentation is more cruel than that of extreme poverty," which was a "pitiful contradiction to our boasted 'inalienable right to life, liberty, and the pursuit of happiness.'"[2] If the Great West could no longer deliver these things, where were Americans to turn?

Whether radical or conservative, western regionalists grappled with the fundamentals of power in America during the 1930s. The debate was brought to a sharp focus by the unprecedented degree of federal intervention into the nation's economic life, though in the West the issue of federal activism was hardly new. As the region's biggest landowner, the federal government had parceled out tens of millions of acres across the West in the three decades since the earlier Plains bust and the supposed "closing" of the frontier. Rose Wilder Lane noted in the opening of her novel *Free*

Land (1938) that of the "total 276 million acres homesteaded during the whole period, 1862–1935," approximately 101 million had been acquired between 1913 and 1926. The Great Plains Committee, who agreed with the conservative Lane on little else, also made note in *The Future of the Great Plains* (1936) that in states like Montana, "the peak years of home-steading . . . were from 1910 to 1917," much of it driven by high wartime food demand and crop prices. As Walter Prescott Webb observed wryly in *Divided We Stand: The Crisis of a Frontierless Democracy* (1937), "The glamour of the frontier concealed the fact from homesteaders that they were all direct recipients of government aid."[3] This taxpayer largesse extended to federal irrigation and hydropower projects under the Newlands Act; construction "loans" were often on such generous terms that they amounted to subsidies to private landowners. On the other side of the coin, the federal government did withdraw from homestead entry millions of acres that were placed under public management and became the national park and national forest systems. But in these cases as well, the government was increasingly involved in tourism promotion (including road building) to underwrite private economic development, especially in the depressed 1930s. And of course, no group in the country felt the federal presence more directly in their lives than the West's reservation-bound Native Americans.

The ideological upheaval of the 1930s occurred as the nature of the federal relationship to the West began to alter in significant ways. Most western state governments simply did not have the ability or political will to cope with the emergency, so the federal government rode to the rescue. Rather than simply parceling out the region's natural resources to private individuals, the government was obliged by the economic collapse to provide jobs and cash payments to help people survive. Some of those jobs came on the immense dam-building projects that were begun or completed in the West during the New Deal years, including Hoover, Fort Peck, and Grand Coulee, all of it to directly spark economic development. At the same time, the Dust Bowl pointed to the necessity of greater federal control over western land-use practices, and so in 1934, the agricultural frontier was officially closed with the passage of the Taylor Grazing Act, which ended homestead entry. Moreover, the federal government took steps to regulate the amount of agricultural production (Agricultural Adjustment Act of 1933) along with the techniques that farmers' used to cultivate their private land. Grazing districts and conservation districts were organized at the local level to coordinate and encourage reforms in land use, especially in distressed areas such as the Dust Bowl. All of this required a more intimate relationship to federal authority than many Americans had ever experienced before, short of wartime.[4]

Such reforms, to be effective, also required changes in individual attitudes and behavior, and an array of New Deal agencies pointed to certain basic American myths and ideals that the Dust Bowl experience in particular was abruptly calling into question. Berkeley geographer Carl Sauer, in a 1934 report for the Science Advisory Board, reiterated Turner's premature 1893 announcement that now "the first cycle of national development is completed for most parts of the United States; the land has been settled. There is almost no true frontier left." The present imperative was to implement a "land program" that was also a "program of cultural balance," unlike the practices of the past. Rejecting Ratzellian environmental determinism like that which guided Webb's thinking in *The Great Plains*, Sauer for the past decade had been arguing for the "cultural landscape" concept—as he put it, "Culture is the agent, the natural area is the medium." Inspired by the "culture area" idea of his Berkeley colleague A. L. Kroeber and Clark Wissler, Sauer's definition of cultural landscape posited that "what man does in an area" could be guided by "tabu or totem ism" or "his own will," but it involved above all the "use of environment rather than the active agency of the environment." In this light, environmental destruction must be laid at the feet of heedless cultural practices such as "commercial production," which predominated in the United States and had resulted in a "gutting and wasting of land without equivalent in history." A land program of cultural balance must entail "the harmonious and constructive development of the natural values inherent in each region," Sauer asserted, rather than the "old, cruel method of trial and error" that had fostered debacles like the "wheat and cotton gamble of the Great Plains."[5]

Fundamentally, settlement there had been misguided by the assumption "That Man Conquers Nature," according to the Great Plains Committee in *The Future of the Great Plains*. In a remarkable chapter titled "Attitudes of Mind," the committee quoted another of Aldo Leopold's landmark essays, "The Conservation Ethic" (1933), which further elaborated what would be necessary for cultural balance: a "state of *mutual interdependent cooperation* between human animals, other animals, plants, and the soils." This new communalism must also extend to relations between humans, the committee concluded. "That What is Good for the Individual is Good for Everybody" and "That an Owner May Do with His Property as He Likes" were two other laissez-faire precepts that "trial and error" on the Plains had tested and found wanting, as evidenced by falling prices, denuded soils, abandoned farms, and widespread public assistance. Definitions of "self-interest" must be revised to uphold the "social interest," as should assumptions of sovereign property rights.[6]

The success of New Deal reform and regionalism as a political possibility both hinged on the likelihood of such changes in attitudes. But these were central articles of America's national civic religion—ideological bedrock, alongside social mobility, female domesticity, and white supremacy. The Dust Bowl and the Great Depression had exposed some of this bedrock, as it were, but the degree to which it might yield was the open question of national politics in the 1930s. As Sauer wrote of the difficulty of solving just the problem of soil erosion, "The control of this form of destruction is going to mean a desperately hard campaign for an indefinitely long period of time."[7]

Rose Wilder Lane understood that Americans, rather than giving up their inherited beliefs, might cling all the harder to the old-fashioned values during times of crisis. Her novel *Let the Hurricane Roar* (1933) was written at the urging of the conservative editor of the *Saturday Evening Post* as a blast from the past against New Deal interventionism. The main characters, Charles and Caroline, live a self-reliant and independent life on their Dakota homestead, enduring plagues of locusts and other hardships without complaint—or public assistance. Caroline admonishes their only neighbor, "No country's going to feed you with a spoon." Lane, intellectually en route to her libertarian philosophical treatise, *The Discovery of Freedom: Man's Struggle against Authority* (1943), exalts Caroline's survival alone with her baby during a long winter in the family dugout in terms of the transcendent power of the individual will—"in its indomitable existence among vast, incalculable, lifeless forces, it was invincible."[8] For Lane, as for most western movies produced during the decade, the West continued to represent independence and freedom; when Charles must look for temporary wage-work back East, it is taken as a badge of shame and dependency. Much the same ethos pervaded Laura Ingalls Wilder's more compelling *Little House on the Prairie*, collaboratively ghost-written with her daughter. Ma and Pa hand-make most everything the family needs; Christmas fits in a stocking, and a new tin cup brings delight. Such scenes were irresistible to readers paralyzed by job and money worries. Nevertheless, though the Ingalls family works hard to build their Kansas farm, in the end the government arbitrarily evicts them from the land.

Writing from the Dust Bowl, Henderson deprecated any such sinister intentions on the part of the New Deal. Despite what the "self-appointed defenders of freedom" were claiming, she wrote, "I have attended nearly all of the wheat meetings in our own district, and the most distinct impression received was the entire absence of anything like standardization or compulsion." In her view, nothing compared to the "loss of liberty" of the homeless, the bankrupt, and the unemployed. Walter Prescott Webb—who lived in Texas, arguably the heartland of the American right—was rougher in his rhetoric, troubled over the resistance of the state's farmers to New Deal regulation. "As individualists they stand, unorganized and practically inarticulate, against the greatest organized forces of the world"—corporations. "They furnish the best soil in which these organized forces can grow," Webb fumed. "They are the manure at the roots of the corporate tree."[9]

At bottom, what divided Lane and Wilder from Henderson and Webb were two competing ideals of freedom: negative versus positive. Under the ideal of negative freedom, the individual is sovereign and self-guided; people rise and fall according to their individual talent and effort; government is strictly constrained to give maximum play to private initiative. Under positive freedom, the individual is a product of his or her social environment; individuals flourish under conditions that foster personal growth; government and other public institutions are charged with nurturing personal development. Philosophers or economists may argue the case for each in their purest form, but in reality the two ideals coexist in unresolved tension within most liberal democracies. The United States, and especially the nationalist West of the frontier myth, has long represented itself as the bastion of negative freedom. But as Webb indicated, much of the settlement of the trans-Mississippi West was predicated on government subsidies to individuals along with corporations, particularly railroads. Public schools and libraries are two long-standing American institutional expressions of positive freedom. Yet Americans have remained committed to a faith in personal independence and self-reliance.

No doubt one of the reasons for the broad appeal of John Steinbeck's *Grapes of Wrath* (and John Ford's film version) was that it so effectively captured some of this ambivalence over negative versus positive freedom. Steinbeck represented the Joad family as upholders of the traditional American values of self-reliance and individual initiative in their decision to head for California to seek new opportunity; staying in Oklahoma and applying for government relief was never portrayed as an option. Along the way west and during much of their time in California, all the Joads hope for are jobs, with the farther-off dream of home ownership. But as the exploitive reality of California agriculture becomes clear, Steinbeck offers a vision of the federally run Weedpatch Camp as an oasis of positive freedom—democratic, humane, safe, healthy, nurturing a sense of self-worth—overseen by a benign manager who, in the film version, overtly resembles FDR in appearance. But the Joads harbor no intention of remaining dependent on the camp and continually look for work outside its sanctuary. They personify the "regimentation" that Henderson pointed to, the pinch of want and necessity, as well as the rejection of any collective or socialized solution that might make them positively free—free from want.

Most readers could come away from *The Grapes of Wrath* with at least their ambivalence about negative and positive freedom confirmed. But the closer that one looked at the world inspiring the novel, there was less reassurance. The "confusion of mind" that attended massive unemployment, the Dust Bowl, the Okie migration, labor violence, fascism abroad, and other facts of life in the Depression era also devolved from real doubt that freedom in either form could endure, and whether America could remain exceptional. The intellectual and artistic construction of homelands for American exceptionalism had been part of the stock-in-trade of American regionalists since Crèvecoeur, and with the nationalist West this tendency had reached its apotheosis. The multiple overlapping crises of the 1930s, however, led many regionalists to begin asking hard questions of their myths. Who had the wealth and power in America and where they were concentrated were issues of the moment as the ideological struggle between "old" and "new" liberalism took shape. History, sociology, economics, investigative journalism—all of these forms of fact-finding offered the promise of objective truth with which to undermine the old order and legitimize the new (or, conversely, to defend the traditional and preempt radical change). When these methodologies fell short in persuasion, there was always the socially conscious novel—like *The Grapes of Wrath*—to press the public's emotional buttons. In some cases, what western regionalists uncovered was the alarming fact that exceptionalism itself might have been a myth.

In *Divided We Stand*, Webb refused to go that far. Where he did go was to an almost dystopian postfrontier account of US history that sharpened Frederick Jackson Turner's sectionalism to a crypto-secessionist point. Tellingly, given his family's southern roots, Webb placed Texas in the South rather than the West under his tripartite division of the nation, pointing the direction of his own politicization. In fact, the "Second American Revolution" of the Civil War became for him the key to understanding the contemporary distribution of power in America, what was essentially a core-periphery model. "The Civil War made the North the absolute ruler and the financial master," Webb wrote. While the potent democratizing force of the frontier still existed, northern domination could not be fully consolidated. After the frontier closed in 1890, Webb argued along with Turner, "the absence of it is now the *sine qua non* of our problem." Since 1890, he wrote, northern corporations were "continually extending their control over society, over the government, over the South and the West." These "feudal lords" had "raped the states of the South and the West of their natural resources"; the "growing fiefs" of their nationwide chain stores had turned their employees into "retainers" and undermined the independence of local businesses and communities. Only half in jest, he proposed a "Good Neighbor" policy among the sections, or failing that, inter-regional tariffs. Webb was hardly alone in making such charges of economic colonialism during the 1930s. The Southern Agrarians in *I'll Take My Stand* (1930) and Bernard DeVoto in "The West: A Plundered Province" (1934) anticipated many aspects of Webb's analysis, if not his feudal analogy.[10] The invocation of feudalism as well as colonialism quite deliberately suggested the waning of exceptionalism that must come to pass in a postfrontier, corporatized America.

This deploying of social terms usually applied to Europe or other foreign settings became a common trope among regionalist social critics, some of whom carried their logic to more radical ends than Webb's. Unlike Webb, they did not assume that there was a common interest among westerners, a monolithic West. Such an analytical point of departure had allowed Webb to sidestep delicate local issues of environmental, class, and racial exploitation. Turning their sights inward, to the local level, these regionalists uncovered the stark social realities hidden behind the frontier myth and the delusions of exceptionalism.

The toll of devastation began with the land itself. Plant ecologist Frederick Clements, using the "climax community" model that he had developed in the 1910s from studies of Nebraska grasslands and Colorado forests, outlined the "process of disturbance" that had been unleashed in the Plains region by "man and his animals upsetting the secular balance between climax and climate," as he wrote with Ralph Chaney in *Environment and Life in the Great Plains* (1936). Over the decades, settlers had heedlessly destroyed the subregion's natural harmony to the extent that the "'Great American Desert' was no longer a myth but a fact fraught with tragic results." As a result, Carl Sauer and the Land-Use Committee reported in 1934, "The United States shows far more extensive and serious destruction of land resource than characterizes the old countries of Europe." This destruction was apparent in the Dust Bowl region as well as the "grazing country of the intermountain West," which was subject to increased erosion and flooding due to overgrazing. The much-vaunted irrigated farms of the West, where the desert had been made to bloom, also brought with them a host of environmental ills, including ground-water depletion, alkalinization of soils, and siltage of reservoirs, Sauer noted. In areas like the bull's-eye of the Dust Bowl, near where Caroline Henderson lived, 40 percent of a farming area of 25,000 square miles had been seriously denuded of vegetation and soil, according to the Great Plains Committee. The "gloomy curtains of dust" prompted University of Oklahoma botanist Paul Sears to reflect in his aptly titled book *Deserts on the March* (1935): "The lustful march of the white race across the virgin continent, strewn with ruined forests, polluted streams, gullied fields, stained by the breaking of treaties and titanic greed, can no longer be disguised behind the camouflage that we call civilization."[11]

The "human erosion" that devolved from this heedless exploitation of nature in the West was the subject of a series of exposés by journalists and social scientists that verified Steinbeck's bleak saga of the Joads. In *An American Exodus* (1939), for example, Berkeley economist Paul Taylor and photographer Dorothea Lange compared the process of farm mechanization occurring in the South and the Plains to the enclosure of common lands in sixteenth-century England, which had uprooted the traditional peasantry. Much like Steinbeck, they traced the migration of the displaced from East to West in terms of a perversion of the mythic westward Overland Trail. On arrival in the "Last West" of California, migrants found that it was a place where individual opportunity had vanished, where one became more dependent and less free: "Settlement and mechanization have transformed our frontier. The land is already occupied, and men work upon it with machines as in factories, or at hand labor in gangs as in industry." What united the South and the West was not, as Webb had argued, their victimization by an imperial North, but their mutual embrace of "large-scale, specialized farming dependent upon landless, propertyless, shifting families"—to use the dread "foreign" word, a "proletariat."[12]

Focusing on the structure of wealth and power within the region itself, particularly in California, Taylor and Lange went further to declare that "in California the old West is gone." There "white Americans" from the Plains, whose ancestors had been "pioneer yeomen" living in a "democracy as evenly based as the surface of their land," were now part of the migrant labor pool that had included a "long succession of races: Chinese,

Japanese, Hindustanis, Mexicans, Filipinos, Negroes." Juxtaposed with photographs of striking cotton and lettuce workers, this racialized rhetoric emotionally underscored the prospect of decline and the crisis of exceptionalism for white mainstream readers, while broadening the list of victims. Perhaps most disturbing of all of Taylor and Lange's observations was that "migration is in all directions"—at midcontinent the uprooted "go again and return again, milling back and forth, seeking opportunity over and over again in Arkansas, Texas, Arizona, New Mexico, even Florida, and above all on the Pacific Coast"—where they learned abruptly that the nationalist West of their dreams, the mythic safety valve, was no more.[13]

This linking of the South and the West, in a bleakly inverted anticipation of the beckoning Sunbelt, connected the West to the South's social pathologies, including its racial oppression. Over the course of the 1930s, a number of western regionalists pushed cultural radicalism beyond economic injustice when they chronicled the West's own long history of racism, further exploding the frontier myth of freedom and equality. What Taylor and Lange had merely sketched about California's migrant laborers in their photo-essay *American Exodus*, for example, journalist Carey McWilliams pursued with much greater depth in works like *Factories in the Field* (1939), the first of his series of exposés of racial inequality. A native Coloradan who had arrived in California in 1922 after his family's cattle ranch failed, McWilliams's interest in regionalism had been piqued by his friendship with Mary Austin, and he went on to write state and regional histories in tandem with his research into what he called the "hidden California." Radicalized by his involvement as an attorney in farm unionization and other reform causes, McWilliams analyzed the two taproots of California-style agribusiness in *Factories in the Field*: "land monopolization and the availability of large units of cheap labor." He found that any chance for small homesteaders in the state had been largely preempted by systematic "force and fraud" as early as the 1860s. The state had very quickly become a virtual "colonial empire" ruled by "land barons."[14] In other words, from the vantage of agrarian republicanism, the most shimmering space of the nationalist West—still luring real-life Joads—had been mostly a mirage rather than the fulfillment of American exceptionalism.

The production system that emerged historically from these large-scale land monopolies made the social reality worse still, according to McWilliams. As he wrote, "The tranquility of rural California is a myth," its history replete with "violence and terror," first directed at the Chinese, then at Japanese immigrants, many of whom had arrived in the state at the turn-of-the-century hoping for a small farm like their American counterparts.

There was no sense of civic obligation or common humanity regarding Asian farm workers in McWilliams's depiction. When the Japanese "through their thrift and enterprise . . . began to exercise their ambition to own land," there was a "hysterical campaign" directed against them, fomented by small white farmers who resented the competition and by large landowners who wished to expropriate their expertly improved land. McWilliams carried his saga of "our Oriental agriculture"—again, the antiexceptional term—through the arrival of the "Hindus," the Filipinos, and the Mexicans. The deliberate strategy of "race exploitation"—to "use a race for a purpose and then kick it out, in preference for some weaker racial unit"—meant that in California the "melting pot," much like the homesteaders' frontier, had "never prevailed." The endpoint of exceptionalism had been reached in the large growers' efforts to quash unionization during the 1930s: "farm fascism."[15] For regionalist defenders of agrarian republicanism, there could be no darker phrase.

If McWilliams's account of California's past threw the historical existence of exceptionalism into doubt, its credibility was undermined more dramatically still by works detailing the plight of those originally on the receiving end of America's "colonial empire"—Hispanics and Native Americans. McWilliams himself, in *Ill Fares the Land* (1941), analyzed the social condition of Mexican migrant workers in terms of a "caste system" alive and well within modern democratic society. The borderland of caste was not quaintly confined to the Southwest, he pointed out, but could be found as far north and east as the fields of Michigan and Ohio. This social and cultural gulf separated Hispanics who had long lived isolated in places such as northern New Mexico, according to Albuquerque-born educator George I. Sanchez in his aptly titled 1940 sociological survey, *Forgotten People: A Study of New Mexicans*. Much of what Charles Lummis, Mary Austin, and other Anglo regionalists had earlier portrayed as folklife survivals Sanchez now recast as evidences of "cultural inadequacy." As he wrote, most rural New Mexican Hispanics were "unprepared to act in their new environment. . . . They have no tradition of competition, of education, or of Western civilization beyond the sixteenth century. The New Mexican is not yet an American culturally." Far from enjoying the blessings of the American way of life, New Mexicans constituted instead "a severely handicapped social and economic minority." Running a counternarrative to the frontier myth, Sanchez invoked colonial status as more than an analogy. New Mexico's Hispanics, he asserted, were to be seen as one of various "subject peoples" like Native Americans, Puerto Ricans, and Filipinos that had been forcibly drawn into the American empire. But unlike those other peoples, New Mexicans' problems had not subsequently received "special consideration" from the government.[16] They had been left neglected in their backwater existence, unready for life in a rapidly changing world, an anomalous rebuke to western enterprise and progress.

A number of writers chronicling the plight of Native Americans followed out the political logic of the colonialism argument, depicting the United States as essentially an illegitimate, alien power. Legitimacy—and the moral high ground—was vested in indigenousness, a claim that would have been familiar to any number of break-away cultural nationalist movements abroad. As Frederic Douglas and René d'Harnoncourt (director of the New Deal's Indian Arts and Crafts Board) declared in their exhibition catalog *Indian Art of the United States* (1941), "Indian art always was and still is regional in the deepest sense of the word. . . . Indian art from coast to coast actually recreates the land, America, in every one of its countless variations." In contrast, John Joseph Mathews, an Osage writer, emphasized the alienness of white culture in his autobiographical novel *Sundown* (1934). A tribal elder observes during a sweat lodge ritual, "White man . . . came out of earth across that sea, and his songs are beautiful there. But he did not come out of earth here. . . . His songs and those things which he thinks, those things which he talks, are ugly here." From this perspective, and with an eye toward Hitler's European *Lebensraum*, Douglas and d'Harnoncourt could therefore depict westward expansion as the "onslaught of the white invader," in which "military conquest was followed everywhere by civilian domination."[17]

Reformer D'Arcy McNickle, a member of the Salish Kootenai tribe born on a reservation in Montana, fictionalized this condition of invasion and subjugation in his 1936 novel *The Surrounded*, in which characters lament "how much greater . . . was the world of priests and schools, the world which engulfed them," and the hero is literally led away in shackles at the end of the story. Mathews attempted to show in *Sundown* that imperial domination could also take subtler and more insidious forms, such as cultural hegemony. When his conflicted hero Chal begins to doubt "all the virtues of the Anglo-Saxon; the romantics and righteousness of their winning of the West, as taught by his history," he finds that he "almost despised himself" and must keep this feeling of doubt "subdued" if he were to "remain in step." Perhaps the decade's most damning indictment of this hegemonic power came from Mathews's fellow Oklahoman, historian Angie Debo. Her book *And Still the Waters Run: The Betrayal of the Five Civilized Tribes*, detailed how the tribes' "communal tenure" was destroyed by the "white man's land system" as prelude to state-building, ultimately leaving in its wake "five extinct Indian republics."[18]

Debo herself was famously subject to the persistent power of this hegemony when *And Still the Waters Run* was rejected as too hot to handle by the University of Oklahoma Press. Leaving behind his dream of an American Indian institute, editor Joseph Brandt published the book after departing Oklahoma to direct Princeton University Press. The Debo episode was one of a range of instances of censorship, fights over academic freedom, vigilantism, strike breaking, and other manifestations of oppression across the West that seemed all the more ominous to the region's artists and intellectuals in light of the rise of fascism abroad. Here was the nadir of faith in American exceptionalism.

Whence the threat of homemade authoritarianism was in the eye of the beholder, to be sure. Rose Wilder Lane and other western conservatives saw it in the collectivist tendencies of the New Deal, which were especially noxious to Lane's concept of radical individualism. "All these 'social security' laws are German, instituted by Bismarck and expanded by Hitler," she declared in some 1943 correspondence that wound up in her FBI file. Lane wrote her libertarian manifesto, *The Discovery of Freedom*, under the cloud of FDR's war state. Carey McWilliams, Lane's opposite politically, was among the few who openly criticized the administration for its wartime internment of Japanese Americans at "relocation centers" across the West, as he examined in books such as *Prejudice: Japanese-Americans, Symbol of Racial Intolerance* (1944).[19] The parallels to Nazi Germany, which eventually helped delegitimize legalized racial segregation in the United States, were plain to be seen.

For McWilliams and many western regionalists, however, the main threat of American authoritarianism arose from the political right rather than the left. Racist, nativist, anti-union, anti–New Deal, pro-corporate, and prone to violence, the homegrown fascism that McWilliams was reporting from California had one of its most baleful chroniclers in Mari Sandoz, who also found it stirring in Plains states like her native Nebraska. There, as in California, it was no new thing, according to Sandoz. In her 1937 novel *Slogum House*, she recast her father Jules's late nineteenth-century Niobrara range war into the lurid tale of Gulla Slogum, a power-crazed empire-builder who plots her future conquests on a county map. Over the decades, Gulla's domain expands and, by the Depression era, seems poised to grow still larger as many of the last holdouts face foreclosure. Sandoz revealed her lingering faith in democratic redress when she ended *Slogum House* on the hopeful note of a mass march on the state capitol that wins a moratorium on foreclosures. But her faith had faltered by the time she wrote *Capital City* (1939)—not the least because *Slogum House* faced censorship. *Capital City* was set entirely in a fictionalized, present-day version of Lincoln, Nebraska. If *Slogum House* had shown that the frontier myth of free abundance was a fiction, and that authoritarianism had a history in the heartland, *Capital City* depicted an entirely unexceptional world in which even the tenuous inspiration of the myth has died away. Demoralized by economic stagnation and splintered by class warfare, the city of "Franklin" has become a place where the rule of law is breaking down, gangs roam the streets, and young men flock to join the "Gold Shirts." *Capital City* ends not with a reprieve for democracy but a perversion of it: demagoguery wins the day, and a strong man is elected governor.[20]

Joining Sandoz, Turner, and Royce before her, Walter Van Tilburg Clark also expressed horror at such consequences of the mass mind. His 1940 novel *The Ox-Bow Incident* deflated the nationalist West to much the same degree that *The Grapes of Wrath* had, if not more so. Cheery "singing cowboys" like Gene Autry and Roy Rogers were busy providing the 1930s and 1940s with an escapist soundtrack of western music on film and radio; in the midst of this, Clark's cowboys struck a very dissonant chord. Playing on familiar clichés of the Old West culture industry, he portrayed the vaunted code of the West—honor, equality, fair play—as hollow, unable to withstand the mob mentality. He echoed Sandoz and McWilliams in questioning the very existence, historically or otherwise, of the exceptionalism that the nationalist West was presumed to embody. The mob perpetrated its crime back in the good old days of nineteenth-century Nevada. Its ringleader, Tetley, was an ex-Confederate rancher—not an outsider but the oldest settler—who lived in a "Southern plantation home," blurring together the West with the homeland of lynching. Clark's cowboys became party to "a kind of American Naziism," as he put it, the "ever-present element in any society which can always be led to act the same way."[21] Like *The Grapes of Wrath*, *The Ox-Bow Incident* was also made into a Hollywood movie starring Henry Fonda, and it helped inaugurate a new era in which occasionally a more problematic and realistic depiction of western history found its way into America's theaters. The relentless questioning of national myths during the 1930s, coupled with the sobering, morally complicated business of waging World War II, at last began to penetrate the formulaic regional identity disseminated by the studios and tourism promoters.

This puncturing of the nationalist West by regionally oriented cultural radicals—and by events such as the Okie migration and the Dust Bowl—was part of a process of redefinition in which the West was no longer the epitome of Americanism but shrank down to become more a region among regions, just "any society" with its own particular issues, problems, and injustices. The political turmoil of the Depression era may have opened the door to the possibility of American fascism, but it also provided a context for other alternatives to New Deal liberalism, including communism and regionalism. Regionalism itself was to be no more than an abortive ideology, since it failed to progress beyond the initial stages of civic proselytizing and cultural radicalism and into practical matters of mass politicking and concrete programs.[22] But this is not to say that regionalist ideas had no impact. A range of regionalist concepts were appropriated by the New Deal, and any number of western regionalists became New Dealers themselves. Regionalism was one means of making the expansion of the welfare state more palatable to localistic and individualistic Americans, especially the New Deal's limited attempts at social and economic planning. It also expressed the ecological consciousness that many New Deal experts shared. Above all, the New Deal's regional approach reflected long-term poverty and underdevelopment in the South and the West, which New Dealers believed must be tackled for the sake of economic recovery. But the fate of those aspects of regionalism that were taken up by the New Deal shows what serious political obstacles a full-fledged regionalist ideology could have faced in the West.

One of the most natural and visible convergences of western regionalism and the New Deal took shape in the realm of the arts. Many of the museums, presses, little magazines, studios, and other cultural institutions that had been established across the West since 1900 already had a civic purpose in mind: to foster regional identity and enrich local community life. It was only a short step from these efforts to the kind of national morale-building that New Deal arts programs sought to restore confidence and instill collective purpose in the midst of the Depression. The focus of the New Deal on the iconography of the common man—an effective rhetorical weapon against corporate-backed political opponents—dovetailed nicely with the regionalists' explorations of the folk and the injustices done to them. The administrators of the New Deal's cultural programs shared the regionalist devotion to a more inclusive, pluralist civic religion for the nation, one reflective of the New Deal's broad constituency and especially pertinent in view of the gathering darkness of fascism at home and abroad.

They were also more frank that such civic celebrations of diversity as the *American Guides* series were intended to promote national tourism. The goal, after all, was economic growth and development.

Folksinger Woody Guthrie's odes for the Bonneville Power Administration (BPA), like "Roll on, Columbia," were among the most famous of the New Deal's appropriations of the folk-regional aesthetic. He was one of many western artists, editors, and writers who were employed by New Deal cultural programs at the state and national levels, particularly those funded by the Works Progress Administration (WPA). It was less a case of exploitation or cooptation than of mutual benefit. Western writers and artists found paying jobs to see them through the Depression, and they now had federal funds to pursue what had previously been state, local, or individual efforts at building regional culture. In Idaho, for example, novelist Vardis Fisher directed the WPA's Federal Writers Project (FWP) for the state, with Caxton Printers of Caldwell, Idaho, issuing several of its publications, including the *Idaho Encyclopedia* (1938) and *Idaho Lore* (1939). (Most of the *American Guide* series volumes were published by big commercial houses in New York; along with Idaho, Oregon, Washington, Nevada, Oklahoma, North Dakota, and South Dakota used local or western publishers.) H. G. Merriam's fading Montana journal, renamed *Frontier and Midland*, was resuscitated by a 1938 special issue featuring western FWP writers and poets. In Oklahoma, the FWP's roster included Angie Debo as well as a young, unknown short story writer, Louis L'Amour. In Nebraska, Loren Eiseley contributed chapters on natural history to the state guide. B. A. Botkin was recruited from Oklahoma to serve as the FWP's national folklore consultant and editor, and D'Arcy McNickle filled a similar national-level role for Native American materials in FWP publications. And like Woody Guthrie's gig with the BPA, opportunities could also be found at other New Deal agencies, most notably the public art commissioned for post offices and other federal buildings. The Navajo painter Gerald Nailor completed an epic mural for the tribe's new council house constructed at Window Rock, Arizona, and he along with Apache artist Allan Houser and Kiowa painter Stephen Mopope were among a group brought to Washington, D.C., to adorn the new Interior Department headquarters with historical and indigenous scenes.[23]

Two of Nailor and Houser's murals could be seen in the Indian Craft Shop at the Interior building, a tangible symbol of the special attention that Native American arts and crafts received during the New Deal. John Collier, who became head of the Bureau of Indian Affairs (BIA) in 1933, was among the most prominent New Dealers to emerge from western regionalist circles, and with him the notion of the redemptive power of indigenous art fully arrived at the capital. Inspired by similar programs abroad in Mexico and drawing on a generation of local experience in cultivating Indian artists at Santa Fe and elsewhere, Collier's Indian New Deal sought to bring into reality the "socially purposeful and businesslike crafts-effort" that he had envisioned in his 1922 manifesto, "The Red Atlantis." Collier saw such an effort as key to creating symbiotic Native industries—marketing primarily to tourists—that would generate new economic prosperity among downtrodden tribespeoples, while enabling them to continue living according to traditional ways. In his poignantly utopian view (which remained the same into the 1950s), the "huge social significance" of places like Taos Pueblo lay in its modeling of a community "consciously living in beauty." Traditional native art was "folk" art, explained Douglas and d'Harnoncourt in *Indian Art of the United States*, because it was "always an inextricable part of all social, economic, and ceremonial activities of a given society," serving a "utilitarian or spiritual purpose that is accepted by the entire group."[24]

The Indian Arts and Crafts Board under d'Harnoncourt was in this sense to be a transculturative agency for injecting these integrated values into the mainstream. Of course, as a number of scholars have pointed out, there was a tension between what white administrators and Native artists considered to be "authentic" art, rooted fundamentally in Collier's romantic belief that modern-day Native Americans must embody ancient traditions. In the end, though individual Native American artists benefited from New Deal arts programs, the market for their productions was definitely of the niche variety and proved insufficient to lift Native communities out of their deep poverty. Yet whatever its practical limits, the Indian New Deal's arts program offered a significant respite from past federal suppression of Native American cultures and helped legitimize them to the mainstream, which in turn buttressed the Native American West as a regional identity. With murals in monumental buildings and exhibitions at major museums, Native American art began to be viewed more as "fine art" rather than simply a product of the folk. *Indian Art in the United States* accompanied an exhibition at the Museum of Modern Art, and as the authors noted, there was now an "Indian art for modern living."[25]

Collier's Indian New Deal as a whole followed a similar pattern, marking a radical departure from past policy while also failing to have the transformative effect reformers hoped for. As originally conceived, the Indian Reorganization Act (IRA) was an astonishing tribute to Collier's reverence for tribalism. For example, the land allotment process of the previous half-century was to be not only halted but reversed—individual allotments were to be returned to tribal ownership. Tribes were to reconstitute themselves as self-governing entities to achieve "civil liberty, political responsibility, and economic independence." But congressional opposition made short work of these provisions. As signed into law, the IRA ended allotment but did not restore previously allotted lands to tribal control; it allowed tribal governments to be organized, but only if members so voted in a referendum. Because they lacked the power to consolidate individual members' lands, these new governments were limited in their ability to conduct their own economic affairs. This limitation stemmed from the role of local agribusiness interests in shaping the legislation (Indian lands were widely leased by non-Indians) and from lingering paternalism at the BIA; tribal leaders were deemed unready to cope with the market economy.[26]

This cultural divide between Indian New Dealers and Native peoples was also evident in the very notion that the "tribe" was to be their unit of government. Collier's regionalist ideal of a unitary, fully integrated community life seated in the tribe missed the more complex, messy, and decentralized ways Native societies organized themselves, often divided along religious, clan, village, and other lines. Collier's prized Taos Pueblo became an unexpected case in point: the leader of the new tribal council was removed after a campaign of persecution against members of the peyote cult (which undermined traditional religious authority) threatened to tear the pueblo apart. Oklahoma's tens of thousands of Native Americans were too "modern" and assimilated to fit Collier's tribal conception and required a separate act. Other peoples, most famously the Navajo, were apparently not modern and assimilated enough to know what was best for them. In the worst case of cultural misreading by Collier and his reformers, the Navajo rejected tribal organization after taking offense at the BIA's heavy-handed attempt to correct overgrazing through a livestock reduction program, which decimated sheep herds that were central to the Navajo way of life.[27]

The Indian New Deal came closest to what might be called "regionalist social planning" in the West, and if the path of reform was not straight (diverted in the 1950s by the appallingly named "termination" policy), it began a long process that eventually led to a real degree of autonomy for many Native tribes and nations, heralding a decentralization of power to Indian country. Regionalist preconceptions about Native American cultures, beginning with Collier himself, had both helped and hindered the launching of this reform. Native Americans tended to be stereotyped as ancient survivals, innate artists, and quaint, virtuous communitarians, and for these very reasons—misplaced or not—Indian New Dealers valued their cultures and fought to preserve them. Yet these same preconceptions constrained what the New Dealers proposed to do to ameliorate the very real social problems that confronted Native Americans as a neglected and downtrodden minority. To save their way of life, Indians should be limited to manufacturing folk handicrafts rather than, say, toasters or auto parts. They should have a tribal government that would express their harmonious oneness, rather than drawing up constitutions that reflected the factions and divisions that actually drove their internal politics.

To a considerable extent, the urge to preserve Native cultures was motivated by the belief that their salvation would come through tourism, and that they must be saved for the tourists, who expected to see an exotic Other for their money. In his book *Forgotten People*, George Sanchez saw much the same attitude at work with regard to northern New Mexico's Hispanic villagers, particularly those living in touristy Taos County. "There is a tendency on the part of newcomers to look upon the *taoseño* as 'local color,' a part of the scenery," he wrote. "From this point of view it is easy for them to ignore social problems and to submerge public welfare under guise of promoting the picturesque, the 'typical.'" But Sanchez maintained that there was no reason to persist in "non-essential and detrimental" traditional ways that added up to "backwardness" in an economic sense. He was confident, more so than many western regionalists, that "agriculture and other practices could well be modernized at no loss to cultural values." New Deal efforts in northern New Mexico to rehabilitate Hispanic villagers remained split between these impulses to reform—and modernize—as well as preserve traditional values.[28]

The traditional values that mattered most to New Dealers were those of agrarian republicanism. The conundrum was that preserving the small independent family farm, particularly in the semi-arid and arid West, would require planning and regulation on a vast scale, not to mention great expense to the nation's taxpayers. Years before the dust began to fly and the Okies to roll, Lewis C. Gray—later a member of the Great Plains Committee and head of the Soil Conservation Service under the New Deal—was the lead author of a lengthy Department of Agriculture report titled "The Utilization of Our Lands for Crops, Pasture and Forests" (1923). Setting aside questions of politics and economic interests, the report applied unusually clear-headed logic to the problems that already beset rural America. The "*let alone* policy of the past few decades has been a source of enormous economic waste, and social misery," Gray and his co-authors wrote. The "evils of over-expansion and mis-directed expansion" had led some farm advocates to propose the "subsidy" as the solution, but unfortunately, the authors noted with alarming candor (perhaps on the assumption that the report would never be read), the "subsidy tends to overstimulate the expansion of the farming area, and this in turn makes the subsidy increasingly essential. Thus, like a drug addict, we must go on and on increasing the dose." What was essential, Gray and others believed, was a "unification in the future direction of our national land policies." By "unification," the report emphasized that the scale must be larger than "individual States," larger even than a "sectional" approach. The current "sectional" policy had brought into being the "reclamation system" of the West, without careful consideration of the "Nation's need for farm land." It was necessary to implement a "national policy" that would balance the "relative advantages of all parts of the Nation for the various uses of land," and would include not only croplands, pastures, and forests but also "wild lands."[29]

Of course, it is not possible to set aside politics and economic interests in such policy making, so logic did not apply. Paying farmers in a rainy region like the South to reduce crop acreage while spending millions in the arid West to create new farmland out of the desert was only the most infamous incoherence of New Deal farm policy and hardly the sole one. In part the illogic stemmed from the farm bloc and other entrenched constituencies that must be catered to, and it also grew out of bureaucratic rivalries within the New Deal administration itself. Efforts to save the family farmer fell under a patchwork of different agencies and initiatives divided not just regionally between the South, Midwest, and West but subregionally within the West. In the Plains states, it mostly fell to the Department of Agriculture through the Agricultural Adjustment Act and the Soil Conservation Service. The USDA also oversaw extensive areas in the National Forest System within the Mountain West, Great Basin, and West Coast states. But out there the Department of the Interior played a larger role, through its management of public lands (including grazing districts), the national parks, and the largesse of the Bureau of Reclamation. The one thing that all of these departments, agencies, and programs had in common was the regionalist assumption that large numbers of small, rural producers were good for the country economically, politically, and morally.[30] Splayed though their efforts were, they strongly reinforced the agrarian West as a regional identity.

The rural resettlement program showed how far New Dealers were willing to go to save agrarian republicanism. The USDA's Resettlement Administration (RA) and its successor, the Farm Security Administration

(FSA), made loans and outright grants to hundreds of thousands of farmers to help them buy equipment or keep up with mortgage payments; these agencies also dispensed technical advice on better farming methods in the Plains and elsewhere. But rural resettlement, the more direct form of regionalist social planning of the RA and FSA, pushed the outer limits of liberal political culture and encountered strong opposition in Congress—much as had John Wesley Powell's proposals four decades earlier. The resettlement farms were the brainchild of Undersecretary of Agriculture Rexford Tugwell, who was also keenly interested in other forms of regional planning, such as garden cities and greenbelt towns (none of which were constructed in the West). Farm sites were carefully chosen, surveyed, and prepared for cultivation—including the construction of irrigation works—before applicants ever arrived; often, new houses were awaiting them as well, clustered closer together to promote community life. On a small scale it approximated what Gray's group of land-use planners had called for: a scientifically directed replay of frontier homesteading. In a limited number of instances, such as the Casa Grande Valley Farms in central Arizona, the experiment was taken further toward full cooperatism, with a central community building surrounded by homes on garden plots, the farming income shared as dividends and the farmers earning wages.

But as is often the case, the resettlement communities on the whole were not as radical an innovation as their opponents made them out to be, despite helping earn Tugwell the nickname "Rexford the Red." At most of the projects, individual resettlers were responsible for paying out their new land (below cost) and furnishing the equipment and livestock to farm it, which many found burdensome. On the other hand, they chafed at requirements such as submitting household budgets and personal bank checks for approval by the project manager as intrusions on their independence. In any event, resettlement proved to be too expensive and controversial (drawing the particular ire of well-connected special interests like the American Farm Bureau Federation) to be conducted on a scale large enough to substantially change the prospects of aspiring small farmers in the West. One recent study of eight Mountain states counted about 1,000 farm families participating. Taken altogether, New Deal programs to keep people on the land did save some, but merely delayed the inevitable departure for many. As a 1946 Brookings Institution analysis put it, "Governmental action permitted many farmers to continue who would otherwise have been forced off their farms and into the labor market at a time when jobs were extremely scarce."[31] During and after World War II, this economic rationale for rural relief disappeared when city jobs became plentiful. The countryside began to empty out.

Rather than resettlement, rural rehabilitation was to be the main thrust of New Deal attempts at reform in the agricultural West. In essence, rehabilitation programs aimed at improving land use and farming practices to make western agriculture more symbiotic with its environment and therefore more economically viable, especially in places like the volatile Plains and the fragile grazing range of the Mountain states. That a new order of things was needed in the West was announced with the passage of the Taylor Grazing Act in 1934. This law came the nearest to closing the frontier as any passed by Congress, since under its authority, President Roosevelt ordered all public lands in twelve western states to be withdrawn from entry for "classification" purposes. (Between 1916 and 1935, 125 million acres of homestead entries took place; after the Taylor Act passed, this figure dropped to just over 800,000 acres over the next ten years.) The stated purpose of the Taylor Act was to "stop injury to the public grazing lands by preventing overgrazing and soil deterioration; to provide for their orderly use, improvement, and development; [and] to stabilize the livestock industry dependent upon the public range."[32]

Clements, Sauer, Sears, and other regionalist critics of environmental abuse in the West could hardly have asked for more. After only a year, 178 million acres in the West—including more than 100 million acres in private hands—were promptly organized into grazing districts, overseen by local advisory boards under the authority of what would soon be known as the US Grazing Service, the kernel of the Bureau of Land Management. Did these developments herald a new era of symbiotic, scientific land management in the West? Not exactly: the local boards were a concession to class and political realities; cooperation with the program would not have been forthcoming without the buy-in of the most prominent grazers in each district. It was no coincidence that the larger ranchers also more than met the "base property requirements" that allowed one to benefit from grazing permits on the public rangelands within the district. The districts regularized use of the range, but often at the expense of smaller and more marginal grazers. The grazing districts conformed more to the local power structure than to the local geography. In later years, the grazing district boards became case studies in the "bureaucratic capture" of regulators by regulatees.[33]

The quandary that New Deal reformers faced in trying to convince western farmers to change their ways, resistance to which Webb had railed about in *Divided We Stand*, was explored fictionally by Kansas-born writer

Alice Lent Covert in her 1939 novel, *Return to Dust*. As someone who had endured the Dust Bowl and once suffered from "dust pneumonia," Covert wrote the novel as an extended New Deal morality play, featuring a crusading editor named Tug who attempts to persuade his neighbors in a small Panhandle town, where government relief checks had become the "major industry," to cooperate with the federal soil conservation program. Not coincidentally, much of the novel was also an extended interrogation of the frontier myth. The "brave men who settled this country . . . made some pretty fatal mistakes . . . that you've got to rectify," Tug exhorts a farmers' meeting. The time had come to "travel a different road than has ever been traveled before." When the farmers still prove reluctant to reduce their planting and return acres to pasture and grass cover, their state senator arrives to speak to them more plainly than a real-life politician ever would have: "The administration wants to help you but, thus far, you haven't allowed it to. . . . You must listen to the advice of men who have made an exhaustive study of this situation! Your methods of farming have failed you! They are ruinous to the land. You cling to them, stubbornly refusing to listen to reason, but demanding that the government help you." In the end, Tug begins to see glimmers of hope, and Covert editorializes through him, "Now, slowly, our people are beginning to turn their faces toward the more intelligent solutions, and salvation might come from their reformed thinking. . . . This conservation and rehabilitation program must grow into a great movement, spreading to the people of other areas. . . . The terrifying tendency of our westerners to destroy wantonly the growth of centuries for the gain of the moment, must stop."[34]

Although Covert's heavy-handed rhetoric somewhat creepily resembled socialist realism, what she was describing was the New Deal's essentially cooperative rather than coercive approach. (Metal signs distributed to participating farmers by the Soil Erosion Service, precursor to the Soil Conservation Service [SCS], actually read "Cooperator.") John Collier later claimed that the idea for soil conservation districts originated from H. H. Bennett's observation of Pueblo councils communally deciding tribal land use in New Mexico, where Bennett was assigned prior to becoming head of the SCS. Whether or not they represented an instance of transculturation, the districts' reliance on individual cooperation often complicated regulation, opened programs up to cooptation by powerful local interests, but left liberty more or less intact. Most Plains farmers in the end did join soil conservation districts, and millions of ruined, submarginal acres were purchased from them to be restored as national grasslands.[35] At a time in history when authoritarian regimes were aggressively expanding their power abroad—including the horrific collectivization of agriculture in the Soviet Union—the soil conservation district represented a new level of government that was neither national, state, nor local, but something of all three. They were decidedly decentralized, locally governed, and dedicated to more symbiotic resource use as compared to the past. Along with the arts programs and the reconstitution of tribal governments, they were one of the New Deal's major regionalist legacies in the West.

What is missing from this legacy is some mention of the most dramatic physical transformation that happened in the western landscape during the New Deal years: the construction of giant multipurpose dams. If any aspect of the New Deal resembled a command economy—as critics like Rose Wilder Lane accused—it was this mammoth program of dam construction. Though projects like Hoover, Shasta, Fort Peck, Grand Coulee, and Bonneville would have great implications for regional economic development during World War II and the postwar years, their main significance in the history of modern western regionalism is what did *not* happen. With power grids and water projects that stretched for hundreds of miles and crossed state borders, none of the dams came to be governed by a regional planning agency after the model of the Tennessee Valley Authority (TVA), the apex of New Deal regionalism nationally. The TVA model, as political scientist C. Herman Pritchett defined it succinctly in a 1946 article on the "transplantability of the TVA," was of a "multi-purpose agency with jurisdiction limited to a particular geographic area, within which it has broad powers to plan and operate a comprehensive and unified program of resource development."[36] In theory, a TVA-style authority could sidestep centralized, single-focus federal agencies and coordinate directly with state and local governments. Nationally, it answered to the president rather than to a Cabinet officer. The TVA also generated its own revenues from the sale of electricity and so was less beholden to members of Congress. Insulated from partisan politics and bureaucratic infighting, a TVA-style regional agency could plan and develop resources in a more scientific, symbiotic, and equitable manner—or so its proponents believed.

This was the future that many western regionalists envisioned in the West but which never happened. The irony deepens when one considers that the original planning for many of the region's multipurpose dams began with river basin surveys in the 1920s under Reclamation Service chief Elwood Mead, the foremost proponent of agricultural land-use planning since John Wesley Powell. Mead had even headed the California State Land Settlement Board, a small-scale precursor to New Deal rural resettlement efforts. As its very name suggests, the Bureau of Reclamation was originally dedicated to projects intended to fulfill the homesteading ideal. Yet during the 1920s, Mead and other reclamation technocrats found that political buy-in was much more forthcoming if they spread their plans around to include multiple states and if they designed those dams to be multipurpose, providing irrigation, navigation, hydroelectricity, and municipal water supplies. So proceeded the erosion of Reclamation's principal directive that federal irrigation projects were to support small farms exclusively.[37]

Having so willingly surrendered to local and congressional influence, Reclamation and other agencies involved in western dam construction (including the Army Corps of Engineers) joined them in resisting any attempt to establish an independent regional authority over their massive constructions. The Pacific Northwest, where New Deal dam projects reached their apotheosis, was a case in point. A "Columbia Valley Authority" (CVA) was first proposed in 1935 but never took shape. Opponents successfully played on public fears of a looming federal autocracy, but one of the main reasons the CVA never happened was the large number of federal agencies already crowded around the subregion's resources. There seemed to be no need for it. According to Pritchett, a former TVA official, the primary difference between the Columbia River basin and the mostly clear field of the Tennessee Valley was the complicated jurisdictional landscape of the Northwest. Because so much of the West was public land, numerous entities were already administering resource programs in the Northwest—some of them for decades—including the US Forest Service, National Park Service, US Grazing Service, and the Bureau of Indian Affairs, not to mention the dam-building agencies. Similarly, in its landmark report *Regional Factors in National Planning and Development* (1935), the National Resources Committee also noted that a substantial planning culture had taken root in the Northwest well in advance of any CVA: "Seventy-five percent of the population lives in cities or counties with planning commissions, and 65 percent of the total area has been covered by organized planning commissions." At the forefront of these efforts and seeking to coordinate them all was the Pacific Northwest Regional Planning Commission (PNRPC), launched in 1934. A federal creation itself, the PNRPC was meagerly funded and purely advisory, but its very existence seemed to provide an alternative to the much more activist TVA model—especially since the PNRPC advocated just such an approach. Director R. F. Bessey, heeding the political headwinds, suggested a regional planning agency that would perform its work on an "over-all, disinterested plane" while leaving construction and operations to the "specialized agencies whose work covers the whole country."[38]

After the CVA idea failed to catch fire, President Roosevelt settled for the enactment of the Bonneville Power Administration in 1937, hoping that it was merely a stopgap until a CVA could be established. The BPA's sole purpose was to distribute federally generated electricity to public and private utilities, "with no responsibility for or control over other governmental programs affecting the same area," as Pritchett observed. But the region-wide impact of what was emerging on the Columbia River was clear from a 1938 map of the "Bonneville System Master Plan," revealing an electrical grid that would stretch eastward across Idaho to Montana and Wyoming, and southward over Oregon to northern California. By 1941, the Bonneville and Grand Coulee dams were powering up to become the largest source of electricity in the world.[39]

As a consequence, the BPA found itself obliged to take on some TVA-style responsibilities, particularly in the area of regional surveys and research, mapping out locations for future industrial plant sites with the help of local governments, and gathering data on labor and natural resources. BPA administrator Paul Raver seemed to envision a much more TVA-like direction for his agency in a 1944 speech, suggesting that "social and cultural betterment and improvement of governmental and cooperative machinery" were now within its purview. Congress begged to differ, and by 1947 appropriations for research were stripped from the BPA's budget. That its annual research budget had been a paltry $220,000 (compared to the $7 million spent by TVA) was the strongest possible signal that there were to be no more TVAs.[40]

President Roosevelt tried futilely to revive the CVA in 1944 as part of a broader proposal to create an AVA (Arkansas Valley Authority) and an MVA for the Missouri River basin. The Missouri basin at that time had become the object of dueling development plans by the Army Corps of Engineers and the Bureau of Reclamation. The MVA enjoyed a considerable level of popular support in the basin states (polls indicated three to one in favor), particularly among organizations such as farmers' unions, women's clubs, the American Federation of Labor, the Congress of Industrial Organizations, some chapters of the Veterans of Foreign Wars, and the occasional local chamber of commerce. The idea seemed to be gathering momentum during 1944 despite the concerted opposition of most state officials, the US Chamber of Commerce, the American Farm Bureau Federation and, of course, the two dam-building agencies. As pro-MVA journalist Rufus Terral wrote in his book *The Missouri Valley: Land of Drouth, Flood, and Promise* (1947), both the Corps and Reclamation regarded the TVA with a mixture of "condescension, terror, and envy," and the prospect of another one on the Missouri forced them to set aside their own rivalry and put forward the compromise Pick-Sloan Plan, which was passed by Congress in 1944.[41]

Encompassing a vast area stretching from central Montana southeastward across the Dakotas, Nebraska, Kansas, western Iowa, and west-central Missouri, Pick-Sloan proposed all the ingredients of multipurpose and comprehensive river basin development, including no fewer than 107 dams for flood control and hydroelectric power, plus irrigation of 5 million acres. To Pick-Sloan's opponents, what was missing was a single independent agency to coordinate, plan, and administer it all—on location—as its sole purpose. Entities like the MVA were "an attempt to operate federal government practically . . . at the place where it was at work rather than at the place where the seat of government was situated," Terral asserted.[42] He and other MVA supporters (like President Harry Truman) refused to let the idea die, and along with similar bills for a CVA, it continued to be introduced in Congress every year into the 1950s.

Regional authority advocates like Terral held faith in a number of unexamined assumptions, most fundamentally, that political legitimation for the TVA model derived from the river basin conceived as a unit of nature. In TVA chairman David Lilienthal's words, the Tennessee River valley was to be conceived "in that unity with which nature herself regards her resources—the waters, the land, and the forests together, a 'seamless web.'" Naturalizing the river basin as a region grabbed the high ground in political debate, yet the river basin—as had been true of Powell's earlier plans— was as much a utilitarian construct as it was an ecological one. "What God had made one, man was to develop as one," remarked Lilienthal. In their zeal Terral and other TVA-model supporters largely ignored alternative administrative units that were already on the ground in the West and demonstrating their utility, such as the soil conservation district and the grazing district. True, both were overseen by separate federal departments, but was this a greater bureaucratic evil than the prospect of multiple "autonomous federal agencies" governing the nation's great watersheds? The state of Montana, split east and west between the proposed MVA and the proposed CVA, might well have become a test case in the ability of the White House to reconcile competing regional authorities, each of them a potential "area of irresponsibility operating without executive control," as Pritchett warned. The prospect seemed as risky as it was farfetched. Hence the sarcasm of Interior Secretary Harold Ickes, who declared that regional underdevelopment in the West could not be overcome "merely by lighting a candle and intoning, 'TVA, TVA, TVA.'"[43]

CHAPTER FOUR

Super-America

It is possible the whole West may try to become a Los Angeles.
LADD HAYSTEAD, *IF THE PROSPECT PLEASES* (1945)

"No, the West of song and story, the West of fable and myth, the West of the colorful books and neon-promotion brochures, as well as the western 'society' of Frederick Jackson Turner, is gone," wrote Ladd Haystead, who covered the region for *Fortune* magazine, in 1945. "It started to wither in the Dust Bowl days. Silently and unnoticed it passed away entirely during the riotous war days."[1] This sense that the West had been transformed by World War II was widely shared among journalists, social scientists, and other observers in the immediate postwar years. As was true of the country as a whole, it seemed a historical divide had been crossed, punctuated by the full stop of the Trinity bomb test. Yet the incursion of the new atomic infrastructure into New Mexico, Washington, and other parts of provincial America was only the most spectacular of a series of dramatic changes to fast-forward the development of the West because of the war.

The movement of eight million civilians into the region, especially to the West Coast states, dwarfed the Okie migration of the previous decade. As many as ten million military personnel were shuttled in and out of the West during the war, and a substantial number returned to live there in the postwar period. The 1950 census reflected the consequences: California alone gained 3.5 million residents in the preceding ten years, a 50 percent increase; the population of the Rocky Mountain states grew by 15 percent; the Southwest increased by 40 percent; and the Great Plains states (still the origin of many migrants) lost 3 percent. Individual cities witnessed explosive growth: San Diego, California, leaped from just over 200,000 residents in 1940 to over half a million civilians and military personnel in

1945. In the same period the Wichita, Kansas, metropolitan area population grew by nearly two-thirds.[2]

Economically, the results of federal war spending were nothing short of astounding in some places, though unevenly distributed regionwide. Hundreds of thousands of new manufacturing jobs opened in the shipbuilding, steel, aircraft, and aluminum industries along the West Coast. California itself received over one-half of the estimated $60–70 billion in wartime contracts awarded in the West. Large cities of the interior also saw spectacular economic growth and development, but much of the region did not take off industrially during the war. Wichita experienced an incredible 800 percent increase in manufacturing jobs thanks to its aircraft industry, which brought in nearly $2 billion in contracts and at one point was adding new workers at the rate of 300 per week. In contrast, the entire state of North Dakota received only $9.6 million worth of military contracts during the war; Wyoming added a sum total of 900 manufacturing jobs to its economy. Nevertheless, World War II did bring boom times even to those subregions of the West that failed to diversify economically and remained primarily farming- or mining-oriented. In some states of the Great Plains, including North Dakota, per capita incomes nearly tripled because of high wartime prices for agricultural products. Not every place in the West could say, as did one city official in San Diego, that "the war has revolutionized the economy," but many westerners were introduced to a level of prosperity (crimped here and there by temporary rationing) they had never known before.[3]

By 1945, prognostications on this developing New West formed a growth industry of their own. Haystead's *If the Prospect Pleases* (1945) was only one of a range of notable regional analyses to appear, including Wendell Berge's *Economic Freedom for the West* (1946), Avrahm G. Mezerik's *Revolt of the South and West* (1946), and Bernard DeVoto's "The West Against Itself" (1947). While bright vistas seemed to be opening for the region, old issues also continued to weigh in, most particularly, economic colonialism. In some ways the theme was a resumption of New Deal political debate interrupted by the exigencies of war. Mezerik had been involved in the formation of the United Auto Workers union in the 1930s; Berge, an antitrust lawyer and native Nebraskan, had been employed in the New Deal's Justice Department. Ostensibly, then, they were predisposed to take up the charge of economic exploitation where Walter Prescott Webb's *Divided We Stand* and DeVoto's own "Plundered Province" article had left it. Mezerik declared at the outset that the "corporate clique in the East [had] strengthened its grip on the economic life of the

South and the West" during the war. Berge also warned of "monopoly and cartel control of the West's vast industrial potential" emanating from the East.[4] But after the regionalist social critiques of the Depression years—the work of Taylor and Lange, Sandoz, McWilliams, Sanchez, Debo, Steinbeck, and others—sectionalist arguments regarding the roots of economic injustice in the West could never again be so simple. If the question remained, Is the West a colony of the East? the answer might now lead in surprising directions.

Haystead, employed by corporation-friendly *Fortune* magazine, admitted as much in *If the Prospect Pleases.* After obligatory chapters on the "rape of the West" by eastern mining companies and the freight rate discrimination ("Add ten cents west of the Rockies") that raised the price of goods flowing in and out of the region, he did not leave the story there, assuming westerners formed a "homogeneous social group," as had Webb and DeVoto had back in the 1930s. With some mild journalistic hyperbole, he depicted an "American Balkans," with western Washington yearning to break free of eastern Washington, Southern California and Northern California each "trying to wreck the other," the eastern slope of Colorado versus the western slope, the panhandles of Oklahoma and Texas planning a joint secession from their states, and the fact that "Nevadans often feel as strongly resentful of San Francisco" as they did of Wall Street. Any pretensions to a regional community of interest dissolved further still when Haystead focused more closely on western social structure and racial attitudes. He would "like to ignore the Steinbecks and Carey McWilliams' of the world," he wrote, but it would be "dishonest" to do so: "Our forefathers and our own generation have not poured out too much of the milk of human kindness for the minorities among us." He outlined a history of homegrown exploitation in the West that began with Native Americans (dispossessed by that "thieving ancestor, whose statue may now desecrate the public square of a small town") and continuing through the Chinese, Indians, Mexicans ("the most abused of all western minorities"), Negroes, Okies, and the forcibly interned "Nisei" Japanese ("legally as much American citizens as the Cabots and Lodges"). For Haystead, this "inside story" of the West was both "sordid" and "shabby," much like empires abroad that "exploit colonies." Unless leaders in the South and West were willing to address this problem, he warned, "all else will probably fail."[5]

Mezerik, as one might expect from someone involved in Depression-era labor organizing, was the most fiery and class-conscious in his prescription for ending western colonialism, economic and otherwise. "Democracy is one integrated philosophy which applies to all of living," he believed, including the economy. Americans should reject the corporations' "authoritarian economic philosophy" that was based on the "fuehrer principle." What Mezerik envisioned as a solution was less radical than these sentiments implied. He called for a western- and southern-based "realignment within the present political-party structure" through that long-standing political will o' the wisp, a farm-labor party. To Mezerik's mind, such a political force would be able to break the stranglehold of patents, tariffs, and other monopolistic practices that still held the South and West and their infant wartime industries in subordination.[6]

Berge, too, recommended a stout dose of federal antitrust action, with no new political parties required. But he was less lawyerly and more rhapsodic in his support of continued multipurpose river basin development in the West, especially the proposed Missouri Valley Authority—on that he, Mezerik, and Haystead all agreed: more cheap power and irrigated farms would be the key to sustaining the West's take-off. If their post-Depression enthusiasm for giant federal water projects may be somewhat mystifying to later generations, Berge's rationale nevertheless revealed the era's technocratic faith in regional planning. When "an area has been attuned to the lives of the people who dwell there," he wrote, "the land is given a new economic balance, often superior to that which existed before men disturbed the soil." Dams for flood control and hydroelectricity brought about an "almost magic change," Berge believed. "Land, industries, and people develop in ways that would not have been possible before." Such an economy was "both free and in equilibrium," no longer subject to market cycles. Berge and others of his generation in this sense yearned for a managed, regularized economy that would never again be vulnerable to the follies that had caused the Great Depression. Regional planning promised a regime of positive freedom enabling individual "activity and accomplishment." Berge saw no contradiction in this federal underwriting of the West's permanent prosperity: "Boulder, Bonneville, and the Grand Coulee," he wrote, had already opened "new vistas for private enterprise." The war had proven that the West, "in terms of potential growth, is still a frontier."[7]

What began to emerge from the pages of books like Berge's and Haystead's, and from chambers of commerce brochures, Bureau of Reclamation reports, and popular farm magazines, was a revivified image of the nationalist West, a region that once again could embody the nation's hopes and dreams. The New Deal had done its part, to be sure; restoring confidence and morale was a not inconsiderable reason behind the giant dams. After witnessing the Dust Bowl and the Okies, America needed the West back, the nationalist West that accorded so well with its liberal-capitalist ideology. Reflecting on postwar change from the vantage point of 1963, San Diego journalist Neil Morgan pointed to the West's aerospace industries, nuclear complexes, and world-class universities and pronounced it the "land of tomorrow"—or more tellingly, the "super-America." The verdict of one of the period's few regionalist conferences (Carmel, 1958), according to attendee Wallace Stegner, was that "we felt pretty much like the rest of the United States, only more so." It was superfluous to ask how the West, particularly the West Coast, might "contribute regionally to the national culture," he declared. "We *are* the national culture, at its most energetic end."[8]

Such avowals of a rejuvenated nationalist West tended to mute the consciousness and expression of the subregional, localist West throughout the postwar years. At a Northwest writers' conference held at Portland in 1946, V. L. O. Chittick, the conference organizer, asserted that the Northwest had "outgrown its colonial status" and "no longer needs to ask for its blessings"—"It can reach up and take them." Historian Lancaster Pollard presented on the theme "The Pacific Northwest: A National Epitome," pointing out how the Northwest "illustrates the history of most American frontiers." Novelist Ernest Haycox wondered, "Is There a Northwest?" to which the answer was, "I think it is more accurate to say that our region . . . is only one more part of the United States." Some regionalist stalwarts from the interwar years, most notably H. G. Merriam, persisted in calling for the Northwest to "think, plan, act regionally" and develop a "recognized community of interests" as a subregional entity. But Chittick summed up the general sentiment that the "dead-hand spell of fanatic loyalty to the local scene and soil was definitely on the discard," an exaggeration indicative of the waning enthusiasm for self-conscious regionalism.[9]

Writing from Carmel a decade or so later, Stegner also reported that he was "not surprised to see regionalism in decline," and not just in decline but in "nearly total eclipse"—"regionalism has pretty well gone." He could not quite put his finger on the cause of it, except to note that regionalism required "conditions [that] involve a relative homogeneity of life in relative isolation over a relatively long period, and that combination is increasingly hard to find." Surely the vibrant, long-standing cosmopolitanism of West Coast cities was part of the reason—such was the serenely self-confident view from Stegner's perch on the Stanford campus. And no doubt Stegner had in mind the growth and development that many parts of the West, especially California, continued to see into the 1950s and early 1960s. As Neil Morgan wrote, by 1963 California was poised to sur-

Figure 5 The West as Super-America. *Scientific, Industrial, and Military Complexes*, from *Westward Tilt: The American West Today*, by Neil Morgan, map by Edward Halsberg, © 1963. Courtesy of Neil Morgan.

pass New York as the largest state, mainly from the additional four million people who had migrated there between 1950 and 1965, voting with their feet that the West was the "land of tomorrow." The Los Angeles metropolitan area alone contained 43 percent of the manufacturing capacity of the eleven westernmost states. Each and every day of the year, 500 new residents moved to Los Angeles proper. The landscape of sprawl fostered by this pace of mobility and growth tended to weaken personal ties to place and "blurs the Westerner's sense of community responsibility," Morgan noted, adding with monumental understatement: "Many problems of city planning in the West are attributable to mobility." As the regionalist philosopher Lewis Mumford warned after Congress passed the act funding a new interstate highway system (1957), "In that tangled mass of highways, interchanges, and parking lots, the city would be nowhere: a mechanized nonentity ground under an endless procession of wheels."[10]

But as important as rapid urban-industrial homogenization was in weakening western regionalism—the urban West identity as well as more traditional varieties—what Stegner failed to acknowledge in his 1959 Carmel postmortem was the role that ideology was playing, both Cold War ideology and old-fashioned states' rights, laissez-faire conservatism. Cold War ideology divided the world into stark, bipolar terms—the "free world" that stood for democracy, economic individualism, and open markets, versus the communist world, which represented autocracy, collectivization, and closed economies. Fear of the threat posed by the "communist monolith" enforced a monolithic mentality on the homefront, because the scale of the threat required a unified national (and international) response. The consequences for regionalism were there to be seen as early as Haystead's 1945 book. The war had "shown that we no longer can afford to have any division here at home for any reason," he wrote—and that included regional divisions, particularly assertions that the West was a separate "society" or "state of mind." V. L. O. Chittick, at the 1946 Portland conference, had also invoked the language of nationalism when he cautioned against anyone becoming a "Northwest cultural isolationist." The "whole nation" must gird itself for "whatever international competition lies ahead," Haystead concluded, especially the challenge posed by "the Bear." Literary scholar Joseph B. Harrison, another Portland conference attendee, quite agreed. "Today, if we are not to perish, change is necessarily toward the inclusion of the smaller units in the larger," he argued in his presentation titled "Regionalism Is Not Enough." Harrison held out the "hope that this process will result in a relationship rather than an obliteration of parts, that cultural variety will survive" in what he called a "period of economic and political integration."[11]

But in the polarized atmosphere of the early Cold War, dissenting and alternative views tended to be stifled—and nationalistic conformity further enhanced—if only because liberal-capitalism seemed an unqualified good when the only comparison was the regimentation of Soviet-style command economies. There was much political hay to be made in likening any domestic curb or regulation of economic activity to the specter of communism. Consequently, in the economic realm, Cold War ideology dovetailed nicely with laissez-faire conservatism. Of course, government subsidies to business were never deemed to be interference, because these could be justified for promoting economic growth and fostering the "American way of life," a generic, largely suburban vision centered on the ownership of cars and single-family homes with profound implications for the landscape. In many cases, particularly in the West, subsidized development could be legitimized with reference to national defense needs. One of the main rationales for building the interstate highway system—passed by the probusiness Eisenhower administration—was its importance to civil defense, including the evacuation of cities during a nuclear attack. Overall, this synergy of prodevelopment forces with Cold War patriotism necessarily had transformative implications for western regionalism. It tended to turn eyes outward to the internationalist perspective and away from the localist, and decidedly away from the frontier roots of prewar western regionalism. As Kansas historian James C. Malin commented in "The Grassland of North America" (1956), "This grassland contained the nerve centers of the military communication systems that defend or strike in its behalf. In such a perspective would anyone be so naive as to insist that the problem of the grassland could be solved by turning it back to the Indian or to the cattleman?" Wilderness, folk, decentralization, agrarianism, pluralism—these earlier articles of regionalist faith had little place in the New West of nuclear tests and missile silos. The "challenges of atomic power indicated a further incorporation into the complex network of areal and cultural interdependence," Malin observed. "Much more, indeed, has become involved than the exclusive interests of the United States as an individual nation." The Plains were now part of a vast "north circumpolar system of political power actually in being."[12]

The landscape of the greater West, identified with futuristic industries like atomic energy and aerospace, became the iconic landscape of the Cold War: Joshua trees silhouetted against rising mushroom clouds. Although this regional identity harkened back to the traditional nationalist West theme of the region as a place of innovation, it also undercut claims to regional distinctiveness because these industries were very much entwined with the military-industrial complex of the emerging national security state. Could the West be both the "land of the free" and the "land of the super-secret military installation"? A whole body of folklore eventually materialized around western nodes of conspiratorial militaristic power, from Roswell, New Mexico, to Area 51 in Nevada. Such a West would have been nightmarish—dystopian—to Mary Austin or Frederick Jackson Turner. Yet if the two decades after World War II were less hospitable to a regionalist sensibility than the interwar years had been, the pervasive conformism of the era began to rekindle—here and there, in modest but significant ways—the very assertions of regional difference that its purveyors hoped to stifle.

Several fronts developed most immediately in the Cold War on western regionalism. One was abstract and scholarly—a critique of Turner's frontier thesis—whereas the others were all too real-world for those most affected: the defeat of proposed regional authorities for the Columbia and Missouri rivers, the opening campaign in a long struggle over who controlled the West's public lands, and the federal government's "termination" policy for Native Americans. The Turner critique struck hardest at the frontier-agrarian version of the nationalist West. The debates over regional planning and public lands invoked both nationalist and localist claims of regional identity. Termination hit at the roots of the localist West's greatest source of subregional diversity: tribal cultures.

The Cold War rewrite of western history questioned Turner's notion of the frontier as an engine of cultural differentiation and emphasized a national narrative in which the West was no longer the "most American" of regions but simply more of the same original (eastern) pattern from coast to coast. Of course, Turner had long had his detractors, but three critics arose in the years before 1960 that sealed the fate of the thesis within the historical profession and largely relegated western history to its fringes until the 1980s: Henry Nash Smith, David M. Potter, and Earl Pomeroy, with a little help from an unexpected source, Walter Prescott Webb.

Smith, a Texas native, was a clear example that the postwar reaction against western regionalism was no plot by outsiders. He had earned his native son credentials as an editor at John H. McGinnis's *Southwest Review* in Dallas during the 1930s, and for a time in the early 1940s he was a junior member of the University of Texas regionalist circle that included

Webb and folklorist J. Frank Dobie. But as the first doctorate produced by Harvard's American civilization program, Smith had imbibed the nationalist ethos of the new field, which saw exceptionalism everywhere except at the regional level (the South alone remained a special albeit pathological case). Smith's blow against Turner was simply to spend the bulk of his magisterial *Virgin Land: The American West as Symbol and Myth* (1950) establishing that the agrarian premises of the frontier thesis had a long history in national literary and political discourse, a discourse that he characterized in terms of "ghosts of outmoded idealisms" ever more divorced from social reality. Chief among these was the vision of a "yeoman society" that had been cast like an "imaginative veil" over a country racing into the Industrial Revolution. Turner's compelling restatement of this mythic vision, which is the subject of the culminating chapter of *Virgin Land*, was a tangle of "metaphors [that] threaten to become themselves the means of cognition and to supplant discursive reasoning," according to Smith. By historicizing Turner this way, Smith presented himself as a "realist" offering the Industrial Revolution as the central narrative of modern American (and therefore western) history. Turner's "problem," in Smith's view, was that he was a "prisoner of the assumptions that he had taken over from the agrarian tradition," and so could not "find a basis for democracy in some aspect of civilization as he observed it about him in the United States" after the turn of the century.[13] That even Smith, formerly a card-carrying regionalist, could have developed such a tin ear regarding Turner's subsequent interest in sections is a good indicator of the unwelcoming intellectual environment that confronted western regionalism in the early postwar period.

Ironically, Webb's hemispheric expansion of the Turner thesis, *The Great Frontier* (1952), did not help matters. In his case the damage was purely collateral. It was David M. Potter, a Stanford University professor who was one of the leading so-called consensus historians, who helpfully pointed out how Webb's book undermined Turner in his own *People of Plenty: Economic Abundance and the American Character* (1954). By redefining the frontier more generically as a "supply of unappropriated wealth" rather than a supply of free land, Webb "everlastingly breaks the link between agrarian thought and frontier doctrine," Potter argued. Incidentally, this redefinition also broke the link between the West and a key regionalist vision of the good society. Rather than Jefferson's "chosen people of the earth," such things were now to be understood in terms of the technological capability to exploit resources. "Abundance in any form, including the frontier form, rather than the frontier in any unique sense . . . wrought some of the major results in the American experience," concluded Potter. Several years later in his essay, "The Historian's Use of Nationalism and Vice Versa" (1962), Potter frankly noted (with a brief nod to Turner) that while postwar historians still recognized sectionalism as "one of the major themes in American history," they nevertheless tended to privilege national frameworks of interpretation because of ideological biases, patriotic triumphalism, and analytical neatness. Without national guideposts, history and geography appeared too "inchoate, amorphous . . . confused" and "indeterminate."[14]

Having laid Turner and his ghosts to rest at the end of *Virgin Land*, Smith had called for a "new intellectual system" with which to interpret the literature and history of the West. Earl Pomeroy, who spent his career teaching western history at major West Coast state universities, took a stab at such a system with his landmark 1955 address, "Toward a Reorientation of Western History: Continuity and Environment." Pomeroy acknowledged that "our own time alerts us to continuity and conservatism" as guiding assumptions for historical analysis. He proceeded on these bases to critique not only Turner and the nationalist West but also expressions of the localist West. "The Westerner," he wrote, "has been fundamentally an imitator rather than innovator . . . often the most ardent of conformists." The Turnerians, with their focus on "environment and radicalism," had neglected the "spread and continuity of 'Eastern' institutions and ideas" in the West. The environmental interpretation had also resulted in an "antiquarian bias for localism," which had "slighted similarities, antecedents, and outside influences generally," Pomeroy insisted—unless those influences were Spanish or Mexican. These had been "exaggerated" (particularly in California) and were, at bottom, "small and uninfluential." Pomeroy's call for western historians to see themselves as "colonial historians," which resonated with later generations, was therefore actually an Anglo-centric retreat from the multi-imperial framework proposed by Herbert Bolton some twenty years earlier; he also studiously avoided mentioning Native Americans. Nor should western historians continue to focus so much on Populism and other outbursts of alleged western "radicalism," Pomeroy asserted. The theme may have been relevant in Turner's time, but necessarily "conservatism in the 1950's" would lead scholars to address more attention to the predominantly "conservative West" of the nineteenth century.[15]

This western conservatism to which Pomeroy alluded certainly made its presence felt in federal land-use policy making after the war, scuttling, resisting, and coopting a wide range of measures. A broader conservative coalition including southern congressional delegations had been chipping away at the New Deal since the late 1930s and continued to do so during the war. James C. Malin, who like Rose Wilder Lane had been born in the midst of the Plains land bust on the Dakota frontier, was among those right-leaning regionalists who applauded such efforts and sought to buttress them intellectually. At the conclusion of *Winter Wheat in the Golden Belt of Kansas* (1944), for example, he stood regionalist arguments in favor of land-use regulation and planning on their head, citing the late nineteenth-century adaptation of hard winter wheat to the Prairie-Plains environment as an example of a "folk phenomenon" of the "common people following their own instincts even against the advice of experts." But, he noted wryly, "this was before the twentieth century, the Triple A, the loss of faith in the common man and surrender to the bureaurocracy [*sic*] of the so-called experts." Malin used the occasion of his 1944 presidential address to the Agricultural History Society to assail New Dealers for invoking Turner's frontier thesis (which he rejected on grounds similar to Webb's and Potter's) as a "justification for totalitarian planning."[16]

Malin continued along the same lines to attack another regionalist hero in his surprising contribution to the major volume *Man's Role in Changing the Face of the Earth* (1956), co-edited by Carl Sauer and Lewis Mumford. "The Grassland of North America" combined insightful observations about the region's ecological complexity with polemical slashes at the "unfortunate propaganda influence" of John Wesley Powell (lately canonized by Wallace Stegner's biography), whose ideas would require "regimentation of society" and limits to economic growth, Malin wrote. He was also happy to question another left-regionalist article of faith and legitimize the contemporary movement to relieve Native Americans of their lands: "Proof is yet forthcoming that imitation of the Indian culture would have been a safe course" and prevented the Dust Bowl, for Malin was skeptical that "aboriginal man was a superior being, endowed with the wisdom of nature" and that "only civilized man was evil." The notion that mechanized overexpansion caused the Dust Bowl was a "brazen falsehood . . . perpetrated on a gullible public." Free enterprise could be held harmless because mammoth dust storms were natural occurrences on the Plains. Natural equilibria were fleeting there, so "why not choose that most favorable to present desires?"[17]

Such libertarian rhetoric has long resonated politically in the United States, and it was also used to good effect by postwar opponents of river basin planning authorities in the West—especially when it could be linked in the public mind to the communist menace. Bills before Congress to create a Columbia Valley Authority (CVA) and a Missouri Valley Authority (MVA) became increasingly vulnerable as the country veered into the McCarthy era. A "citizen's pamphlet" about the MVA produced by Malin's own University of Kansas reflected the types of arguments wielded against it: "a threat to free enterprise" that would "establish for the people of the Missouri Basin a physical, social, cultural, and economic pattern over which they would have little or no control"; or variously, "the creation of a superstate" that would mean "autocracy—the substitution of arbitrary power for democratic processes" under which "state sovereignty would be challenged." Oklahoma-based farm journalist Elmer T. Peterson, in his book *Big Dam Foolishness* (1954), denounced the "authoritarian" TVA model flatly as "total socialism" and linked it to similar developments in the Soviet Union.[18] It did not help that the Army Corps of Engineers and the Bureau of Reclamation continued to oppose the creation of regional authorities, as did numerous congressmen hoping to fund water projects for their individual states. Cold War ideology provided inflammatory political cover to cloak their actual motives.

An MVA bill was submitted to the House of Representatives every year between 1945 and 1951 but never left committee. One last attempt to create a CVA by the Truman administration in the late 1940s provoked similar accusations that a "dictatorial" and "autocratic" board of planners would rule over the region's natural resources until it, too, was finally dead in the water. North Carolina sociologist Howard Odum, one of the national gurus of regionalism during the interwar years, probably did the proposal no favors with his overzealous contribution to the postwar era's lone major national conference on regionalism (Madison, 1949), during which he spoke of his dream of "total American planning." But Philip Selznick's classic account of the Tennessee Valley Authority, *TVA and the Grass Roots*, published that same year, could have allayed any fears of a coming superstate. His "study in the sociology of formal organization" showed how susceptible TVA-style planning was to capture by entrenched local interests, a failing that a more robust national oversight of TVA's activities might actually have prevented.[19]

Native Utahn Bernard DeVoto was already sounding much the same alarm about certain other public trusts out West, specifically the public lands and national parks. With earlier works such as his remarkable essay, "The West: A Plundered Province" (1934), DeVoto had well established himself as a defender of the colonial West against eastern monopolists and "manipulators." In that earlier essay, he argued flatly that westward expansion had "made the East wealthy" at the expense of the West. Alluding to the nationalist West hegemony in the mass media, he observed bitterly that "a creditor seeking by tariffs" or other means "to expedite the plundering of the West" was treated as a "person of patriotic vision." But any attempt to resist and "slow up the rate of exploitation," such as participation in a sectionalist political movement like Populism, had been depicted as though "you are just an anarchist pushing the Republic over the cliff in the name of Utopia." At most, DeVoto fumed, the perpetually bankrupt West had "sometimes been tipped a fractional percent of its annual tribute" through public works funding.[20]

A mid-1940s tour through several beleaguered national parks apparently caused DeVoto to begin to look closer to home for the origins of western exploitation. His postwar sequel to "Plundered Province" was "The West Against Itself" (1947), delivered from his nationally prominent editorial post at *Harper's* magazine. Here and in a subsequent series of polemics, DeVoto dissected the rhetoric of western boosters and politicians bent on seizing publicly owned resources for "liquidation by the West itself." No longer did colonialism emanate solely from the East. The pending land grab in the interior West threatened that a California-centered "coastal dictatorship would merely be substituted for a trans-Mississippi one." The first stage in the liquidators' campaign, according to DeVoto, was to break those resources free from federal control by smearing sustainable management as a "system of paternalism which is collectivist at base and hardly bothers to disguise its intention of delivering the United States over to communism." The next step was an array of measures put before Congress by western lawmakers acting on behalf of lumber companies, big ranchers, and other "despoilers" hoping to accomplish an epic land grab: "The plan is to get rid of public lands altogether, turning them over to the states, which can be coerced as the federal government cannot be, and eventually into private ownership." Stands of old-growth timber in national parks such as Olympic National Park in Washington; millions of acres of grazing lands in the national forests in Idaho, Utah, Nevada, Arizona, and New Mexico—these were just some of the most immediate plums that, if ceded to the states, would "end our sixty years of conservation of the national resources." DeVoto called attention to the irony that the special interests behind these measures were again "skillfully manipulating" evocative nationalist West myths and values to win support, including rugged individualism and the cowboy archetype. To counter this rhetoric, DeVoto resorted to a curious argument for a regionalist. Appealing to a national audience, he himself invoked the nationalist West in its baldest form: "This is your land we are talking about"—the western landscape embodied a special heritage of the whole of the American people. Others in the gradually coalescing environmental movement made a similar plea in later years, and DeVoto was still making it when he died in 1955, believing the western landscape not yet safe from that segment of the West "hellbent on destroying" it.[21]

But absent a regional authority or political will at the state level, there seemed to be no alternative to federal control as a means of securing western resources. The paradoxical situation arose in which national corporate interests working toward capitalist consumption of the western environment could pose as defenders of decentralization and localism, while western regionalists must embrace centralized, national power. Unfortunately, with the election of the Eisenhower-Nixon ticket in 1952 (winning every single western state), that power changed hands to what DeVoto, in one of his final broadsides, called the "Business Administration in Washington." His appraisal of their first two years in office was bleak: "They have reversed most of the [conservation] policy, weakened all of it, opened the way to complete destruction."[22]

"Termination," or what Mari Sandoz called the "unlanding" of Native Americans, was pursued concurrently with the broader campaign to seize western public lands generally. This policy of aggressive assimilation was pressed by western congressmen who not only wanted tribally owned resources for their benefactors but also were offended ideologically by tribal loyalties and communalism. In the Cold War context, the Native American West regional identity represented balkanization. Tribal ownership of land by Native Americans was especially suspect given the communitarian rhetoric of John Collier's Indian Reorganization Act. One western senator labeled reservations "natural socialistic environments." Historian Karl Wittfogel, in his study of the repressive "total power" structure fostered by irrigation-based societies, *Oriental Despotism* (1957), used Pueblo Indians as a case study, while carefully avoiding mention of the vast hydraulic infrastructure powering the Pacific Northwest where he lived. Liberal-capitalism was being touted as a universal good; individual opportunity under the American way of life was said to be unlimited. This ideal of national unity and homogeneity could cut both ways: the same ideological atmosphere also spurred demands for individual equality among returning minority veterans, who wanted to know what they had been fighting for. In New Mexico and Arizona, for example, Native Americans were still denied the right to vote (as late as 1962 in New Mexico). So-called progressive factions in some tribes also wanted to end what they deemed paternalistic federal control over their political and economic affairs, allowing

them to join the mainstream. But most of the impetus behind the termination policy nevertheless came from western congressional conservatives
(the "terminationists") backed by local powers-that-be who hoped to gain
Indian lands or at least the right to exploit them.[23]

So in the years following Collier's departure from the Bureau of Indian
Affairs in 1945, calls were made to "liberate" Native Americans from the
"concentration camps" of their reservations. The use of such language by
terminationists, along with words like "freedom" and "emancipation" that
alluded to the nascent civil rights movement, was much like the rhetorical
world-turned-upside-down of the public lands fight. In fact—telegraphing
the direction of future policy—the House and Senate committees overseeing Indian Affairs were merged with the public lands committees beginning in 1946. By the mid-1960s, 14 termination bills had been passed by
Congress, affecting 106 groups of Native Americans. Twelve of the bills
terminated tribes or groups in western states, including California, Utah,
Texas, Oregon, Oklahoma, and Nebraska. Other measures sought to end
federal trusteeship over Indian lands and facilitate the process of "relocation" of individuals away from reservations. In 1955, for example, Sandoz
reported that trust lands in the Pine Ridge reservation were being sold off
at the rate of eighty-seven acres a day. By 1960, over 1.3 million acres total
had been removed from federal oversight nationally. Tribes such as the
Klamaths of western Oregon, who were relieved of valuable timber lands,
became case studies in land grabbing. The Fort Peck tribes of Montana
reportedly lost a quarter of a million acres to non-Indians. In this atmosphere, it was no wonder that Army Corps of Engineers officials were less
than solicitous of the 900 Sioux families who were displaced by five Pick-
Sloan dams in Nebraska and the Dakotas during the 1950s and 1960s,
when 550 square miles of bottomlands on seven different reservations were
inundated by rising reservoirs. This same period saw more than 30,000
individuals participate in the Voluntary Relocation Program, primarily to
big cities. But a far larger number moved off-reservation without benefit of
government help. For Native peoples, it represented a drastic demographic
shift: nearly half of all Native Americans lived in urban areas by the 1970s,
up from less than 15 percent in 1950.[24]

The experience of this massive uprooting, which reverberated through
all aspects of Indian life because of their spiritual ties to the land, found its
classic literary expression in Kiowa novelist N. Scott Momaday's *House
Made of Dawn* (1968). It told the harrowing story of Abel, a World War II
veteran drifting back and forth between his New Mexico reservation and
Los Angeles, a lost soul unable to make a home for himself, spiraling

downward to alcoholism and jail. "Once you find your way around and get used to everything," Abel reflects bleakly on city life, "you wonder how you ever got along out there where you came from. There's nothing there, you know, just the land, and the land is empty and dead."[25]

Paradoxically, Momaday's novel, which won the Pulitzer Prize (the first ever by a Native American writer), was framed by an optimistic prologue and conclusion that suggested the redemptive power of place. Abel is ultimately depicted as reintegrating his identity with the landscape and traditions of his deceased grandfather: "The land was very old and everlasting. . . . The land was still and strong. It was beautiful all around."[26] These declarations were symptomatic of other gestures of resistance and defiance offered in the postwar years, showing that there was life still in western regionalism despite all of the ideological, economic, and cultural forces arrayed against it.

Surely the framers of the termination and relocation policies failed to anticipate the reaction to their crash assimilation program. Although Native Americans in the West and nationally still confronted enormous social problems by the late 1960s, whole tribes and factions of tribes resisted the termination process, proclaiming their right to self-determination and sovereignty—demands that became more vociferous as their cause was drawn into the vortex of the larger civil rights movement and global decolonization. As was true of many independence movements abroad, Native American rights advocacy groups were distinguished by their identification with reservations (and associated land claims) as "ancestral homelands." Congress inadvertently abetted Indian nationalism by legally defining the jurisdictional boundaries of what became known as "Indian country" in 1948. D'Arcy McNickle and the National Congress of American Indians subsequently proposed that the federal government extend its Point Four Program (aid to developing countries) to America's Indian reservations; others called for a domestic Marshall Plan. Many of the terminated tribes eventually regained federal recognition, though the process could be long; for the Klamaths, it did not end successfully until 1986. Congress did not officially repudiate the termination policy until 1988.[27]

On balance, the rhetoric of Indian nationhood reinforced localist expression of western regionalism. As early as 1948, for example, sculptor Korczak Ziolkowski—a former assistant to Gutzon Borglum at Mount Rushmore, recruited by Lakota chief Henry Standing Bear—began work on the larger Crazy Horse Memorial in South Dakota's Black Hills, finally honoring a native son of the region. Mari Sandoz, Crazy Horse's biogra-

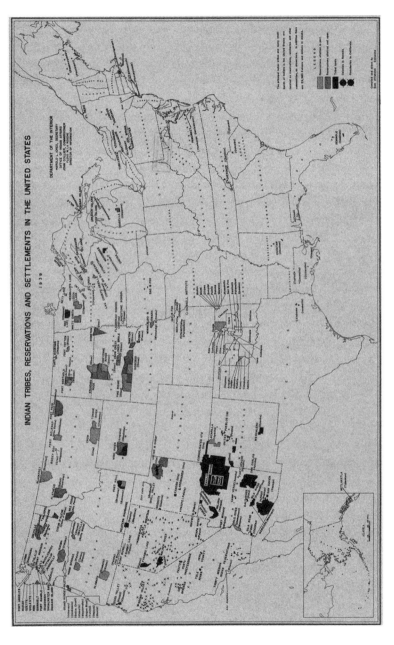

Figure 6 Indian country. *Indian Tribes, Reservations and Settlements in the United States*, by Sam Attahvich, Comanche, Department of the Interior, Office of Indian Affairs, 1939. Courtesy of Library of Congress Geography and Map Division.

pher, called it "a great monument to the American Indian rooted in the heart of the continent." Momaday's *The Way to Rainy Mountain* (1969) was another example of the localist impulse, bringing the epic story of the Kiowa people, his family, and himself to focus on a single, modest, sacred knoll. This growing sense of the particularity and complexity of Native cultures was also captured by academicians of the time. In 1955, for example, University of California anthropologist Julian Steward published *Theory of Culture Change: The Methodology of Multilinear Evolution*, its insights—particularly on the relationship of natural environment to technology, work, and social structure that he called "cultural ecology"—based in part on fieldwork that he had done in the 1930s among the Shoshone and Paiutes in the Great Basin subregion.[28]

Several years later, University of Arizona anthropologist Edward H. Spicer published his own landmark book, *Cycles of Conquest* (1962). Subtitled *The Impact of Spain, Mexico, and the United States on the Indians of the Southwest, 1533–1960*, the book was very much a testament to the endurance and agency of Native American cultures in the face of multiple attempts at assimilation and acculturation. Reversing perspective on Turner's and Bolton's frontiers, Spicer asserted: "Indian cultures did not disappear through replacement by Spanish, Mexican, or Anglo-American cultures. . . . Cultural conquest was not achieved by the three successive invasions." Instead, "cultural growth" of Native groups occurred across "cultural frontiers" of adaptation and interchange. Attempts to assimilate and acculturate had produced not homogeneity, Spicer argued, but the opposite effect—"heterogeneity" and "differentiation." If Turner's frontier thesis embodied the nationalist West, Spicer's "cultural frontier" seemed to provide a nonethnocentric way of conceptualizing the myriad subregions of the localist West.[29]

Out beyond and surrounding Indian country, the subregional localist West was given further expression in a smattering of intrastate and multistate portraits that emerged from under the nationalist West mantle during the Cold War years. Some were more critical than others, but all evinced a more mature and present-minded orientation toward understanding western issues. These works included Joseph Kinsey Howard's *Montana: High, Wide, and Handsome* (1943), Carey McWilliams's *Southern California Country* (1946), Morris E. Garnsey's *America's New Frontier: The Mountain West* (1950), Carl Frederick Kraenzel's *The Great Plains in Transition* (1955), Johansen and Gates's *Empire of the Columbia* (1957), Oscar Winther's *The Great Northwest* (1947), and Earl Pomeroy's *The Pacific Slope* (1965).[30] Each of these works implicitly challenged national homogeneity by their very existence, but the pressure to mute localism and yield to the trope of nationalist unity was also clearly evident.

Howard's book on Montana, for example, began with some of the starkest colonial language of the era. "Montana is a remote hinterland about as well known to the average eastern seaboard citizen as East or West Africa, and quite a bit like such ill-starred captive 'empires' in other ways," he wrote in his introduction; Montana was a "subject colony" and an "object lesson in American domestic imperialism." Yet by the end of his story, Howard succumbed to the requisite narrative of progress to note "wartime trends toward decentralization" that might deliver to Montana the possibility of "integration of some small-scale industry with its agriculture" and "bring acknowledgement of the region's great natural resources, its spaciousness, its ability to provide a better life for workers." He was particularly excited about the prospect of a pan-American highway. The less edgy *Empire of the Columbia*, written more deeply into the Cold War years, incorporated Montana into its overview of the prosperous Pacific Northwest and declared triumphantly that at midcentury, "The country as a whole was knit together and the Pacific Northwest was one with the nation as never before."[31]

Even the estimable Pomeroy could not resist a bow to the nationalist West. In his acclaimed *Pacific Slope*, he declared that "the West itself as an area separate and different from the rest of the United States is disappearing." Not only was the West "becoming representative of the nation," but—echoing Stegner at Carmel—"the most dynamic parts of the West were those where national trends were strongest." Significantly, this was not Pomeroy's last word; later in his concluding chapter on the "Trend of the Far West," he wrote that the Pacific Slope states still comprised "a distinct region with significant intraregional ties and resemblances." Flying in the face of all the nationalizing trends, there was a "stubborn persistence of Far Western ways," Pomeroy believed.[32] Perhaps by 1965 the conformist implications of his "Reorientation of Western History" address had begun to sink in.

Western contributors to the 1949 Madison regionalism conference had far fewer qualms about claims of subregional distinctiveness than nationally published portraitists like Johansen and Gates or Pomeroy, possibly because they were able to present them in the friendly intellectual confines of the University of Wisconsin. North Carolina sociologist Rupert Vance, more sensitive on the subject of separatism, sounded a cautionary note for the symposium with his assertion that the region "gains its significance only from its relation to a total structure" such as "nation or world."

But Oregon historian Lancaster Pollard, who at the 1946 Portland confer-ence had described the Pacific Northwest as the "national epitome," now made a subtler and stronger case for regional differentiation. The North-west, he wrote, displayed "qualities typical of all United States regions," which he saw as evolutionary and dynamic. Any region, as Lancaster de-fined it, was "an area of coherent, relevant change" delimited by "com-mon problems and interests." The Northwest had witnessed a series of regionalisms, each disrupted by socioeconomic change such as the in-migration of outside ethnic or regional groups. Over time, "area-kinship" reemerged as alternate group self-consciousness lessened and different peoples related together and to their shared place—the melting pot, but on a regional rather than a national scale. Similarly, editor John W. Caughey of the *Pacific Historical Review* noted all the contemporary na-tionalizing and homogenizing forces at work in the United States, admit-ting that "no section has a chance to gather much moss of provincialism." Nevertheless, the "measurable distinctiveness" of the Southwest (which he defined as stretching from central Oklahoma to southern California) "constitutes it beyond cavil as a region." Significantly, Caughey perceived state loyalties rather than nationalism as more subversive of regional con-sciousness.[33] The problem was not a looming national uniformity but dis-integration and further differentiation into smaller and smaller scales than the major subregions.

This phenomenon was precisely what was observed by anthropologist Evon Z. Vogt, who made the case for western subregional diversity more prominently than any other analyst in the postwar period, anchoring it in the best contemporary social scientific methodology. Vogt had grown up in western New Mexico on his family's sheep ranch, where his neighbors were Zunis, Navajos, Mormons, and Hispanics. In 1949, after joining the faculty at Harvard, Vogt helped launch what he described as a "six-year study of the value systems of five distinct cultural groups in western New Mexico: Navaho, Pueblo, Spanish-American, Mormon, and Texan home-steader," which "coexist in the same relatively small ecological area . . . yet have developed over time and continue to maintain distinct value sys-tems." Vogt's depiction of this localist subregion in his 1955 book, *Modern Homesteaders: The Life of a Twentieth-Century Frontier Community*, was no multicultural rural idyll. Part of the reason for the Homesteader com-munity's distinctiveness was that little "value transmission" was occurring with their diverse neighbors; they looked on the Native Americans and Hispanics with "contempt," while there was a "religious barrier" between them and the "clannish" Mormons.[34] Nor did *Modern Homesteaders* tell the required nationalist tale of postwar progress; in Vogt's view, the community was in decline socioeconomically.

As depicted, the Homesteaders were not an isolated "enclavement," to use Edward Spicer's term. Anticipating geographer Donald Meinig, Vogt saw a broader subregional complex, a "Texan (and 'Okie') subcultural continuum which now extends from Texas and Oklahoma across the Southwest to California." Refining this analysis in 1966 with *People of Rimrock*, Vogt and coeditor Ethel M. Albert realized that the peoples in the area identified as Rimrock were not segregated from each other but did "form a *de facto* intercultural system" that resulted in "some intercultural borrowing," though which also led to a "tenacious retention of distinctive values." It seemed that each cultural group—Zuni, Navajo, Mormon, Hispanic, Texan—tended to have an "ethnocentrically flattering" view of themselves, while looking on the others as "excluded from or inferior to true humanity." As Vogt and Albert wrote ruefully, it was a "first-rate preservative of uniqueness and difference."[35]

Cultural chauvinism had always had its role in fostering regional consciousness, but in the constant cross-comparisons of the five cultures, the larger power differential among the groups could sometimes be obfuscated in *People of Rimrock* (a fact of life that would have been the point of departure for the next, post-1960s generation of scholars). As Guy J. Pauker finally pointed out in his contribution to the volume, "Texans and Mormons can and do view themselves as full members of the American community into which they are integrated on a basis of equality, but for the other three groups, Zuni, Navaho, and Spanish-Americans, the relationship is one of subordination to a more powerful but still alien nation." Despite the relative occupational equality of the five groups—all of them small fry when compared to the "big ranchers" of the vicinity—the racial caste system of the West designated the Texans and Mormons as superior.[36]

Localist and pluralist expressions like *People of Rimrock* further weakened the hegemony of the nationalist West and the Old West culture industry that perpetuated this caste system, however, opening up more cultural space for alternative viewpoints. Already in the 1950s, films like John Ford's *The Searchers* (1956) were showing the strain of upholding Western movie conventions while beginning to incorporate a heightened consciousness of racial injustice. Ford's film adaptation of Mari Sandoz's book *Cheyenne Autumn* (1964)—the final release of his career—was more explicit in trying to shift to a Native American perspective, but it foundered under too many stereotypes and inaccuracies. Once the legitimacy of the conquered's worldview began to be acknowledged, conquest became less entertaining. Conventional films like *How the West Was Won* (1962), *True Grit* (1969), and series like *Gunsmoke* (1955–75) might still predominate at the movies and on television, but now viewers could see more problematic and contemporary fare like *The Treasure of Sierra Madre* (1948), *Giant* (1956), *The Misfits* (1961), and *Hud* (1963)—the latter based on Larry McMurtry's debut novel with a more explicitly postfrontier title, *Horseman, Pass By* (1961). As the genre fragmented, struggling for novelty and relevance, some strange incongruities crept in, like Burt Bacharach's pop music soundtrack for *Butch Cassidy and the Sundance Kid* (1969), or the disorienting European locations for director Sergio Leone's so-called Spaghetti Westerns (1964–66).[37] By 1970 the reign of Westerns as a staple of American theaters was largely over, choking off a primary conduit of Old West symbols and motifs in defining the West's regional identity.

Nevertheless, the appeal of the Old West hardly went away, itself refusing to yield to Cold War conformity. Since the late nineteenth century, the concept of the nationalist West had tended to undercut regional distinctiveness. It not only proposed the West as the space for enacting all-American ideals, its very cultural jingoism also tended to suppress any counterclaims of subregional differentiation, especially those of Native Americans and other minority groups. But if it was regionalism at its most generic, nationalist West rhetoric at least proposed some diversification of unitary American nationhood. In the face of the rapidly changing trends in popular and academic culture, adherents to Old West regional consciousness mounted essentially conservative, rearguard actions to create a vibrant subculture, latent within the mainstream and still full of meanings and associations for the postwar generation.

In 1945, for example, a new national membership organization of frontier lore and history enthusiasts, Westerners International, began forming "corrals" and "posses" across the country. In 1955, the National Cowboy Hall of Fame and Western Heritage Center was established in Oklahoma City. In 1961, the leader of the remaining Turnerian stalwarts, Ray Allen Billington, and a group of like-minded scholars founded the Western History Association at Santa Fe. Billington's standard frontier history textbook, *Westward Expansion* (1949), remained virtually unchanged between its first and third (1967) editions, offering up the frontier thesis unapologetically. Louis L'Amour, whose Western novels sold millions of copies in the postwar period, also failed to get the memo that the Old West was out of fashion, as did more serious Western novelists like A. B. Guthrie Jr. and Jack Schaefer. Dude ranches remained staples of local tourism promotion, more accessible than ever because of the new interstates. In the same period, professional rodeo increased greatly in visibility and popularity, thanks to champion cowboys like Oklahoma's Jim Shoulders and Oregon native Larry Mahan. Along with television staples like *Gunsmoke* and *Bonanza* (1959–73), all of these expressions of western nostalgia seemed to indicate that the Old West culture industry still had a following.[38] But the time when frontier mythology remained largely unchallenged in American culture was over.

The growing contestation of the frontier myth as part of the West's identity—and the continuing rise of alternative brands for the region—could be traced to another sea-change in attitudes happening in the postwar period: the decline of producerist values regarding work and nature. Producerism glorified thrift, industry, and manual labor, and it looked on nature as raw material, as a place for generating wealth; the producerist hero (generally male) was the self-made individual who controlled his own destiny through ownership, such as a homestead. The 1930s was the last decade in which a significant portion of Americans (often out of desperation) still thought of the West as a site for homesteading. The wartime and postwar boom in blue- and white-collar employment was decidedly urban centered, and many Americans from other parts of the country chose to migrate to western cities in search of a mode of easy living that seemed more elusive in the northeastern Frost Belt states: benign climate, close proximity to outdoor recreation, spacious modern housing, suburban amenities geared to the automobile.[39] In the urban West, it seemed, play, leisure, and nature could be integral with daily life. The wilderness West might boast natural spectacles—the Grand Canyon, Old Faithful, Yosemite Valley—and in the postwar years, the urban West also beckoned fantastically and larger than life: Hollywood, Las Vegas, Disneyland.

It was jobs, war production jobs, that first lured the influx of people westward, and during the war western cities struggled to provide adequate housing and services. Worse than the problems associated with chaotic growth was the possibility that it might all go away at war's end. This dread of a return to the Depression, and the need to sustain local economies through a postwar reconversion into a prosperous future, drove many cities in the West to engage in substantial planning for the first time. The sense of urgency was clearly seen in a 1943 program overseen by the National Resources Planning Board (NRPB) and encapsulated in a pamphlet, *Action for Cities: A Guide for Community Planning*. The NRPB picked three western cities to participate in the program—Corpus Christi, Salt Lake City, and Tacoma—and supplied each with a technician along with a copy of *Action for Cities*, which was a kind of quick-fix, how-to manual for urban planning in outline form. Although *Action for Cities* was seen as a stopgap when planning professionals were scarce, it did an admirable job of summarizing many of the larger goals of American planners circa 1940, such as "relating the community to the region of which it is a part," and "open spaces: greenbelt protection for residential areas, open space for control of densities, preservation of natural beauty spots." There were also glimpses of a vision or two that remained pie-in-the-sky for most US cities into the postwar period: "Whenever possible, planning should be done for the whole urban region," preferably via a "metropolitan planning agency." But the example of Corpus Christi showed the direction in which most western cities desired to go in the postwar years and what they expected planning to accomplish: "The Corpus Christi strategy is for a fast-growing city which is expected to retain its wartime growth."[40]

Multiplied across the urban West, the "Corpus Christi strategy" produced the astounding level of creature comfort and affluence known as "western living," inducing many who had moved there to marvel how they had left behind the grime, squalor, and congestion of the East for an exceptional place where problems like these were unknown (at least until such wake-up calls as the 1965 Watts riots). From this western suburban plane of being, a growing middle class with leisure time and disposable income came to view nature less in terms of profit and production than beauty and recreation. Neil Morgan in *Westward Tilt* described this "transition" in the "philosophy of Western natural resources" in terms of the "rising power" of those "interested in preserving areas where they can fish, hunt, hike, swim, ski, and camp," versus the "declining" power of "those who exploited its natural resources—its timber, oil and minerals, its grass, water and farmland." From the vantage point of 1963, Morgan underestimated the political fortunes of western producers, many of whom were part of well-organized and -financed trade associations with hardball lobbyists. But he was quite accurate that the "new leisure power" was ascendant though splayed among "diverse" interests. How to mobilize this vast but amorphous constituency for what Morgan called "the fight to save the West" became one of the main challenges for environmental activists in the postwar era.[41]

But save the West from what? DeVoto had already answered that question: itself. Two contemporary planners, Christopher Tunnard and Boris Pushkarev, elaborated in their book, *Man-Made America: Chaos or Control?* (1963): "The fully urbanized society which we have now attained requires a consideration of the entire land area of North America as being covered by overlapping fields of urban socio-economic influence, emanating from the major centers." Carl Abbott, a scholar of planning history, later brought this point closer to home in his book *How Cities Won the West* (2008), referring to the "physical appropriation of the empty West by the urban West. . . . City people utilize outlying lands and resources to stoke and serve the urban metabolism."[42]

Not all observers of the postwar West were alarmed by this prospect. The iconoclastic cultural geographer John Brinckerhoff Jackson reveled in many of the changes that he saw occurring around him in the Southwest from his vantage "down three miles of dirt road" near Santa Fe. In his journal *Landscape: Human Geography of the Southwest*, which he began self-publishing in 1951—itself indicative of the low ebb of regionalism's fortunes—Jackson wrote a wide array of essays on subjects ranging from suburban front yards to trailer houses to gaudy commercial strips; the latter, in his view, expressed a vital new modern vernacular. He embraced highways and automobiles along with the new urban forms that they required much more than most western regionalists. Jackson also did not disdain the producerist West but found value in machine-strewn farmyards and one-light High Plains county seats that were "part of the landscape—one might even say part of every farm," as he wrote in a 1952 article, "The Almost Perfect Town." The West provided confirmation to Jackson that "an inhabited landscape is neither beautiful nor sound unless it makes possible an unfolding of the individual in work and social relationships as much as in health and recreation."[43] Such ideas later endeared Jackson to advocates of cultural landscape preservation. But contemporaries who were less sanguine about the more immediate consequences of the West's explosive urban-industrial growth looked on what Jackson saw as fun and kitschy with different eyes. Where he perceived dynamism and exuberance, wilderness defenders and planning advocates saw only sprawl, destruction, and blight.

The writer Wallace Stegner was among those who joined the fight to save the West from itself, turning to activism near the time of his friend DeVoto's death in 1955. Stegner's works about the West, which included histories of the Mormon subregion where he had grown up, bridged the cultural transition that Morgan wrote of, particularly his magnum opus, *Beyond the Hundredth Meridian: John Wesley Powell and the Second Opening of the American West* (1954). Widely regarded as one of the most important books ever written about the West, *Beyond the Hundredth Meridian* told the story of a man who was deeply rooted in the petty producerist worldview and eagerly sought to foster agricultural development in the region. But several themes in the book resonated with contemporary readers and their awakening environmental concerns: western aridity and the limits it set on urban-industrial expansion; the need for planning to harmonize development with natural systems; and, most immediately evocative for the battles of the mid-1950s to the early 1960s, the sublime wildness of the canyons that Powell encountered during his 1869 descent of the Colorado River through the Grand Canyon. Obscure to most Americans, Powell was resurrected in Stegner's pages and spoke again, becoming a modern environmentalist icon: "We have an unknown distance yet to run; an unknown river yet to explore. What falls there are, we know not; what rocks beset the channel, we know not; what walls rise over the river, we know not."[44] There were places in the West that could still provide some semblance of this wilderness experience, and this was what beckoned millions of tourists. That such places were under threat and rapidly disappearing was the message that motivated thousands of activists in the burgeoning environmental movement, including Stegner.

DeVoto's theme that public lands and national parks in the West constituted the collective heritage of all Americans remained a key nationalist West refrain for wilderness advocates. Indeed, Stegner went further in his influential "Wilderness Letter" of 1960 to make a full-fledged Turnerian argument in support of preservation. Wilderness, he wrote, "was the challenge against which our character as a people was formed." Wilderness represented the "remainder" of the frontier that had made the quintessential American "such a democrat, such a believer in human individual dignity." But Stegner and his erstwhile allies in the preservation movement, including David Brower of the Sierra Club, found an equally effective rhetorical strategy in the detailed, localist depiction of particular locations as more than just points on a map, most famously exemplified in the battle to prevent dam construction inside Dinosaur National Monument on the Colorado–Utah border. *This Is Dinosaur* (1955), edited by Stegner, provided a lyrical, historical, and scientific portrait of the 325-square-mile monument, underscoring what would be lost in the inundation.[45] Such "picture books," often featuring the work of board member Ansel Adams, became a standard tactic of the Sierra Club and other organizations to convey to voters a concrete sense of place and arouse an aesthetic attachment and emotional response—and hopefully, an outpouring of letters and phone calls to Congress.

Wilderness had been a significant component of the West's regional identity since before 1900, and these mid-century preservationist campaigns raised its visibility still higher—ironically for one of the most heavily urbanized regions in the country. As Neil Morgan pointed out, "Of the one hundred and fifty regions to be preserved under the wilderness bill considered by Congress in 1962, one hundred and thirty-nine were in the West." The postwar content of *Sunset: The Magazine of Western Living* was built essentially around two themes: refined suburban lifestyles, and travel to the West's parklands. A 1954 article urged readers to "visit Dinosaur soon if you want to be sure of seeing it" and included an arrow on a photograph of Steamboat Rock showing the level of the planned reservoir, along with the address of the Sierra Club. This type of growing public awareness was instrumental to the eight-year effort to pass the landmark Wilderness Act (1964). Unfortunately, there was less effort among policy makers to correlate the environmental impact of refined suburban lifestyles with the fact of disappearing western wilderness. The federal Colorado River Storage Project (1956) was charged with "comprehensive" river basin development to support those lifestyles, including flood control, water supply, irrigation, and hydroelectric power. From this infamous basin plan, Stegner, Brower, and other activists rescued Dinosaur National Monument, only to surrender equally worthy places like Glen Canyon in Arizona.[46]

The politics were complex. At times, Stegner must have wondered if he had walked into the pages of *Beyond the Hundredth Meridian*, as he confronted much the same irrationalities that had bedeviled Powell. The intellectual hubris that Stegner expressed at the 1958 Carmel conference, when he pronounced regionalism dead and California the capital of American culture, becomes all the more puzzling in this context. Here he was at the same time scrambling to protect western hinterlands from destruction by West Coast and other western centers of urban-industrialism, as Haystead and DeVoto had foretold in their analyses of intraregional colonialism.[47] To accomplish this end, preservation advocates needed federal intervention to expand and protect wilderness areas. But many western Congress members were prodevelopment at all costs, ideologically opposed to "locking up" natural resources, and seeking sweetheart deals for local and state constituents. The federal natural resources bureaucracy, such as the Forest Service and Park Service, was at best underfunded and at worst coopted during the Truman and Eisenhower years, and so was not the most reliable ally. The powerful Bureau of Reclamation hatched aggressive and grandiose dam-building schemes to keep the appropriations flowing, but its "comprehensive" river basin plans were never comprehensive enough—they omitted amenities such as wild canyonlands and wild rivers, even as they sought to fulfill the public's mandate for suburbanism.

Such things required water, lots of it, and electricity. As yet in the postwar period, there were few who were willing to call attention to the necessary trade-offs.

Wilderness advocates were obliged to focus their limited resources on their single issue as they fought to contain the environmental damage caused by the very government on which they must rely to save the West from itself. Stopping a dam in Dinosaur, they got one at Glen Canyon. Scuttling a later plan for two dams in the Grand Canyon, they saw coal-burning power plants built nearby in the Four Corners, hazing the views. David Brower admitted years afterward that he had missed an opportunity to save Glen Canyon because he had never visited it and did not know the beauty of the place. Stegner had been there, and he journeyed there again once the waters of Lake Powell were rising behind the dam in 1966. He confessed in an article that it would make a pretty lake, but while there he jotted privately, his earlier hubris dashed: "Altogether what will be lost is sense of sanctuary."[48]

The map of the new National Wilderness Preservation System established by the Wilderness Act looked much like the scattering of Indian reservations comprising Indian country—disjointed subregional bits and pieces of what remained (or had been abandoned) after a century or more of industrial-capitalist expansion. But these bits and pieces marked and enhanced—added value to—the regional identity of the West well beyond their actual square miles. Secretary of the Interior Stewart Udall, who had helped pass the Wilderness Act along with a plethora of other measures during the more environmentally friendly years of the Kennedy and Johnson administrations, was among the most prominent policy makers to recognize that truly comprehensive regional planning would be necessary to ensure that these places endured. In his book *The Quiet Crisis* (1963), which he wrote with his friend Wallace Stegner's assistance, Udall pointed to other encouraging but piecemeal accomplishments in the postwar years, such as California's "open space" law of 1959. His emphasis, however, was on the limitations of the single-issue approach: "Our mastery over our environment is now so great that the conservation of a region, a metropolitan area, or a valley is more important, in most cases, than the conservation of any single resource." All uses and plans must be "evaluated comprehensively by those who make the over-all decisions," Udall wrote, because it was "inevitable that incompatible plans involving factories, mines, fish, dams, parks, highways and wildlife, and other uses and values will increasingly collide." He advised that "those who decide must consider immediate needs, compute the values of competing proposals, and keep distance in their eyes as well."[49]

The phrase "those who decide" came to the heart of the conundrum facing regional planning in the West in the postwar period and subsequent decades: how to "evaluate comprehensively" given the division of authority among local, state, tribal, and federal officials; how to "compute the values" when powerful vested interests could influence the outcome; how to look in the distance when election cycles set the timetable. As Neil Morgan noted in 1963, in California, where planning culture seemed ostensibly to have taken hold the deepest, "Each . . . county is required by law to maintain a planning commission and develop a master plan for land use. All major California cities do the same. But the plans become hopelessly ensnarled in metropolitan areas like Los Angeles County, which has seventy-three incorporated cities within its boundaries."[50] Postwar political culture as a whole, riven by Cold War ideology and laissez-faire dogma, squelched prospects further still that "those who decide" would be regional planners.

This outcome suited J. B. Jackson well enough; real estate developers and mining companies were not the only ones who found fault with planning. Jackson was among a growing contingent of planning critics who argued that "those who decide" did not always decide well, or tolerantly, or democratically. They seemed to have a "distrust of everything vulgar and small and poor," Jackson wrote. The workaday, vernacular West that he cherished was the creation of ordinary people, not planners or civic leagues, and likely to be beautified out of existence if they had their way.[51] Yet here the conundrum tangled further: if not planners answerable to the public, who should decide what happened to the landscape—lobbyists, corporate boardrooms, next-door neighbors with questionable taste? Taken in this light, the subregional bits and pieces that managed to be saved by Native Americans, wilderness advocates, and open-space crusaders might be seen as a signal achievement.

Besides these tangible if partial physical legacies, other accomplishments of postwar western regionalism, some of them largely unheeded in their own time, took the form of intellectual bequests to later generations. These included some new ways of understanding the *region* as a concept, such as Malin's environmental history, Spicer's cultural frontier, Steward's cultural ecology, and Jackson's vernacular landscape. There was also Stegner's "Wilderness Letter" (the text of which is posted to this day on the Wilderness Society's website), which did something more than reprise the

Turner thesis. Stegner suggested that previously devalued western landscapes such as prairies and deserts deserved preservation equally with alpine vistas; these areas were also part of what he called the West's "geography of hope."[52]

That concluding turn of phrase became increasingly important to students of the West after 1970, as they began to come to grips with what had happened to the region during the postwar years. Stegner felt it, too, and he had John Wesley Powell "symbolically" survey that terrain at the end of *Beyond the Hundredth Meridian* "and with some confidence wait for the future to catch up with him." For if Stegner's gospel of Powell was not to be the guide, there was another mid-1950s way of looking at the West that was somewhat less than hopeful: Wittfogel's "hydraulic civilization." His essay on the subject appeared with Malin's on the North American grassland in the 1956 volume *Man's Role in Changing the Face of the Earth.* Despite the fact that Wittfogel never explicitly pointed to the contemporary West in this or his book-length analysis, some telling phrases were there, applicable depending on one's degree of hope, such as "hydraulic civilization" itself, or "centralized works of water control," or "agrarian monopoly despotisms."[53] A fuller hearing of his ideas and the other bequests of postwar western regionalists had to await the more open political and intellectual climate of the 1960s and 1970s, especially the change in environmental consciousness precipitated out of the "quiet crisis" that came to be known, appropriately, as the "quiet revolution."

CHAPTER FIVE

Quiet Revolution, Angry West

I am bone-deep in landscape.
MARY CLEARMAN BLEW,
ALL BUT THE WALTZ:
ESSAYS ON A MONTANA
FAMILY (1991)

"It is quite possible that loss of meaning is the problem of our time," social scientist Raymond Gastil wrote at the conclusion of his 1975 book, *Cultural Regions of the United States.* "But if so, what do we do about it?" This "crisis of meaning" was not a new one, he noted, recalling that the 1920s had first witnessed the modernist "failure" of cultural coherence. Subsequently, according to Gastil, the Great Depression, World War II, and the Cold War had imbued Americans nationally with a powerful sense of mission, distracting them from the deeper fragmentation of values and belief. The 1960s and 1970s had undermined this "frail self-confidence," he wrote, and "eroded any sense of personal mission." Americans in this tumultuous period discovered widespread poverty and environmental degradation in their midst, watched their cities erupt in riots, witnessed the assassination of their most inspiring leaders, lost a war, and saw a president quit in disgrace. Not without reason, a contemporary history of the era was titled *The Unraveling of America* (1984). In Gastil's view, people were now filling the void of "purposelessness" with the "standardized, consumer world of convenience, comfort, and commercialism," resulting in what he saw as a "chilling uniformity" of national life.[1]

Published at the very moment when American pride and unity should have been peaking—the years surrounding the Bicentennial celebration—Gastil's was one of a number of regional surveys of the 1970s that were instead symptomatic of the weakening of nationalism and cultural consensus, evidence of a search for an alternative seat of individual and collective identity. "This all started as a kind of private craziness," journalist Joel Garreau confessed in his 1981 book, *The Nine Nations of North America*. Paraphrasing an unnamed Texas "folklorist and regionalist," Garreau declared that "if Washington, D.C., were to slide into the Potomac tomorrow under the weight of its many burdens and crises, the result would be okay." The "healthy, powerful constituent parts" of the country would continue functioning "no matter what violence is done to the federal system." The essential thing, Garreau wrote, was for people to realize that "your identity is shaped by your origins." Daniel J. Elazar's analysis of American sectionalism, *American Federalism: A View from the States* (1966; 3rd ed. 1984), offered a comforting conclusion to readers looking for rootedness and continuity—America's disparate political cultures "arose out of very real sociocultural differences . . . that date back to the very beginnings of settlement and even back to the Old World."[2]

For many groups in American society, their search for identity dovetailed with political demands for social justice. The so-called cultural consensus, after all, had required their subordination under a male WASP establishment. The search was carried on most intensively and self-consciously in academia, where women's studies, Native American studies, Chicano/a studies, and Afro-American studies departments became all the rage. Folklife studies or "regional ethnology" was also part of this larger trend. As folklorist Don Yoder wrote in his introduction to *American Folklife* (1976), the field was motivated by "the present concern of Americans, particularly American youth, to determine their identity as it relates to ethnic, national, and world loyalties" and "their meaning in the larger picture."[3] Much in this vein, various regional centers began to be established across the country, including the American West Center at the University of Utah (1964), the Center for Great Plains Studies at the University of Nebraska at Lincoln (1976), and the Center for the Study of Southern Culture at the University of Mississippi (1977).

Even within such staid disciplines as geography, there were calls for a more socially conscious orientation. "Geography places too much emphasis on describing and explaining our sorry reality and too little on improving it," wrote David M. Smith in *The Geography of Social Well-Being in the United States* (1973). He believed that "professional geography has a vital and revolutionary role to play in the creation of a new society," particularly through mapping what he called "territorial social indicators," which would reveal "extreme inequalities at all spatial levels." Smith contended that in issues of social justice, an individual's "race, color, or *region*" must be taken into account. Gastil, too, found hope in the role that "regional culture might play in contributing to a national and personal revival." Elazar echoed Josiah Royce in calling for individuals to "gather together in communities . . . on a more restricted scale—as a prelude to renewal of public conscience for our larger civilization." Garreau stated simply that "to come away with a new understanding of regionalism is to come away with a better understanding of yourself." That integration of self and place would serve to make everyone "more confident of our future," renewing a sense of purpose.[4]

There were any number of hurdles to the attainment of this "new regionalism," as it came to be known after the postwar lull. First and foremost, there was the perennial and almost universal assumption that regional distinctiveness was in decline and therefore not the surest fount of identity. For example, in his book *Assimilation in American Life* (1964), sociologist Milton M. Gordon noted that "regional differences" were "doubtless decreasing" because of "the accelerating onslaught of rapid transportation, mass communications, and the increasing mechanization of a vast array of productive enterprises." Similarly, historical geographer Donald Meinig, in spite of his status as one of the period's ablest scholarly promoters of western regionalism, observed that "federal laws and broad educational trends, mass communications and population mobility, economic affluence and corporation networks, a broadening world outlook and a deepening social consciousness" were bringing about an "increasingly cohesive and uniform national pattern."[5] Much the same arguments had been made by Josiah Royce and Frederick Jackson Turner decades earlier, and Meinig was among those who once again had to make the case that regionalism was real and persistent.

But the region was also being challenged methodologically, both as a means of analysis and as a form of personal and group identity. Some members of Meinig's profession were doubtful about the region and the "descriptive, mechanical, inventory nature of much of its content," according to J. P. Cole and C. A. M. King in *Quantitative Geography* (1968), who pointed also to the "dubious nature of the limits of many regions used." Some geographers "condemned [the region] completely," Cole and King reported, whereas others "simply ignored it." This latter trend was perhaps the greatest hindrance to regionalism: in the civil rights era, there were too many other modes of identity and analysis vying for hearts and minds. Race, ethnicity, religion, class, and gender (among others)— each offered its own compelling way of seeing the self and the group, and of understanding America's past and present. Regional differences were "doubtless decreasing," Gordon concluded, while such identities as "ethnic group and social class" would become "increasingly important" in defining a "subsociety with its subculture." Don Yoder called it the "re-ethnicizing of America," and Gastil, in *Cultural Regions of the United States*, recognized the implications for regionalism. "Ethnic, religious, class, and professional" identities were "community-splitting" in relation to the places where people actually lived, he believed, and might undermine regional loyalties. Worse still for the regional community of interests, there was also the atomizing, apolitical, self-obsessed individualism that marked the era, well into the 1980s, as the "Me Decade," what historian Christopher Lasch labeled the "culture of narcissism."[6]

To counter these tendencies, the region represented a stable, fulfilling, shared form of meaning, something to "relate to" in a personal and concrete way, Gastil and others argued. "For the more a person sees the natural and human past of the environment that immediately surrounds him," he wrote, "the more he is able to relate his life to the present and future of that same environment."[7] Establishing the empirical validity of the region as something that was "really real" and expressive of a genuine dimension of American culture—the importance of *place*—became the central task of geographers, sociologists, historians, journalists, political scientists, and other analysts of the new regionalism during the 1960s–1980s period, with the West providing crucial if sometimes ambiguous evidence.

Broad strokes were the order of the day in many of these analyses—some poll data, a few anecdotes, a stereotype here and there. In a 1967 article appearing in *Public Opinion Quarterly*, for example, sociologists Norval D. Glenn and J. L. Simmons addressed the critical question, "Are Regional Cultural Differences Diminishing?" Using Gallup polls and similar national surveys, they found quite the opposite—"many kinds of differences have increased," in particular, "the South has diverged from the other regions, and the other regions have diverged from one another." The status of the South as a conservative outlier became a common theme of these regional overviews, and in fact, the South played a key role in first arousing general interest in the "new regionalism." The southern states' distinctively blatant form of legalized racial segregation, together with their very public defiance of federal measures to end it, seemed to point to the inescapable fact of regional differentiation. But rather than contrasting the South with the North or Northeast, as one might expect, Southern difference was often defined in relation to the polar opposite of a purportedly "liberal" West, as in Glenn and Simmons's study. According to their figures, social attitudes in the West were changing at the fastest rate and in the most liberal direction in the nation, "with the West farther 'ahead' of the other regions and the South farther 'behind.'"[8]

Likewise political scientist Ira Sharkansky, in his book *Regionalism in American Politics* (1970), asserted the "power of regional norms to persist over time" but found a greater degree of subregional variety especially in the West, where the state political cultures of the "Plains, Mountains, and Southwest stand out distinctively from their neighbors." Overall, western states were "high spenders," with higher party competition and more voter participation than other regions, again in marked contrast to the "low turn-out, competition, and service" of southern governance.[9] Using the latest tools of social science, the traditional nationalist West identity of the region as the land of the future, on the cutting edge of progress, was reconfirmed.

Glenn and Simmons divided the country broadly into four regional groupings of states; Sharkansky's "empirical analysis of regions" discerned as many as seventeen subregions nationally, four in the West, but still made individual states the unit of construction. Not all analysts found such neat boundaries to be a satisfactory reflection of reality, nor did they accept the facile contrast between a backward South and a progressive West. The most prominent challenge took the form of a new region, the Sunbelt, usually credited to political commentator Kevin Phillips in his book, *The Emerging Republican Majority* (1969).[10] The idea, if not the catchphrase, dated back much further, of course, but in the past agrarianism was the common cause that united westerners and southerners against an aggrandizing North, as in Walter Prescott Webb's *Divided We Stand.* Now it was suburbanites rather than farm folk who would fight the good fight, this time against an over-reaching federal government instead of northern corporate overlords.

An amorphous band of rapidly growing metropolitan areas stretching from Georgia and Florida out across Texas and Arizona to southern California, the Sunbelt concept did capture the real social phenomenon of the relocation of people and industry from the so-called Frost Belt or Rust Belt states of the Northeast. The Sunbelt also allowed the conjoined South to share in the patina of progress of the golden West. But despite its "widespread popular currency in the 1970s," as historian Raymond A. Mohl noted in *Searching for the Sunbelt* (1990), some analysts questioned whether the Sunbelt was more public relations slogan than anything else. As Blaine A. Brownell observed in the same volume, "The fact was that most residents of the Sunbelt were not aware of their new regional identity or good fortune, and even the prime beneficiaries of the new trends did not recognize the Sunbelt as a real place."[11] On balance, it seemed more akin to the grandiose trade areas promoted by western city boosters in the late nineteenth century, but on a vaster scale—and a form of regionalism nevertheless.

Joel Garreau also attempted to think outside the box of traditional American regions with *The Nine Nations of North America*, recombining them in unconventional ways and extending them across international borders. The South was relegated once again to the "Dixie" region, whereas the greater West was dismembered in a variety of directions: an "Ecotopia" occupied the West Coast from San Francisco to Juneau; a swath of borderlands stretching from California to Texas was linked into "Mexamerica"; the Plains states joined the Midwest as the "Breadbasket"; and the Mountain states were lumped into a vast region reaching to Point Barrow called the "Empty Quarter." Garreau disdained "hard theory" and number crunching in defining his regions, as his broad strokes certainly showed, but his construction explicitly questioned the nationalist- as well as state-biased frameworks in which much American regionalism had long operated.[12]

Other analysts, less averse to theory and statistics, also sought new ways of measuring and defining America's regions, the West included. As its title implied, Daniel J. Elazar's *American Federalism: A View from the States* seemed ostensibly to embrace the conventional division of the country into blocs of states within "three great historical, cultural, and economic spheres . . . the greater Northeast, the greater South and the greater West." Although his West excluded Oklahoma and Texas and incorporated Iowa and Minnesota, Elazar's true revisions lay in the fine print. When the predominance of "moralistic," "individualistic," or "traditionalistic" political cultures were tracked in different combinations, Elazar's states began to dissolve into a much more complex "internal diversity" of subregions. In Richard Franklin Bensel's *Sectionalism and American Political Development: 1880–1980* (1984), state borders disappeared altogether, replaced by a subregional patchwork of "trade areas" centered on hub cities like Denver and often stretching across parts of several states. Applying Immanuel Wallerstein's core-periphery model of the world system within the United States, Bensel portrayed the West as splayed politically between the core "industrial-commercial pole" anchored in the Northeast and Midwest, and the peripheral "interior-hinterland pole" that was strongest in the South. Some western trade areas, especially those centered on the big West Coast cities and some in the Plains, actually worked in political concert with the core, whereas other areas, including some in the Mountain states, seemed willing to bargain between the sides to further their own local advantages.[13] Bensel in this way offered a much more nuanced depiction of American sectional alignments than the more slapdash Sunbelt concept, but again, it was doubtful if his "trade areas," for all of their explanatory power vis à vis congressional voting patterns, reflected any popular level of regional identity or consciousness.

The same might be said of the work of geographer Donald Meinig, who among practitioners of the new regionalism achieved perhaps the highest level of sophistication in his mapping and devoted the most detailed attention to conceptualization of the localist West. Meinig grew up on a farm in the intricately varied Palouse country of eastern Washington, and he counted Carl Sauer and A. L. Kroeber as important influences. Through a series of works that he considered parts of a whole, in the 1960s Meinig began to construct a general theory of region formation. Like western regionalists dating back to John Wesley Powell, he used the cohesive Mormons of Utah as his point of departure. In his 1965 article "The Mormon Culture Region: Strategies and Patterns in the Geography of the American West, 1847–1964," Meinig sought to move beyond the "cultural geographer's generalization" of regions as "static uniform patterns" and toward seeing them as "dynamic areal growths." His region consisted of a gradation from a concentrated, homogeneous "core" surrounded by a larger "domain" where a culture is more diluted but still dominant, and outward from this, a "sphere" of "outer influence" where the culture is present but in the minority. Meinig applied much the same model in the widely read *Imperial Texas: An Interpretive Essay in Cultural Geography* (1969), tweaking it to include a diffuse "Secondary Domain" of regional culture and, at the farthest remove from the core, a "Zone of Penetration." Apparently, the model could not be retrofitted to the complexity of his Washington "homeland" as depicted in *The Great Columbia Plain* (1968), which was based on work he had done in the 1950s. Nor did it seem that the model could be applied across the epic scope and time frame—not to mention the page limit—of his short book, *Southwest: Three Peoples in Geographical Change, 1600–1970* (1971), but that work did bring to the fore the importance of transportation networks in region building.[14]

Meinig culminated this period of his thinking with a major synthetic essay, "American Wests: Preface to a Geographical Interpretation" (1972), in which he introduced an entirely new terminology, defining six major cultural "nuclei" in the historical West: Northern California, Southern California, Colorado, the Oregon Country, the Mormon Region, and Hispano New Mexico. Under this new scheme, each of these nuclei underwent regional development across four different categories: "population (numbers and areal distribution), circulation (traffic patterns within and

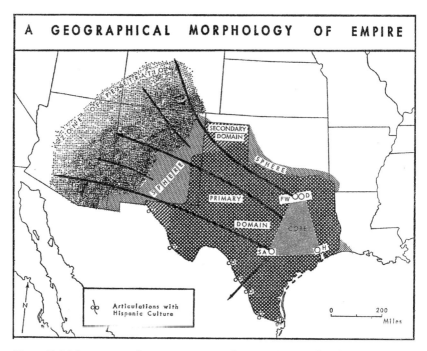

Figure 7 Making a case for western regionalism. A *Geographical Morphology of Empire*, from *Imperial Texas: An Interpretive Essay in Cultural Geography*, by D. W. Meinig, © 1969, renewed 1997. Courtesy of the University of Texas Press.

between regions), political areas (basic jurisdictional territories), and culture (selected features characteristic of the local society and its imprint upon the area)." Within each category, the region evolved through four stages. For example, the "circulation" of the region changed from "isolation" to "regional system" to "interregional network" and finally, "intermetropolitan national network." And so on. By 1978, having pushed social scientific definition of the localist West to its limits—like a nuclear physicist finding quarks within what were thought to be "elementary" particles—Meinig seemed to retreat from the overwrought complexity of it all, admitting, "Regions are abstractions, they exist in our minds . . . as tools of thought." He announced a new scheme under which regions could be broken down into "subcomplexes such as cultural landscapes, social geographies, and spatial systems." Ironically, in this same 1978 essay, "The Continuous Shaping of America," Meinig invoked his original terms of "core" and "domain" only at the safely ambiguous scale of the nationalist West: "The subordination of the South and the West to the economic, political, and cultural power of the Northeast" in the decades after the

Civil War should be "studied as a major geographical topic," he proposed.[15] Walter Prescott Webb would have approved.

While Meinig struggled valiantly to put the new regionalism on a more scientific basis, other analysts took a different path toward defining regions—away from demography and historical data and toward psychology and perception. Inspired by the civil rights movement, this methodological shift paralleled the emergence of the "new social history," in which historians and scholars in other fields paid more heed to the lives of ordinary people as shapers of history, setting aside the elitist, top-down approach to understanding the past and present. In the broadest sense, it was also an expression of the "linguistic turn" away from modernism and its hope of finding a ground of certainty in external reality and toward a "postmodernist" sensibility that accepted the indeterminate, created nature of reality. The protean character of the region seemed to epitomize the insight that "language helps to constitute its object," as historian Dominick LaCapra put it. Thus in his important article "Perceptual Regions in Texas" (1978), geographer Terry G. Jordan defined what he called the "vernacular region," which was not the "intellectual creation of the professional geographer" or "based on carefully chosen, quantifiable criteria," but rather "the product of the spatial perception of average people" . . . "the mental maps of the population."[16]

Wilbur Zelinsky had begun trying to capture this lived reality of regional America in *The Cultural Geography of the United States* (1973), hoping to inject what he called "self-consciousness" into the regional concept. His definition of the "culture area" required that it be "distinguished from others on the basis of genuine differences in cultural systems," that these differences by "manifested physically and behaviorally," and that there be a "condition of self-awareness on the part of the participants" in the culture. In *Cultural Geography*, Zelinsky mapped out five major American regions including a West that began roughly halfway across the tier of Plains states, excluding west-central Oklahoma and Texas. Within the larger West he identified nine subregional core areas, including the Upper Rio Grande Valley (Taos, Santa Fe, Albuquerque, and their environs), the Willamette Valley, central and southern California, Puget Sound, the Inland Empire (eastern Washington), Colorado Piedmont, Central Arizona, and the Mormon region, drawing most of his evidence from studies such as Meinig's. In a 1980 article, Zelinsky went further in trying to grasp the "vernacular region," using telephone or city directories from metropolitan areas across the United States and Canada, compiling the frequency with which regional terms appeared in the names of local nongovernmental entities. He found fourteen vernacular regions nationally by this method. Besides a broad-ranging "Western" region, Zelinsky also mapped the Southwest, the Pacific, and the Northwest cutting across the western states. He noted, "The territory claimed by the Greater West is several times larger than that within the Greater East. . . . We have here further evidence, if any is still needed, of the extraordinary grip of the idea of the West on the North American popular mind."[17]

Just how much the nationalist West still gripped the American consciousness remained to be seen, but surveys like Zelinsky's seemed to show that the localist West was also alive and well. When everyday respondents in the West were asked to name their local regions themselves, the maps fragmented into a variegated tapestry of dozens of sub-subregions. Zelinsky, Jordan, and others had been inspired by the research of Ruth F. Hale, whose dissertation "A Map of Vernacular Regions in America" (1971) was based on postcard surveys mailed to newspaper editors, county agents, and postmasters across the country, asking the simple question, "What name is commonly used to refer to the region(s) in your state in which your county is located?" Her national map revealed no fewer than 288 such vernacular regions—"many of them quite minute," Zelinsky commented—including some 45 shown in a published map of the Great Plains. Using much the same methodology and mostly polling college students, Jordan himself tallied twenty-nine "perceptual" regions in Texas alone, not counting the ubiquitous (in the South and southern Plains) "Bible Belt." These findings seemed to confirm the fate of Meinig's "Great Columbia Plain": far from being absorbed into a greater regional or national uniformity, this subregion dissolved into as many as seven smaller constituent subregions over the course of the twentieth century. "For regions exist in the minds of men," Meinig observed, "and maps mirror their times."[18]

Jordan, Meinig, Zelinsky, and other academic exponents of the new regionalism during the 1970s may have provided ample evidence for the persistence of regionalization in the West and elsewhere in America, but something seemed to be missing from their analyses when compared to the "old" regionalists of the 1920s and 1930s. In his 1978 essay, "The Continuous Shaping of America," Meinig deprecated this earlier generation, the "Odum School of regional sociology" and the "Turnerian historians," for their "static subregions and blocks of states" and "broad sections."[19] Yet in the hands of that interwar generation, regionalism had become, at the very least, a nascent ideology, dedicated to decentralizing power and establishing a more symbiotic and communitarian social order. Meinig and their successors, whether because of professionalization or post-1960s political exhaustion, viewed regionalism largely as a "tool of thought." Cultural radicals they were not, except to the extent that they ran counter to the widespread assumption that regional America was being homogenized out of existence.

If they failed to heed David M. Smith's call for a "revolutionary" geography, the new regionalists nevertheless contributed to the burgeoning identity politics of these years by authoritatively establishing the cultural reality of regions. It is true that many of the regions and subregions uncovered by new regionalist analysts were either innocuously descriptive ("High Plains") or clearly the creature of local boosters ("Golden Triangle"). Western regionalism had always fed off of the promotion of homesteading, town building, and tourism. But it could also be put to more transgressive uses by those who chose to do so, as Mary Austin, D'Arcy McNickle, Rose Wilder Lane, and others had shown. Their heirs in the post-1960s West similarly looked to the region to gain footing to leverage social and political change. As an alternative space for those aggrieved by the nation-state, regionalism served three very different groups of westerners into the 1970s and 1980s: Native American activists, radical environmentalists, and the Sagebrush Rebels.

In her 1993 autobiography, Cherokee leader Wilma Mankiller remembered the trauma of her family's relocation by the government from Oklahoma to San Francisco when she was ten years old: "One day I was living in a rural Cherokee community, and a few days later I was living in California and trying to deal with the mysteries of television, neon lights, and elevators. It was total culture shock."[20] In 1969, when she was twenty-four, activists began an eighteen-month occupation of San Francisco's Alcatraz Island, a case study in the contemporary search for identity—and the central role that place could serve in that search.

Most of the several thousand Native Americans who participated in the Alcatraz protest were, like Mankiller, urban dwellers from the Bay area, uprooted relocatees or the children of relocatees, and a substantial percentage were college students. As Sioux scholar Vine Deloria Jr. noted in *Custer Died for Your Sins: An American Indian Manifesto* (1969), "Urban Indians have become the cutting edge of the new Indian nationalism." Without a reservation "homeland" to call their own, the protesters rushed into the vacuum of meaning that occurred when the federal government closed the infamous prison on Alcatraz, declaring that the site had now become "surplus" federal land and therefore, under an obscure nineteenth-century treaty, open to be reclaimed (symbolically) as part of Indian country. In a sardonic proclamation, they imbued Alcatraz with a variety of pointed meanings: virgin territory that Native Americans had "discovered" and for which they offered fair payment ($24 in beads and cloth); a space to provide a reservation for Alcatraz's white residents, overseen by a "bureau of Caucasian Affairs"; an ideal location for an Indian reservation, since the island lacked water, natural resources, industry, schools, and health care; and the future site of multiple community centers devoted to Indian culture, religion, ecology, and job training. Alcatraz therefore revealed the power of place to provoke a movement culture into being, built around a growing self-consciousness of sovereignty. One of the leaders of the occupation, a Mohawk student named Richard Oakes, remarked that the goal was "not so much to liberate the island, but to liberate ourselves for the sake of cultural survival." Mankiller herself joined the protest and recalled the electrifying effect that such Red Power occupations had on her sense of identity. "Alcatraz articulated my own feelings about being an Indian. It was a benchmark. After that, I became involved."[21]

Inspired by Alcatraz, the sites of subsequent occupations during the early 1970s were carefully chosen to ratchet up their symbolic value. In the summer of 1970, Mount Rushmore became the target of John Trudell, an Alcatraz organizer, along with Russell Means and other members of the American Indian Movement (AIM). Camping on the summit, the group issued a statement that sought to collapse the nationalist West monument down to the localist grievances of the "Sioux Indian people of South Dakota," focusing on treaty violations, the desecration of the Black Hills subregion, and the villainy of the four white demigods toward native peoples. A second takeover of Mount Rushmore and the hovering threat of more to come—especially in the years leading up to the Bicentennial—required the Park Service to beef up security at times to absurd levels, including SWAT teams and the FBI.[22] Yet the point was made: force of arms was necessary to maintain illegitimate American rule there.

After the astonishing seizure (and trashing) of BIA headquarters in Washington in 1972, AIM activists the following year took this line of argument to a more radical level at Wounded Knee, another piece of sacred ground. Under siege by federal law enforcement, the self-declared Independent Oglala Nation, complete with temporary visas for "foreign visitors" and demands for negotiations with the White House, dramatically addressed the critical issue of Native sovereignty. In the wake of these early 1970s protests, the federal government did accelerate the process of yielding greater autonomy to Indian country through a series of congressional acts and court opinions, including the Indian Self-Determination and

Education Act of 1975. Increasingly, for example, block grants were issued to tribal governments to administer social programs themselves, rather than relying on BIA administrators under Washington control. Considered as an expression of regionalism—the term "federalism," which applies more to the states, did not quite capture it—this shift toward Native American sovereignty, however piecemeal, represented a true decentralization of power.[23] This was no mere "tool of thought" but had real consequences in the lives of Native peoples and individuals. Mankiller, for one, became a community organizer and eventually returned to Oklahoma to be named principal chief of the Cherokee Nation in 1985, under the new constitution ratified during the push for greater self-determination in the 1970s.

Contemporary "bioregionalists," as another wing of post-1960s regionalism referred to themselves, would have seen the various Native American occupations—temporary though they were—as examples of "reinhabiting" America, one of the bioregionalists' key concepts. The reaction of constituted authority to the Indian protesters was one indicator of just how radical this idea could be. Bioregionalism in the West emerged from much the same countercultural ferment that had helped spawn the spirit of Alcatraz. Activist Peter Berg and poet Gary Snyder are usually credited as its founding fathers. Berg first arrived in Haight-Ashbury during the mid-1960s and formed The Diggers, a street theater troupe, proselytizing anarchism, communalism, and a localistic, moneyless economy. It was Berg who earliest synthesized these ideals with ecology, particularly from the vantage of rural Black Bear commune in Northern California's Klamath region, where he resided in the late 1960s. Such experiments in alternative living suggested the doctrine of reinhabitation that came to be prominent in Berg's writings on bioregionalism. "THESE NATION-STATES CAN BREAK DOWN & FADE OFF THE LANDSCAPE," he declared in "Reinhabitation Message from Pacific Coast, North America" (1974). Snyder, too—who grew up on a farm near the Puget Sound—noted in a 1970 interview that "especially in the Far West, the lines are quite often arbitrary and serve only to confuse people's sense of natural associations and relationships." As he later defined it, reinhabitation was the effort to "regain self-determination in place after centuries of having been disenfranchised by hierarchy and/or centralized power."[24]

Reinhabitation thus might require the bioregion to become a "separate state," capable of organizing "watershed governments appropriate to maintaining local life-places," as Berg projected in "Reinhabiting California" (1978). According to Snyder, the outlines of such bioregions were taken from works such as Kroeber's *Cultural and Natural Areas of Native North America*. "Bio-" was intended to distinguish bioregionalism from the functionalist brand devoted to metropolitan planning, but Berg also alluded to Carl Sauer as an influence, and other "old" regionalists were invoked by Kirkpatrick Sale in *Dwellers in the Land: The Bioregional Vision* (1985) to define their intellectual tradition, including Frederick Jackson Turner, Lewis Mumford, and Howard Odum. Such a lineage enhanced their legitimacy in light of their demands for local sovereignty. In any case, the numerous bioregionalist groups that sprang up across the country into the 1980s, like the Shasta Bioregion in Northern California, could still exist as a kind of shadow government without an actual revolutionary redistribution of power that reinhabitation seemed to necessitate. As Berg described the process in 1986, bioregionalist adherents could find meaning and engage communally through a whole range of grassroots activities short of full-fledged bioregional government. "A bioregional politics originates with individuals who identify with real places," he wrote. "Involving close by watershed neighbors creates a 'socialshed,'" and several "socialsheds" could organize "co-ops, community gardens, renewable energy, bioregional education, recycling" and other projects, thereby "rightfully claiming representation for the closely shared place itself."[25]

This shift in spatial perception toward an ecosystem framework was hardly limited to the ideological margin represented by the bioregionalists. During the 1970s, the concept of ecosystem protection also began to gather momentum within the environmental establishment, driven by the habitat requirements of the Endangered Species Act (1973) and the once-in-a-lifetime opportunity to preserve whole wilderness ecosystems in Alaska under the Alaska National Interest Lands Conservation Act (1980). There was recognition of the need to preserve larger and larger parcels of land for ecosystems to operate viably. Hard scientific criteria—climate, plant distribution, soil types, and other measurable elements—also promised to ground regionalism in an objective certainty lacking in definitions that relied on cultural or psychological analysis.

Although a western regionalism rooted in natural watersheds reached back to the time of Powell, and whole-cloth wilderness areas dated to Leopold in the 1920s, the remapping of the West into a variegated array of localist ecosystem subregions or "ecoregions" saw official light of day in 1976 with the publication of a US Forest Service map titled "Ecoregions of the United States," by Robert G. Bailey, a geographer at the Intermountain Region office in Ogden, Utah. Based on regional commonalities of climate, vegetation, fauna, soils, and terrain, the map divided the country into four regional levels, each successively more localistic, beginning with "domains," "divisions," "provinces," and the finest degree of detail, "sections." The West fell into two domains (Dry and Humid Temperate), seven divisions, eighteen provinces, and at least thirty-four named sections. The rationale for the map, according to Bailey, was to aid in ecosystem classification for "regional and national long-range planning." Bailey's effort was followed in 1987 by a competing version issued under the auspices of the US Environmental Protection Agency (EPA), "Ecoregions of the Conterminous United States." The latter was the work of James M. Omernik of the EPA's Environmental Research Laboratory in Corvallis, Oregon. Numbered consecutively from west to east beginning with the "Coast Range" ecoregion (where Omernik resided), the map divided the continental United States into no fewer than seventy-six irregularly shaped ecoregions, with the West incorporating wholes or parts of forty-eight of them. Omernik also noted the map's potential usefulness for "national level planning, management, and analysis."[26]

These expectations were more than academic in the wake of measures like the Federal Land Policy and Management Act (FLPMA, 1976), which in the eyes of some observers was the true closing of the western frontier. The FLPMA was part of what has been called the "quiet revolution" in land-use planning that began in the early 1960s at the state level, most notably in Hawaii. A major 1972 report that first characterized the revolution concluded that the "states, not local governments, are the only existing political entities" able to deal effectively with problems like pollution and environmental degradation. But the report also noted that "concern over the interrelatedness of land uses had led to a recognition of the need to deal with entire ecological systems rather than small segments of them." Places such as San Francisco Bay and Lake Tahoe were increasingly seen in ecoregional terms, "as single entities rather than as a collection of governmental units." The Hawaiian model lauded by the report's authors divided the islands into intrastate subregional districts defined by land-use types, crossing multiple jurisdictional and private boundary lines. The focus by the report on state "governmental units"—in a bow to federalism— was intended to set the stage for the National Land Use Policy Act, a much sought-after reform that would have mandated and funded land-use control by the states. The bill was introduced in Congress repeatedly between 1968 and 1975 and never passed, but the FLPMA was enacted the following year, a law potentially just as momentous for the western states.[27]

The FLPMA was partially the outgrowth of another landmark federal report, *One Third of the Nation's Land* (1970), which had recommended that the long-standing policy of "large-scale disposal of public lands" to private use and ownership be "revised," with the future presumption of "retaining in Federal ownership." The FLPMA made nearly this exact wording the first in its list of policy declarations, but further along it also sought to reassure commercial users of the public domain that the public lands would be "managed in a manner which recognizes the Nation's need for domestic sources of minerals, food, timber, and fiber." Yet besides the shift from disposal to retention, what seemed new and potentially revolutionary in the FLPMA was the stipulation that there would be a "land use planning procedure" to balance competing interests, applied now not merely to highly visible parcels like the national parks and forests but to the far vaster and long-neglected holdings of the Bureau of Land Management (BLM). Among the other interests to be taken into account would be "scientific, scenic, historical, ecological, environmental, air and atmospheric, water resource, and archeological values," as well as "outdoor recreation." Of course, a "multiple use" doctrine had in some form been a part of federal land management deliberations for decades, doing little to curb the prodigious exploitation of public lands by ranchers and other commercial users. The FLPMA recognized that there were other players that it was now politically wise to include, not to mention the fact that the BLM, the Forest Service, and other land-managing agencies were obliged to submit environmental impact statements to the EPA (sometimes at the behest of a federal judge). Maps of western ecoregions were good information to have in such cases. The authors of *One Third of the Nation's Land* said more in their recommendations, however: "Comprehensive land use planning should be encouraged through regional commissions," which must include the involvement of the "regional public" as well as the concerns of the "national public," resource users, state and local governments, and the federal government both as "sovereign" and "proprietor."[28]

Everyone understood that by "national public" the authors meant, in a concrete sense, the increasingly influential mainstream environmental organizations that claimed to speak in their name, such as the Sierra Club, the Wilderness Society, and the National Audubon Society. Certainly these groups, echoing Bernard DeVoto, frequently legitimized their demands in the baldest nationalist West terms by invoking the "American public" as owners of the public lands. They also continued the time-honored nationalist theme of the West as wilderness wonderland for all Americans, an argument made more convincing thanks to the easy accessibility provided by the recently completed interstate highway system, linking the western landscape with the family sentimentality of millions of vacationing voters. At the same time, the broader cultural "crisis of meaning," which sent middle-class Americans to the West in search of the peace and stability of nature, seemed to find an objective correlative in the "energy crisis" of the 1970s, heralding a new era of limits in which there was an imperative to husband what remained of America's beauty and bounty. The potency of such arguments was shown not only in the place made for the mainstream environmental organizations at the policy-making table but also in their growing memberships. The Wilderness Society increased from 7,600 members in the mid-1950s to nearly 200,000 in 1988; during the same period, the Sierra Club grew from 7,000 to almost half a million members. Their clout was evident in statistics like these: the number of acres within the National Wilderness Preservation System grew by nearly 800 percent between 1964 and 1980, almost all of it in the West, including Alaska.[29]

The "regional public" referred to in *One Third of the Nation's Land* may have included urban-dwelling westerners who themselves cherished wilderness experience and were sympathetic to the mainstream environmentalist agenda, but it also meant (in the authors' words) "those who live in or near the vast public lands" and who "have a special concern that the public lands help to support them and their neighbors and that the lands contribute to their overall well-being." Besides this general local interest in economic growth, the more direct interests that must be accommodated were the "users" of the public lands, which assuredly included recreationists, but especially "those seeking economic gain"—there must be "equal consideration" for them along with all other users.[30] Perhaps the most important of these commercial users from the standpoint of western regional identity were the public lands ranchers.

In the 1970s and 1980s, the cowboy archetype still held considerable sway in the American mind, despite the fact that the Old West culture industry was not what it once was. Western TV series like *Gunsmoke* and *Bonanza* had gradually disappeared by the mid-1970s. Devastating parodies such as the film *Blazing Saddles* (1974) also did their work, as did more realistic films ranging from *McCabe and Mrs. Miller* (1971) and *The Last Picture Show* (1971) to *Unforgiven* (1992). Yet Americans had a hard time relinquishing their nationalist West myths, especially the cowboy. Texas writer (and rancher) Larry McMurtry, who built his own personal culture industry of novels and screenplays around this ambivalence, scored his biggest success with *Lonesome Dove*, a melancholy but respectful celebration of cattlemen that began life as a screenplay for movie idol John Wayne and evolved into a Pulitzer Prize–winning novel (1985) and ac claimed TV miniseries (1989). The hit movie *City Slickers* (1991) also played it straight, depicting a group of dude ranch guests who must meet the challenge of a real cattle drive, reviving Old West clichés that dated back to Owen Wister. Gretel Ehrlich made ample use of them as well in *The Solace of Open Spaces* (1985), her best-selling paean to contemporary western sheep- and cattle-raisers. She herself replayed Wister's therapeutic rest cure in Wyoming (fleeing the West Coast rather than the East), where she found "vigor, self-reliance, and common sense . . . anchored by a land-bound sense of place." Small wonder that two economists (A. H. Smith and W. E. Martin) reported in a 1972 study that the allure of ranching remained so strong that while many arid West ranches operated at a loss, their owners refused to sell "almost regardless of the market price of ranches," because "maintaining the ranch as a home and way of life is the rancher's most important goal."[31]

Increasingly, mainstream and more radical environmental groups were calling western ranching into question, particularly that form of it requiring tens of millions of acres of arid public lands. Their critique necessarily pitted the wilderness West regional identity against that of the agrarian West, for at stake were the large contiguous parcels of the remaining public domain overseen by the BLM—large enough to support a pastoral "way of life" on sparse grasses, and also large enough to provide a semblance of primitive wilderness experience as well as ample room for wildlife habitat. Critics pointed first of all to the sheer scope of public lands devoted to ranching, which by 1977 occupied 170 million of the BLM's acreage along with 100 million acres in the National Forest System, but which produced only 2 percent of the nation's livestock. That small percentage still amounted to several million cattle and sheep grazing, trampling, and defecating often on dry, rocky, sandy, easily eroded, and barely vegetated ranges—much of which constituted what federal officials once called "frail lands." A 1975 study by the BLM acknowledged that 50 percent of federal rangelands were in only fair condition, and an additional 33 percent were in poor condition.[32]

Environmentalists invoked Garrett Hardin's widely read essay, "The Tragedy of the Commons" (1968), a meditation on irresponsible individualism, to explain the widespread degradation. Edward Abbey called it "cowburnt." Most critiques, including the public lands survey *These American Lands* (1986) issued by the Wilderness Society, also highlighted the fact that this vast territory was under lease—at one-quarter of the market rate—to roughly 30,000 ranchers at most during the 1970s and 1980s, a tiny fraction of the total number of stockraisers nationally, and dwarfed by the millions of recreational visitors to the public lands. Radicals like Abbey and other activists consequently zeroed in on the cowboy myth as the debate over the disposition of BLM lands intensified in the 1980s. In a prominent *Harper's* article published in 1986, Abbey referred to public lands ranchers as "welfare parasites." One local activist in Arizona, Lynn Jacobs, self-published a polemic titled *Waste of the West: Public Lands Ranching*, in 1991. Jacobs depicted stockraisers as a kind of aristocracy who had "more power over the rural West and its people than any other group." The western cowboy, he declared, "personifies the glorification of violence" as well as the "perpetuation of machismo and all it entails—might is right, man over Nature and woman . . . brutality towards animals, and a generally wasteful, over-exploitive attitude." Ranching, Jacobs concluded, "is not natural to the wild West but is instead its most deadly enemy," and he yearned to see "a West free from ranching."[33]

Extreme sentiments like these were alarming to western stockraisers, needless to say, but there was something to their accusation that wilderness advocates hoped to use federal power to impose the wilderness West regional identity on the locals. For example, the authors of *These American Lands*, as the title implied, explicitly employed nationalist West arguments to sway their audience, embracing Turner's frontier thesis for having "legitimized wilderness" and its "shaping of the American character," and declaring Turner a major figure in the intellectual tradition leading to the wilderness preservation system.[34] The agenda of *These American Lands* included a substantial expansion of that system, and one step in this direction was supposed to be the long-term review then being undertaken by the BLM to determine if up to 25 million acres of its inventory might be added.

The glittering possibilities—and stark political obstacles—of the BLM's so-called Wilderness Study Areas (WSAs) were evident in a sample environmental impact statement written in 1988 for a 200,000-acre subregion encompassing the Ely, Las Vegas, and Winnemuca districts in Nevada, one of dozens of such statements the BLM had been ordered to make. Phrases like "outstanding opportunities for solitude" and "primitive and unconfined recreation" appeared, which certainly in decades past had not been part of the BLM's institutional culture. In addition to ranching, the whole gamut of economic activities in the rural West came under review. Concerns were expressed over the "natural perception" of certain WSAs if utilities were strung; "scarification of topography and the sights and sounds from heavy equipment" would occur if mining and other development went forward; "crucial desert tortoise habitat" might also come under threat. Yet out of fourteen WSAs reviewed for the statement, twelve were recommended for the "No Wilderness/No Action Alternative," whereas only two were proposed for the "Partial Wilderness Alternative." The "All Wilderness Alternative," under which mining, drilling, utilities, and motorized vehicles would be "forgone" and "unavailable" (in the dismal language of the statement), was left on the table. In fact, even under the purely hypothetical "All Wilderness" proposals, little mention was made of any restrictions on ranching activity, except in one case where the construction of two stock tanks would have been forbidden, and local cowboys would be required to ride horses rather than motorbikes "to accomplish livestock trailing." It is no surprise that the authors of *These American Lands* saw this type of WSA evaluation as essential to beginning the land-use planning process that had been mandated by the FLPMA, but at the same time invoked the historical lesson of Powell's earlier failure. "The political realities of his time defeated Powell," they noted, "but after a century of the kind of waste and misuse that his ideas might have prevented, it is perhaps necessary for us to revive at least some of his concepts and do with them what we can . . . to revolutionize our future utilization of the public lands."[35]

Among the contemporary political realities curtailing these attempts to expand land-use planning was the conservative insurgency known as the Sagebrush Rebellion. For a time in the late 1970s and early 1980s, the Sagebrush Rebellion seemed to provide sensational confirmation of the "resurgence of sectional feeling" that Daniel Elazar predicted would be a "major force in the post-1976 generation." Colorado governor Richard Lamm may have overstated the case in 1978 when he claimed that "feelings of sectionalism and regionalism are the most intense of any time since the Civil War," but certainly Sunbelt–Frost Belt animosity enjoyed a good deal of currency in the media—an important part of the context of resentment out of which the Sagebrush Rebellion emerged. The OPEC-inspired spike in energy prices caused parts of the West to boom but helped throw the industrial Northeast into the economic doldrums, exacerbating the longer-term trend of out-migrating people and industries. Frost Belt politicians began to wonder aloud why such prosperous states were still a net importer of their hard-squeezed constituents' tax dollars. Western politicians, for their part, gave voice to fears that East Coast liberals—jealous of the West's success—were attempting to take national their region's high-tax regulatory regimes, sabotaging western growth with a proposed "windfall profits tax" and environmental laws such as the FLPMA.[36]

Thus a traditional West-versus-East theme became a pronounced (albeit background) element of Sagebrush rhetoric. In their contemporary and not entirely sympathetic account of the movement, *The Angry West* (1982), Lamm and coauthor Michael McCarthy cited several examples. The governor of Montana likened easterners to foreigners, declaring that "we don't want to . . . turn over control to outsiders, and that means OPEC, Washington, and the East." Another western state official rejected a water project because its "basic philosophy unfortunately is patterned after the values of the East." Senator Orrin Hatch of Utah referred to the "confining attitudes and overregulated approaches of the East."[37] Two could play the regional culture war game, it seemed, but the branding of "eastern" as alien and illegitimate was only the beginning of the Sagebrush counterattack against the environmentalist assault on "welfare cowboys."

Rather than focusing resentment—and political pressure—on an amorphous "East," the Sagebrush Rebels took more careful aim at the federal government in Washington, DC. Much like the wilderness advocates, they fielded their own regional identity for the West in the debate over public lands: aggrieved colony. In *The Angry West*, Lamm and McCarthy rehashed charges of economic colonialism similar to those put forward by Garland, Webb, DeVoto, Howard, and other westerners in decades past, recounting the West's history of exploitation and dependence at the hands of eastern corporate monopolism. But what really aroused their ire, and that of the bulk of the Rebels, was the *political* form of colonialism. Lamm and McCarthy portrayed the West as "Washington's child," at the mercy of "suffocating federal power" that for more than a century had treated westerners with "paternalism and disdain . . . arrogance," and "ignorance." Its public lands, they noted, were "managed, regulated, and overseen" by no fewer than "seventeen federal agencies."[38]

Wilderness preservation was just one of a range of issues that had brought matters to a boiling point, according to Lamm and McCarthy. The energy crisis, with all of its geopolitical implications, had spurred great corporate and federal interest in the oil shale lands of Colorado, Wyoming, and Utah, pushing aside traditional small-time users. The proposed MX missile system, to be situated across 24,000 square miles of Nevada and Utah, promised to consume vast quantities of scarce water for construction and operation, would oust many agricultural users, and would preclude energy exploration on the lands in question, not to mention making the Great Basin subregion a principal target of the Soviets. As Lamm and McCarthy noted, Utahns in particular had long-standing suspicions of federal power, reaching back to nineteenth-century discrimination against Latter-day Saints members, and refreshed most recently by revelations that the health effects from nuclear testing in the 1950s had not been as harmless as the government claimed. Most oppressed of all in the West were the stockraisers, many of them driven out of business by permits, fees, and an ever-tightening web of federal regulations since the Taylor Act. The "war touched off between cattlemen and the federal government," wrote Lamm and McCarthy, "has not ended to this day." As a Nevada rancher who leased 290,000 acres from the BLM—but was barred from half of it to protect an endangered species—told *Newsweek* magazine, "I never figured I'd be fighting my own government to defend my way of life."[39]

Texas economist Gary D. Libecap elaborated on this point in his 1981 study, *Locking Up the Range: Federal Land Controls and Grazing*, in which he detailed western subordination to an imperial Washington bureaucracy. Smith and Martin had argued in "Socioeconomic Behavior of Cattle Ranchers" that arid lands ranching was such a losing proposition that it could hardly be considered "part of commercial agriculture"; Libecap, to the contrary, held up public lands ranchers as living embodiments of Economic Man. Ranchers, he wrote, "bear the costs" and "receive the benefits of their actions" according to "market signals"—BLM bureaucrats did none of these things. Insulated in salaried positions, they sought to aggrandize the power and budgets of their agencies and from their lordly position handed down only those land-use policies that were the most "politically rewarding" to themselves. The bureaucrats refused to grant private property rights or simple security of tenure to the ranchers. Rejecting "market processes," the BLM had embraced "central planning" for multiple use, guided by "biological rather than economic criteria," according to Libecap. Gone were the golden days of the 1940s and 1950s, when western stockmen largely governed themselves through the local grazing advisory boards. Since 1960, the BLM had worked steadily to "weaken the control of the livestock industry over federal land," and the only solution, in Libecap's view, was once and for all to grant "secure private property rights to the western range."[40]

Senator Hatch agreed that something must be done to restore and maintain the West as the "last great preserve of free enterprise," a neofrontier utopia that resounded through the rhetoric of the Rebellion. It offered a stark contrast to the oppressive reality that ordinary westerners now allegedly confronted. William Perry Pendley, head of the Mountain States Legal Foundation, which first emerged in the late 1970s as the legal arm of the Sagebrush Rebellion, looked back in a 1992 speech and concluded that in the previous twenty years the West had been used as a "laboratory for controlling and limiting growth." Virtual expropriation had been taking place, Pendley argued, "as the cattleman, the rancher, the wool-grower, the miner, the timberman, the water developer, the ski resort operator, the oil and gas explorationist, and all of the little towns and communities that depend upon such activities are being pushed off the land."[41]

Control, Lamm and McCarthy concluded, was the "central issue in the Sagebrush Rebellion"—seizing control away from the Washington bureaucrats and their environmentalist allies and ending the West's colonial status. Most observers dated the beginning of the rebellion to June 4, 1979, when the Nevada legislature passed a law asserting state control over the 48 million acres of BLM lands within its borders. A month later, county commissioners in Moab, Utah, celebrated the July 4 holiday by running a bulldozer onto a nearby "roadless" wilderness study area in defiance of the BLM. Within the next year or so, Wyoming, New Mexico, Utah, and Arizona passed measures similar to Nevada's, and other western states (including Hawaii) considered them. Their legal reasoning again invoked the West's quasi-colonial status, focusing on the western states' lack of "equal footing" with the states of the East, which had not been forced to relinquish claims to public lands as a condition of statehood, as had many in the West. They did so on the implicit assumption that the federal government would continue to convey public lands to individual ownership, a long-standing policy that seemed to have been halted by the FLPMA. The import of a law put forward by Orrin Hatch in 1979 became clear—the Western Lands Distribution and Regional Equalization Act proposed to transfer more than 500 million acres of federal public lands to state oversight.[42]

Despite the fact that the bill did not pass, the Sagebrush Rebels believed they had a champion in the White House when former California governor Ronald Reagan was elected president in 1980. Reagan explicitly identified himself with their cause on the campaign trail, and he appointed James Watt, then head of the Mountain States Legal Foundation, to be secretary of the Interior. Yet the Rebellion itself was divided over its fundamental goal. There were those like Hatch who simply wanted to transfer oversight to more business-friendly state governments, but after 1980 there was also an increasingly vocal group who believed like Gary Libecap (with some lip service, at least, from Watt) that the lands should be directly privatized. This outcome might have been philosophically satisfying to conservatives, but it did not necessarily make the best economic sense to ranchers and other commercial users, who presently could run their operations on lands below the market rate and did not have to bear the full burden of state property taxes. Lamm and McCarthy were among those seeking a third alternative, fearing that outright cession to the states would result in a vast corporate land grab, pushing out small businesses and farmers. The Sagebrush Rebellion, they wrote, is "a movement of the few" that could end in the "final corporatizing of the West"—merely exchanging one form of colonialism for another. To prevent this scenario, they envisioned what Utah governor Scott Matheson termed a "positive regionalism," which would involve the "restoration of federalism," with Washington retaining ownership but decentralizing authority, giving western states and localities a greater say over what occurred on public lands.[43]

There was never a dramatic cession of public lands to the western states as some Rebels had dreamed, but the Sagebrush Rebellion ultimately "got a great deal of what it sought," according to a 1983 analysis by planning scholar Frank J. Popper. Many of these gains were due simply to having more business-friendly public lands administrators during the Reagan years—as the wilderness-poor example of the 1988 BLM environmental impact statement showed. If commercial users could get the favorable rulings they wanted from federal managers, there was little point in testing their luck with a different set of state-level officials. Public land cessionists were mollified somewhat when the Reagan administration also launched a comparatively modest program under which federal agencies could sell their "surplus" lands; the amount Popper counted was roughly 50 million acres rather than the 500 million acres the Rebels originally demanded.[44]

This denouement of the Sagebrush Rebellion was a far cry from that which convulsed neighboring Canada after a similar uproar in that country's West in the 1970s. There, too, the Prairie Provinces and British Columbia had long-standing grievances against eastern (Ontario) domination and colonialism. Ottawa's resource, transportation, and economic policies increasingly chafed as energy prices spiked and many areas of the West experienced rapid development. But Canada's western unrest, rather than being channeled and dissipated by largely bureaucratic concessions, helped precipitate a prolonged period of constitutional turmoil, culminating in the formation of the western-based Reform Party in 1987. The signal difference between the US and Canadian experiences, of course, was the presence of Quebec, which far more than the West was the driving force behind the very visible expression of regionalism in Canadian politics. (The "peculiar" American South, lacking its degree of cultural and linguistic distinctiveness, does not compare.) Indeed, as one Quebecois group put it in 1991, "Quebec is not a region, it is a nation." The West had its role in this dynamic, simultaneously resisting too much autonomy for

Quebec while benefiting from a greater acknowledgment in the central government of the need to accommodate regional differences. Canadian nationalism remained strong in the West into the 1990s, but Canada, far more than the United States, looked openly to regionalism as a way of holding its nation together. As Prime Minister Pierre Trudeau said in 1976, " 'Unity,' for us in Canada, cannot mean 'sameness.' "[45]

The western United States was not entirely peaceable in this period, even if its skirmishes were more political theater than determining the fate of nations. If the Sagebrush Rebellion had failed to produce the environmental Armageddon that some activists had feared, it was successful enough as a public relations effort to help radicalize a vocal minority of wilderness defenders—though the Rebellion was hardly the only reason for their outrage. As wilderness advocates well knew, the BLM and other federal agencies presumptively favored economic exploitation over other uses of western public lands, regardless of presidential administration. The advocates' every victory for multiple-use planning, more so for wilderness designation, was compromised, limited, and hard-won. Out of despair over the limitations of politics as usual, this more extreme wing of environmentalists erupted in the West, brandishing their own radical conceptualization of the region. Known as Earth First!-ers, eco-warriors, or to some, eco-terrorists, these direct activists turned from mainstream environmental organizations as those groups grew too corporate in size, budget, and temperament. They sacralized nature, and though they drew on the long regionalist tradition of the wilderness West identity, their devotion could also be to a very specifically beloved local place, which they strove to defend not only from developers but also bureaucrats, tourists, or any potential violators of its biocentric wholeness.

Their spiritual leader was the writer Edward Abbey, who described a sojourn in what he called "Abbey's country" in his 1968 book, *Desert Solitaire*. This localist West covered 33,000 acres in southeastern Utah— Arches National Monument, where he worked two seasons as a part-time ranger. Abbey's persona in the book was as the anti–Charles Lummis: rather than the tireless promoter and institution-builder entering the western wonderland, he was the cranky loner trying to keep it all to himself. His solo excursion in the West was avowedly "not a travel guide but an elegy," seeking to take the Thoreauvian depth of this single, small, threatened place.[46] Among gentler chapters on local geology, flora, and fauna, he interspersed passages that demythologized both cowboys (wage-workers in pickup trucks) and Indians (isolated rural poor with no good options). This puncturing of the icons of the nationalist West amplified Abbey's broadcast of a virtually apocalyptic sense of environmental crisis, which Earth First! shared. He gave voice to the anxiety and anguish of someone looking squarely at what Raymond Gastil had more dispassionately described as the "loss of meaning." Abbey wanted the reader to *feel* that crisis—particularly if he or she entertained any illusions that there was a certainty that could be anchored to pristine nature.

Nature in a pristine condition was scarcely to be found in the modern West, Abbey had discovered, and any institutional solution to that problem was so inherently compromised, so given over to liberal-capitalist values, that it must destroy what it was trying to save. The most visible manifestation of this paradox was the "Industrial Tourism" that brought hordes of automobiles to spoil western wildernesses like Arches, increasing visitors there from 3,000 to 300,000 annually in a few short years once the roads were paved. Industrial Tourism was only a localized symptom of an economic "monomania," of "growth for the sake of growth," that was a "cancerous madness," Abbey wrote. Such a mindset drove the equally destructive campaign to engineer grassy suburban sprawl in the arid region. After describing some of the rich and delicate ecosystems that lived off the limited waters of the desert, Abbey observed, "There is not lack of water here, unless you try to establish a city where no city should be."[47] Wallace Stegner, David Brower, and others had begun sounding such themes well before Abbey, and he followed them down the Colorado River to the construction site at Glen Canyon Dam, before warning signs stopped him dead.

It was this beleaguered sense of no political way out that finally pushed Abbey and others like him toward more radical solutions. In *Desert Solitaire*, his erstwhile employer, the National Park Service, stood in for a federal government that aided and abetted ruthless development. Stegner and Brower still had faith enough in the establishment to continue seeking redress through conventional political means. But Abbey and others who formed Earth First! and the environmentalist far left had no such confidence. For them, there were stark and fundamental issues that the "mainstream" environmental movement did not address: "Unless a way can be found to stabilize the nation's population, the parks cannot be saved. Or anything else worth a damn," Abbey wrote. "Wilderness preservation . . . will be forgotten under the overwhelming pressure of a struggle for mere survival and sanity in a completely urbanized, completely industrialized, ever more crowded environment."[48]

The degree of Abbey's political despair was shown in later works wherein he countenanced the practice of "monkey-wrenching," or sabotage of development. So he was credited by Earth First! founder Dave Foreman, who invited Abbey to speak at his group's own bit of political theater a year or more after the officials in Moab rolled out their bulldozer. On the day of the spring equinox in 1981, activists stood atop Glen Canyon Dam and unfurled a 300-foot banner in the shape of a giant black crack down the face of it. Foreman recalled Abbey's words on the occasion in his book *Confessions of an Eco-Warrior* (1991): "Oppose. Oppose the destruction of our homeland by these alien forces from Houston, Tokyo, Manhattan, Washington, D.C., and the Pentagon. And if opposition is not enough, we must resist. And if resistance is not enough, then subvert." Actually the guerrilla sensibility of Abbey's novel *The Monkey Wrench Gang* (1975) was already well in evidence in *Desert Solitaire*. In language that now evokes Ruby Ridge and backwoods supremacists (proving once again that the political extremes eventually meet), Abbey suggested the "value of wilderness . . . as a base for resistance to centralized domination" by a coming "dictatorial regime"—all successful insurrections in modern times had such a hinterland sanctuary, he argued.[49] The West could be a neo-frontier not of free enterprise, but of sovereign individualism. What is remarkable is that in the latter twentieth century, the potency of the wilderness West as a regional identity remained so strong that it could yet serve as a canvas for such fantasies. People still went there and tried to live them out.

While Abbey and the Sagebrush Rebels (and a few still further outside the margins) imagined their Wests of ideological purity—pristine wilderness, open range, mother lode, fatherland—a political neo-frontier of an entirely different sort was actually opening in the state of Oregon. Abbey had grasped that suburban sprawl was indirectly responsible for the West's disappearing wildlands, but his anarchic extremism veered him away from any viable solution to it. Similarly, most Sagebrush resolutions expressed genuine frustration over thwarted desires for home rule, but few if any offered concrete proposals or budgets for state-level land management. While these two extremes ranted and postured, the "quiet revolution" in land-use planning was still going about its work, as Frank Popper pointed out in a major 1988 article. As of 1975, no fewer than "thirty-seven states had new programs of statewide planning or statewide review of local regulatory decisions," Popper marveled. What he saw was a pragmatic consensus rooted in the fact that the "public's support for land use and environmental regulation has remained high and constant throughout the 1970s and 1980s, and shows no signs of wavering."[50]

Rather than engage in posturing for the true believers, Oregon's political leaders worked hard to build a locally based popular consensus around what was admittedly a left-of-center political middle in their state, but a middle ground nevertheless. Arguably, whether one agreed with their approach to land policy, it was Oregon that made the most responsible case for turning federal public lands over to the western states. For example, in the same year (1979) that officials in Nevada and Utah were seeking figuratively and literally to bulldoze federal land-use restrictions, regional planners in Portland were instituting an Urban Growth Boundary (UGB) around their own city. It was the culmination of a decade of intensive effort in Oregon to establish a system of state-mandated land-use planning, the most thoroughgoing in the nation. Their Shasta bioregionalist neighbors to the south might hope that states would fade off the map, but state government in this case was crucial.

What lay behind this remarkable experiment was a sense of Oregonian exceptionalism that was more than the usual state boosterism. Subtly and overtly, political leaders played on the state's frontier heritage as a promised land inhabited by virtuous agrarians morally superior to the get-rich quick crowd who had taken the trail fork to California. Oregon, said pro-planning Republican governor Tom McCall, "should not be a haven to the buffalo hunter mentality." The promised land was physically embodied in the verdant 11,000 square miles of the Willamette Valley where upward of three-quarters of the state's population were increasingly crowded together, with farms, cities, and industries having to share the same very visibly limited space. That Portland itself must avoid the plight of Los Angeles or rival Seattle became a rallying cry of those seeking to control growth and revitalize the central city as a site of richly urban experience. Surprisingly, substantial impetus for comprehensive planning also came from outside the city—from Willamette Valley farmers, who had watched while half a million acres of farmland disappeared from the mid-1950s to the mid-1960s.[51]

When an additional 30,000 acres was consumed by development in 1973 alone, McCall—in the speech of his career—demanded that the legislature rein in the "grasping wastrels of the land," the purveyors of "sagebrush subdivisions, coastal condomania and the ravenous rampage of suburbia in the Willamette Valley."[52] With the farmers joined by environmentalists, quality-of-life suburbanites, and urban revitalization advocates, the political momentum was there to propel passage of the landmark Senate Bill 100 (SB 100), which required every city and county in the state to draw up land-use plans in accordance with statewide goals and subject to approval by a state agency, the Land Conservation and Development Commission (LCDC).

Cities and counties in Oregon and elsewhere in the West had possessed the power to plan and zone for decades. California required localities to plan beginning in 1965. But Oregon's law to coordinate and enforce land-use planning statewide was an innovation—and controversial. It became not only an experiment but a microcosm of regionalism and its fate in the US political system. SB 100, for example, originally proposed fourteen intermediary regional councils of governments to oversee planning in different parts of the state. This idea was bound to be a hard sell in the Pacific Northwest, which had already rejected the more grandiose Columbia Valley Authority two decades earlier. Local politicians, fearful of losing authority, raised the traditional western refrain of "colonial government" even against these smallish intrastate regional planning districts, and the measure was eliminated from SB 100 in favor of the existing local–state distribution of power. In effect, each city, town, or county would become its own sometimes diminutive, and usually arbitrarily defined, region.[53]

It soon became clear that this jurisdictional scale would not be adequate for all circumstances, especially the Portland area with its multi-county sprawl. In 1978, the second major innovation of Oregon-style planning was approved: the Portland Metropolitan Service District, or "Metro," as it came to be known, which would plan land use for three counties encompassing twenty-five cities in the Willamette Valley, overseeing issues such as housing, transportation, waste management, and zoning. Several other cities around the state also established metropolitan-scale planning—as did other large cities in the West—but the master stroke of the Metro's charter (as amended through 1992) was to make its council a popularly elected body—to date, the only popularly elected regional government in the United States. The CVA had been attacked as a potential cabal of appointed experts who would impose their will on the locals with impunity. The LCDC was itself a creature of governor appointees, though pains were taken to make it representative of disparate regions of the state (especially the rural and arid eastern portions). The Metro's framers sought to avoid ideological challenges to planning's legitimacy by anchoring it completely to the local popular will—those most immediately affected by the council's decisions. As Carl Abbott, the Portland-based scholar of urban planning, noted admiringly, the "Metro council districts are designed to cut across city and county boundaries and reinforce Metro's direct relationship with the voters." Conversely, because land-use planning in Oregon was state-mandated, Metro council members could still use the po-

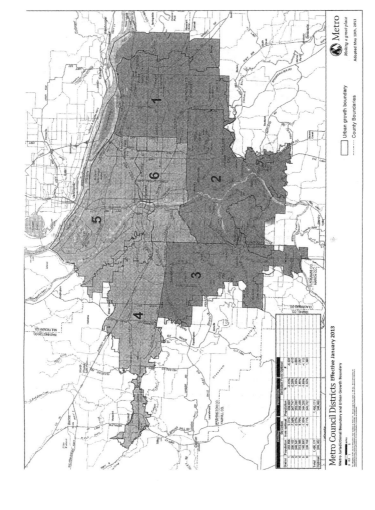

Figure 8 Legitimizing regional government through direct elections. *Metro Council Districts Effective January 2013: Metro Jurisdictional Boundary and Urban Growth Boundary,* Portland, Oregon, 2011. Courtesy of Metro.

litical cover of "the LCDC made me do it" to pass necessary but less popular measures against NIMBY and other forms of local resistance.[54]

Such questions of legitimation were important as Oregon and the nation entered an era of greater skepticism about government, while at the same time the magnitude of urban growth–related problems increased apace. But not everyone decried western urban development as "sprawl," and not all of its defenders were real estate tycoons and chambers of commerce. In their provocative book *Learning from Las Vegas* (1972; rev. ed. 1977), architects Robert Venturi, Denise Scott Brown, and Steven Izenour made a case that was to gain currency in planning and architecture circles in years to come—that western cities, including their suburbs, represented new forms of urbanization. Their arguments evoked the long-standing theme of the West as the land of the future, while at the same time savvily tapping into the animus against expert planning. For Venturi and his coauthors, the urban neo-frontier was the commercial strip that reached its spectacular "archetype" in Las Vegas, a postmodern "process city" encompassing a "brutal automobile landscape of great distances and high speed." The chaotic yet dynamic "commercial vernacular" of places like the Las Vegas Strip should be embraced rather than squelched under "an order dominated by the expert," Venturi and his associates believed, echoing J. B. Jackson. "Commissions produce mediocrity and a deadened urb," they wrote. "What will happen to the Strip when the tastemakers take over?"[55]

Although the spirit of their polemic led Venturi and his colleagues to declare that "sprawl and strip we can learn to do well," others were less confident about the direction of western urbanization.[56] Certainly western cities were to have plenty of practice at sprawling and stripping while they continued to grow at an astounding rate in subsequent decades, with Las Vegas leading the way. As westerners lived with the consequences, there were signs of renewed interest in regional approaches to deal with sprawl and also with related issues like rural depopulation and water infrastructure. Oregon remained a bellwether, and into the 1980s, there were no fewer than three statewide ballot initiatives that effectively sought to repeal state-mandated land-use planning. Though all were defeated, the repeated attempts were indicative of the limited room available for regional governance within American political culture. An experiment or two were allowed, it seemed—a Metro here, a TVA there—but no more. It remained to be seen whether there might still be elbow room for regionalism in the West.

CHAPTER SIX

Hell of a Vision

Though Regionalists are marginal, Regions have no margins.
MAX CAFARD (A.K.A. JOHN P. CLARK),
THE SURRE(GION)ALIST MANIFESTO (1989)

In 1990, the nation was treated to a spectacle unique in the history of American regionalism: the "Buffalo Commons" road show, starring Frank and Deborah Popper. The two Rutgers University professors were touring the Plains states—sometimes in the company of network TV news crews, sometimes with police escorts—to speak to civic groups about their entirely hypothetical plan to restore much of the region to the condition of open bison range. The Poppers had first proposed the idea in a 1987 article for *Planning* magazine, "The Great Plains: From Dust to Dust," and they were riding a wave of sudden fame unexpectedly released from the zeitgeist. As one colleague later declared, the Buffalo Commons had "caught fire unlike any other title I can think of in the history of land-use management." Another marveled, "The Poppers accomplished with one article what few in academia can accomplish with multiple books. . . . They've gotten people to think about the Plains as a region and address problems from a regional perspective."[1] Whether the response had such positive direction is difficult to say, but the Buffalo Commons debate surely seemed to indicate that regional consciousness was alive and well in the late twentieth-century American West.

Not all of the "fire" that greeted the Poppers was enthusiastic, as they soon discovered; much of it was angry. Writer Anne Matthews, who chronicled the road show in her book *Where the Buffalo Roam* (1992), depicted scene after scene of regional resentment erupting out of discussion of the Poppers' proposal, at least once to the point of physical threat. During one meeting, Matthews reports, a woman in Oklahoma City remarked, "These

Easterners, coming in here, saying, 'The land is all of ours. One nation.' We're not used to thinking that way, is all." A man in Nebraska who had to be ushered out of a gathering yelled, "Don't try to come in and use our land for common property for people from New Jersey and California. *Don't you do that!*"[2]

That so much ire could be vented against two academic experts with no official governmental standing was curious on the face of it. In part it was a product of American celebrity worship, which conflated fame with power—the Poppers were on national TV, so their ideas must carry weight and be taken seriously (such things loomed larger in the years before the Internet). The reaction also expressed an alarming sense of powerlessness and disconnection from the federal government and the national establishment in general. A decade or more of post-Watergate, Reagan-era rhetoric declaring the federal government to be essentially harmful had taken its toll on the nation's political will and unity. In all of this, the Poppers themselves—two middle-class college professors with an idea—were totally obscured. The focus was on what they represented: the wave front of cultural change attending environmentalism, which must radically challenge much that Americans traditionally held dear—unlimited growth, sovereign property rights, command over nature, individual liberty. As had occurred during the Sagebrush Rebellion, the threat to these sacred, inherited traditions was spatialized as an alien force from the East, a conspiracy by quasi-aristocratic, elitist outsiders. It also didn't help that the Poppers were of Jewish heritage, confronting one of the most Protestant, ethnically homogeneous regions of the country with some unpleasant facts and a "revolutionary" plan.

The Buffalo Commons concept itself seemed perfectly calibrated to press a wide variety of mythic and ideological hot buttons. The Plains were the setting of "the largest, longest-running agricultural and environmental miscalculation in American history," the Poppers wrote in their original article. Twice before, the busts had been so bad that the region was severely depopulated—in the 1890s, when Rose Wilder Lane and her parents fled Dakota to go back East; and in the 1930s, when Caroline Henderson held on for dear life in the Oklahoma Panhandle. Now the Plains were in another downward spiral that could leave them "almost totally depopulated." Rather than renew the cycle of economic futility, the Poppers suggested that "the region be returned to its original pre-white state, that it be, in effect, deprivatized." Much of the Plains would be reinhabited (to use the bioregionalist term) by bison and other wildlife, becoming "the world's largest historic preservation project, the ultimate national park." The figure used in *Where the Buffalo Roam* was an area of 139,000 square miles.[3]

Already the Poppers were treading beyond the policy innovations that had provoked the Sagebrush Rebellion. Then the dispute had been over public lands, who would manage them, and whether they would remain public. *Deprivatization* was unquestionably more radical, and to throw fuel on the fire, the Poppers suggested that it be carried out by a "regional agency like the Tennessee Valley Authority or a public-land agency like the Bureau of Land Management, but with much more sweeping powers." By the time of the 1990 road show, the Poppers were backing away from this aspect of the plan and, significantly, beginning to speak of the Buffalo Commons as a "metaphor," a theme they amplified in subsequent articles, most notably "The Buffalo Commons: Metaphor as Method" (1999), as the bitter reaction and the overwhelming complexity of the undertaking sank in. It seemed that some people had mistaken the Buffalo Commons for a "formal plan that purposefully laid out the location of particular land uses, but it remained primarily a metaphor" that was "inescapably ambiguous," thereby creating a "public dialogue" on the future of the Plains, the Poppers now asserted.[4] They praised gradualism and private initiatives.

What becomes clear about the "dialogue" recounted by Matthews was the degree to which Plains dwellers and Poppers were talking past each other. Matthews herself had her share of regional biases; at times she seemed surprised that people who spoke with twangy southern Plains accents could speak at all. The Poppers' premise was that Plains farmers were short-sighted capitalists in ecological denial, an interpretation compellingly put forth by University of Kansas historian Donald Worster in his book, *Dust Bowl: The Southern Plains in the 1930s* (1979). With prodigious academic condescension—which was not lost on their audiences—the Poppers saw themselves as "therapists for an entire American region," helping it come to terms with the error of its ways. "All the Plains states are terrible ideas, ecologically speaking," Frank Popper told a road show crowd with a glibness appropriate to the seminar room.[5] Cultural radicalism of this sort is usually best not expressed in face-to-face interaction; it is no wonder that the Poppers came away chastened from the furious response they provoked.

The Poppers never seemed to grasp that many of the people to whom they were speaking were the Caroline Hendersons or the descendants of the Caroline Hendersons, the ones who had endured on the Plains generation after generation and were strongly tied to particular places. For them, land was a private domain, not a public amenity. Community was on a local scale, a bond between neighboring landowners, who shared churches and schools. Land and animals must be well cared for not only because they were the family's livelihood but because they were something inherited and passed on. "Agriculture is not an extractive industry!" a rancher in Montana shouted at Deborah Popper.[6] At every presentation of the Poppers' maps, such people always craned to see their home counties. To suggest that this heritage was one huge mistake needing to be erased was deeply offensive, made aggravatingly and intimidatingly so by its extensive play in the national media. The Poppers thought their opponents were paranoid, but crazier things had happened on behalf of the snail darter and the spotted owl; what might the government do for an iconic beast like the bison? Here certainly lay one of the reasons the Buffalo Commons seized the nation's attention. The Poppers' metaphor had struck one of main tripwires of the conservative critique of environmental "extremists"—that they valued plants and animals more than human beings.

The question that the Plains dwellers had no good answer for was asked by Frank Popper at the Denver stop of the road show: "If the Plains are such a wonderful place, why do so many people leave?" Perhaps the most intriguing aspect of the Buffalo Commons concept from the perspective of western regional identity was this vision of a Plains neo-frontier that was no metaphor and no utopia—it was actually happening, unbidden. Vast stretches of land were emptying of people and returning to the demographic definition of the frontier that had been good enough for Frederick Jackson Turner: two people per square mile. Indeed, earlier in his career Frank Popper had begun tapping this theme. "The frontier survives," he wrote in a 1984 analysis of the Sagebrush Rebellion, focusing on the greater nationalist West. As of 1980, "seventeen percent of the country—383 million acres of Western public land—has never even been surveyed," Popper observed. In the 1980 census, over a quarter of the country's land area could still meet the two-per-square-mile test. "We are no longer a frontier nation," he declared with some Turneresque dramatic flair, "but we are a nation with a frontier."[7]

The Buffalo Commons idea delivered this message to the masses, coupling it with a potent symbol, the bison, that embodied the frontier, the restoration of which promised both racial and environmental redemption. (Native Americans in the region—at least those with reservations—seemed to be strongly in favor of the idea, especially the part in which the homestead system was rolled back.) Whether concrete plan or fuzzy metaphor, it touched something deeply in supporters across the ideological spectrum, those who also comprised the audience for a mini-renaissance of sorts in Plains-related writing during the late 1980s and early 1990s. What had formally been derided as fly-over country seemed now by that very fact to capture the imagination: neglect and invisibility had shielded this unspoiled, novel, and exotic land in their midst, now revealed and poetized by the Poppers, Ian Frazier (*The Great Plains*, 1989), Kathleen Norris (*Dakota*, 1993), and William Least Heat-Moon (*PrairyErth*, 1991). As Frazier noted, "For fantasies, the Great Plains are in many respects the perfect place. They're so big that you could never know all there is to know about them—your fantasies could never wear them out." For example, in her "spiritual geography" of the Dakotas, Norris found "traditional people, country people . . . second-, third-, and fourth-generation Americans who have lived on the land for many years, apart from the mainstream of American culture," and who had "become one with their place: this is not romanticism, but truth." Or, if symbiotic folk cultures were not to one's taste, the Plains also offered boundless solitary freedom. "The land, the 360 degrees of unobstructed horizon, invites you to keep walking," Norris wrote. "As when I was a child, I want to remain in the open, becoming something other than human under the sky." On the tallgrass prairie of Kansas, Heat-Moon found "a paradigm of infinity, a clearing full of many things except boundaries, and its power comes from its apparent limitlessness."[8] This was what it felt like to have a frontier. The Poppers called up the same yearnings.

"The West's real crisis is one of inertia, of will, and of myth," environmental journalist Marc Reisner concluded in his book *Cadillac Desert* (1986, rev. ed. 1993), citing Wallace Stegner's career-long effort to move the West out of the shadow of the cowboy. Such preconceptions had real consequences, as Reisner showed; in the 1990s, more water was used in the West to grow alfalfa for livestock than went to fill the daily needs of urban dwellers. Yet to assert that the West was primarily urban rather than cattle country, and that its water use might be reprioritized, remained a tough sell. It was difficult to imagine in 1993, but as recently as 1981, Stegner—the foremost literary figure in the modern West—had been prominently misidentified ("William Stegner") and disrespected in a widely read article on western writers appearing in the *New York Times Book Review*. Hamlin Garland and Frank Norris would have nodded knowingly at the resulting furor against the eastern literary establishment, which despite his Pulitzer Prize in 1972 (a controversial selection, with the *Times* again leading the attack) had never fully acknowledged Stegner's stature in American letters, or that of any other postwar western writer.[9] The Plains people who railed at the Poppers were not alone in their resentment of eastern elites; many western elites felt the same way.

Over the course of the 1980s, the colonial status of the West, certainly this colonial *mentality*, seemed to abruptly reverse. It was all part of the same cultural moment that had produced the Buffalo Commons road show, breaking open a broader debate over nationalist West myths and the West's regional identity. As historian Patricia Nelson Limerick characterized a major 1989 symposium on the West: "Many westerners realize that we cannot take ourselves and our present challenges seriously until we take our history seriously. We cannot live responsibly in the American West until we have made a responsible and thorough assessment of our common past."[10] That reassessment of the West continues to this day, with regionalism playing a crucial role.

The "crisis of myth" had been brewing since the 1960s, precipitated not only by environmentalism but also by the other signature consciousness-raising movements of that decade: civil rights and women's liberation. These revealed how deeply embedded racial and gender inequality were in American institutions, culture, behavior, and attitudes. In the 1970s and 1980s, this already potent social critique was sharpened to a finer point by a body of ideas known as postcolonialism. Scholars like Edward Said originally formulated postcolonialism to analyze the impact of European colonial empires in Africa, Asia, and the Middle East, but Americanists, including those studying the West, soon enough realized that postcolonial concepts could be applied closer to home. They also partook of the intellectual revolution known as postmodernism, which greatly heightened self-consciousness about language, now seen as both indeterminate (an unstable multiplicity of meanings) and loaded (encoding society's power structures). The frontier myth provided an especially big target for such critiques, and several widely regarded and influential attacks on it began appearing before academic trends like postcolonialism had a name. Vine Deloria Jr.'s *Custer Died for Your Sins* anticipated one of postcolonialism's key insights—how romanticized depictions of indigenous peoples reinforced imperial regimes. Dee Brown's best-selling *Bury My Heart at Wounded Knee* (1970) retold American history as an example of another word that was not quite current yet: genocide. The first volume of Richard Slotkin's massive historical trilogy on the frontier myth, *Regeneration through Violence* (1973), began to make the case for its centrality in American culture since the 1600s and how the frontier myth legitimized pervasive violence as well as class and racial domination in America.[11]

Slotkin's second installment, *The Fatal Environment* (1985), was timed perfectly to land among the upwelling of works in the 1980s that constituted what may be called the New West renaissance. Suddenly, it seemed, most of the best writing in the country was focused on the region. A conversation opened in which some authors tried to salvage or update western myths, while others peered at them with a stark new light. Three arrestingly unromantic depictions of the historic and contemporary West that also happened to be literary achievements of the first order appeared all at once: Louise Erdrich's novel, *Love Medicine* (1984), which won the National Book Critics Circle Award; Evan S. Connell's best-selling biography *Son of the Morning Star* (1984); and Cormac McCarthy's novel *Blood Meridian, or, The Evening Redness in the West* (1985). Harold Bloom, a pillar of the eastern literary establishment, declared McCarthy's novel to be the finest by a living American writer.[12] Gretel Ehrlich's *Solace of Open Spaces*, another best seller, was also published in 1985, offering comfort from the agrarian West. So too did Larry McMurtry's epic *Lonesome Dove*, which straddled realism and romanticism and was the 1986 winner of the Pulitzer Prize for fiction. ("National" recognition for western writers still required prizes from East Coast institutions, it seemed.)

McMurtry's ambivalent, remorseful tone in *Lonesome Dove* seemed a perfect overture to the wave of historical revisionism announced in 1987 with the publication of Patricia Nelson Limerick's influential book, *The Legacy of Conquest: The Unbroken Past of the American West*. The productions of the "New West" historical school frequently appalled McMurtry (a reaction that he now dispensed as a regular contributor to the *New York Review of Books*). While some New West scholarship could be heavy-handed, western history as a whole became one of the hottest fields in academia, thanks to an array of gifted historians who took it up in the 1970s and 1980s, including Donald Worster (*Rivers of Empire*, 1985), John Mack Faragher (*Women and Men on the Overland Trail*, 1979), William Cronon (*Nature's Metropolis: Chicago and the Great West*, 1991), and Richard White (*"It's Your Misfortune and None of My Own": A New History of the American West*, 1991). Revisionism ramified into other fields as well. In literary studies, for example, the equivalent of Limerick's *Legacy of Conquest* appeared in 1992—Annette Kolodny's essay "Letting Go Our Grand Obsessions: Notes Toward a New Literary History of the American Frontiers." New multidisciplinary centers for the West and its subregions also were founded, such as Limerick's Center of the American West at the University of Colorado (1986) and the Center for the Study of the Southwest at Texas State University, San Marcos (1990).[13]

The nonfiction Plains books of Frazier, Norris, and Heat-Moon, each romanticizing western nature or culture in greater or lesser measure, rounded out the literary renaissance in the early 1990s, but the upsurge of acclaimed works dealing with the West was hardly limited to the printed word. The soundtrack of the renaissance, as it were, was provided by Montana writer Ivan Doig, five of whose books were read over the air by the "Radio Reader" on National Public Radio between 1979 and 1990. On television, historian William Goetzmann's major PBS documentary series on western artists, *The West of the Imagination* — its very title instructive — aired in 1986, followed in 1989 by the hit CBS mini-series *Lonesome Dove*. The full-length series *Dr. Quinn, Medicine Woman*, which premiered in 1993, offered a more feminized view of the West to a mass audience. At movie theaters, Lawrence Kasdan's popular film *Silverado* (1985) was a quite self-conscious attempt at "revitalizing scenes and images" that were "so well-loved" from the Old West culture industry, as *New York Times* reviewer Janet Maslin wrote. Director Jonathan Wacks's off-reservation comedy *Powwow Highway* (1989) was a Sundance Film Festival winner that went into wide distribution. Kevin Costner's *Dances with Wolves* (1990), though burdened with the cliché of the Indianized white man, ventured further than virtually any mainstream film to depict whites as invaders, winning the Academy Award for Best Picture, as did Clint Eastwood's grim shoot-'em-up, *Unforgiven*, in 1992. If these series and films did not add up to a "New West culture industry," they certainly indicated a receptive critical and popular audience for new takes on the West. A case in point was the unveiling of Apache sculptor Allan Houser's "As Long as the Waters Flow," a direct allusion to Indian dispossession, on the steps of the Oklahoma state capitol in 1989, marking the centennial of the state's famous land run. In 1992 — the quincentennial of Columbus's arrival — Houser was honored with the National Medal of Arts by President George Bush.[14]

Thus Marc Reisner had reason to wonder at the persistence of the cowboy myth by 1992, but what was arguably the culminating event of the New West renaissance suggested the complexity of cultural change: the furor over the 1991 National Museum of American Art exhibition, "The West as America: Reinterpreting Images of the Frontier, 1820–1920." The exhibit featured works by Catlin, Bierstadt, Russell, Remington, and other canonical artists, accompanied by text panels that gave viewers a bracing dose of academic deconstruction — and New West revisionism undiluted. One panel welcomed visitors with the admonition that the "paintings in this gallery and those that follow should not be seen as a record of time and place," but were "contrived views" that "justified the process of nation building," some of which "predicted the destruction of all who contested white settlers." In the catalog, curator William Truettner elaborated on this theme, drawing on Slotkin's frontier interpretation: "No major artist was part of the moving frontier, and historical references in paintings of the nineteenth-century West create only the illusion of authenticity." The art was propaganda not for white pioneers but for "those who stood to gain most from the westward movement—the leaders of the industrial East."[15] Rather than participants in a folk migration, as the conventional frontier myth would have it, settlers were recast as shock troops of imperial expansion.

Truettner's tendency to provocative overstatement was typical of the show, stuck in the manifesto mode in which New West interpretation still found itself. Postcolonial in intent, seeking to uncover how class self-interest, white supremacy, and misogyny were encoded in what had once seemed the most harmless of genres, western art, "The West as America"—as the title implied—ironically reinforced the regional identity of the West as a colonial extension of the East, a nationalist West projection of eastern "hopes and desires." Beneath this mask of ideology was the true western expression of America, the "hell of a vision" of revisionist scholars: imperial power and violence, environmental destruction and expropriation, class conflict and exploitation, racial and gender oppression. In effect, they had inverted the Turnerian nationalist West of previous generations; rather than the beckoning realm of American exceptionalism, a place of starting over and progress, the West was just more of the same old depressing thing.

A substantial number of visitors to the exhibition seemed inclined to accept the assertion of the essential unreality of the Old West and embraced the curators' iconoclasm. As a visitor from Houston, Texas, commented, "It is embarrassing, sad, and scary to hear the truth sometimes—especially when you must admit that you have wronged someone else. . . . It makes me wonder what country I am living in." Other visitors, along with many conservative pundits in the media, denounced the show for its so-called political correctness. One outraged visitor asked simply, "Do you hate the United States?" What is striking in these two reactions and many similar from other viewers, as well as the resultant storm in the media, was the staying power of the nationalist West: the West remained central to America's self-image. Perhaps for this reason, some visitors to the show, while they accepted certain aspects of the curators' interpretations, had qualms about relinquishing everything that the frontier myth stood for. "I will always imagine myself as a pioneer or a railroad man settling the West," one commented with a relativism that may have taken the curators aback. "The propaganda in them does not destroy my dream—the reality of the West is not available to us or to the curator of this exhibit." Another visitor wrote defiantly, "Granted it wasn't all a 'dream,' and inequalities were there—but it took guts and spirit to go westward." In the following year, such people comprised a readership for Cormac McCarthy's breakthrough novel *All the Pretty Horses*, wherein he retreated from the near-nihilism of his earlier (and some later) works, including the frontier abattoir of *Blood Meridian*, to tantalize readers with a romantic story set in a bilingual borderlands neo-frontier of the recent past. It was the publishing sensation of 1992, winning the National Book Award and the National Book Critics Circle Award.[16]

One achievement of "The West as America" exhibition had been to announce to the broader American public that western history and regional identity were now openly contested. As part of this ongoing reinterpretive process, Patricia Limerick may be excused for proposing to sidestep the enormous ideological baggage of the term "frontier" by turning to the concept of "region." As she wrote in the introduction to *Legacy of Conquest*, "In rethinking western history, we gain the freedom to think of the West as a place" rather than a "process," and as a "center," not an "edge." In a later manifesto, she noted that the term " 'frontier' is nationalistic and often racist," whereas "region" could accommodate a more pluralist vision of "the convergence of diverse people . . . and their encounters with each other and with the natural environment." Richard White famously refused to include the word "frontier" in his massive "new history" of the West, *"It's Your Misfortune and None of My Own,"* and a subregional orientation was prominent in other works of his concerning the Pacific Northwest, from a single Washington county to the vast transnational expanse of the Columbia Basin.[17]

Critics questioned the validity or desirability of abandoning the frontier concept, however, and a "frontier versus region" debate ensued during the 1990s. Kerwin Lee Klein, a noted historian of the frontier concept, argued in a 1996 article that regionalists like Limerick (the principal straw-woman in the debate) "hope that if we tip the 'West' upside down, shake it hard, and empty it of its history, we can escape all the old ethnocentric meanings the word [frontier] has acquired over a millennium. . . . Of the two words, frontier is better structured to lead us into multicultural dialogue." Klein may have protested too much—Limerick's animus was directed particularly at the nationalist West frontier myth of Frederick Jackson Turner, rather than more ethnologically neutral frontier concepts such as that of Edward Spicer. In fact, many scholars studying the West still found room in it for both "frontier" and "region." In "Letting Go Our Grand Obsessions," Annette Kolodny sought to bring literary history to a postmodern Spicerian frontier "as a locus of first cultural contact, circumscribed by a particular physical terrain in the process of change . . . all of it inscribed by the collisions and interpenetrations of language." The more that Kolodny described her frontier, the more "regional" it seemed, variously a zone, territory, or borderland. She denounced conventional American literary studies for its tendency to "characterize all productions outside major urban cultural centers as *merely regional*" (emphasis in original), and she called for a "literary history that privileges no group's priority and no region's primacy."[18]

A number of western historians also arrived at the region via the frontier, notably William Cronon, George Miles, and Jay Gitlin in their 1992 essay, "Becoming West: Toward a New Meaning for Western History." They outlined a set of processes that people experienced while living on the frontier, most especially "self-shaping," or the definition of "boundaries" and distinct "communities" that produced "special cultural identities" tied to specific regions or subregions. The frontier experience in itself proved to be one of the most important forms of self-shaping regional identity in the West, they argued, and for this reason the nationalist West could embody the myths and values of America as a whole—frontier experience was embedded in the cultural memory of groups in every region of the country. Both Clyde Milner and David Wrobel, blurring together frontier and region in their own analyses, pointed specifically to the old pioneer historical associations that sprang up in many western localities, often immediately on the heels of the frontier era, to enshrine it in memory. As historian Michael C. Steiner pointed out, recent scholars were in good company with this line of argument. Several decades earlier, Turner himself, in attempting to move western history beyond the frontier to a regional framework, had suggested that the experience of pioneering might imprint on regional culture for generations to come. "Turner's sectional thesis visualizes the American West as a complex place in the modern world," Steiner concluded, "and anticipates much that is valued in western history today."[19]

Most regionalists in the historical profession made their peace with Turner, even as they rejected the racism and ethnocentrism that suffused his thesis. That still left them and other regionalist scholars open to further criticism—for being regionalists. Their cardinal sin was to attempt to de-

fine the regional characteristics of the West (aridity, wide-open spaces, predominant federal ownership of land, etc.). To do so was to "essentialize"
the West—to fix its characteristics as a given, an essence—which to the
postmodern, poststructuralist mindset of the 1990s was the gravest of
scholarly errors. "Regionalists believe that if we nail the word to the map,"
Kerwin Lee Klein wrote, "all those 'other' meanings will not creep back
in." Their definition of western regional identity and history was a "process
of exclusion," he asserted, which was as "Eurocentric" in its own way as
the Turnerian frontier. Historian Virginia Scharff declared that to "claim
any object, idea, place, process, or people for the category 'West' is to fix
things, thoughts, social processes, and lives that are, historically, only con-
tingently, contradictorily, and discontinuously Western." Most modern-
day people living in the West, especially those who were members of racial
and ethnic minorities, had no sense of being "western" as the regionalists
used the term, Klein believed. Particularly damning was a growing body of
scholarship that documented the ways Anglos imposed their own definition of region on Hispanics living in New Mexico and elsewhere in the
Southwest. John R. Chávez traced the history of this process in *The Lost
Land: The Chicano Image of the Southwest* (1984). Andrew Leo Lovato
found today's Hispanics still subject to "other-defined stereotypes" in
Santa Fe Hispanic Culture: Preserving Identity in a Tourist Town (2004).
"The issue is one of power and self-determination," Lovato concluded,
and western regionalism was implicitly conservative, or so wrote historian
Robert D. Johnston in a 1998 article criticizing prominent regionalists like
Limerick and Worster. In his view, their "reified regional frameworks,"
filled with rugged individualists and overweening federal bureaucrats,
seemed to deny the possibility of radical social and political change in the
West.[20]

Other scholars begged to differ with this assessment of regionalism,
continuing to find it a potent source of cultural radicalism. Conceptually,
their focus was on the subregional localist West. That was their very point,
to borrow some of Annette Kolodny's language: to destabilize and decen-
ter cultural production from artificial "national" containers, to privilege
no dominant region such as the East as arbiter of what constitutes the literary, and to call into question the imperialist motives underlying constructions like the nationalist West. In a Boltonian hemisphere-wide setting, the
frontier subregions that Kolodny envisioned, for example, were "multilin-
gual, polyvocal, and newly intertextual and multicultural," she wrote, and
they must challenge the "singular identities and unswerving continuities"
of accepted literary canons and traditions. The earlier generation of Gar-

land and Norris had looked to regionalism to buttress cultural nationalism and break free of what they saw as a Europeanized cultural hegemony, but Kolodny's generation of postcolonial literary scholars—all too aware of the devastation wrought by nationalism since Garland's time—increasingly used regionalism to question the very idea of a national literature. Judith Fetterley and Marjorie Pryse opened a genderized front in this revolt with their major work, *Writing Out of Place: Regionalism, Women, and American Literary Culture* (2003). Spotlighting western women writers such as Cather, Austin, and Zitkala-Ša, Fetterley and Pryse declared that "regionalism is in effect a women's literary tradition," and that these regionalist writers were already calling into question "nationalist visions of an 'American' literature" in their own day. Regionalism was therefore "an alternative and oppositional tradition, one that worked against the construction of nation and empire and that challenged the constructions of masculine and feminine that underwrote the projects of nation and empire."[21]

This historicizing of regionalism was, ideologically, a double-edged sword. As scholars began to explore how regionalism had shaped the culture and politics of the West, they started to appreciate more how regionalism, like nationalism, was an invention, and how "alternative and oppositional" were in the eye of the beholder. This was found to be especially true of the regionalist mecca of Santa Fe and the modern infatuation with Pueblo cultures. The titles of Chris Wilson's *The Myth of Santa Fe: Creating a Modern Regional Tradition* (1997) and Audrey Goodman's *Translating Southwestern Landscapes: The Making of an Anglo Literary Region* (2002) spoke for themselves. Not only had such places been restored and interpreted to fulfill the cultural and psychological needs of modern American tourists, but so had the very "rules for claiming authority and authenticity" of southwestern culture been laid down by a relative handful of twentieth-century artists and intellectuals, as Goodman wrote. Similarly, Leah Dilworth in *Imagining Indians in the Southwest: Persistent Visions of a Primitive Past* (1996) and Elizabeth Hutchinson in her book, *The Indian Craze: Primitivism, Modernism, and Transculturation in American Art, 1890–1915* (2009), found that "even though modernists glorified the primitive, hegemonic relationships haunted all contact between Indians and the modernists who represented them," in Dilworth's words.[22] Given this self-consciousness of how culturally problematic and democratically compromised twentieth-century regionalism may have been, what role (if any) could regionalism still serve as America entered the twenty-first century?

Increasingly during the 1990s and 2000s, the terms "postregional" and "postwestern" began to crop up in the discussion. Partly this trend was a restatement of the trope of homogenization that stretched back to Josiah Royce's time. William Leach's *Country of Exiles: The Destruction of Place in American Life* (1999) was the most widely cited current expression. "Worldwide economic interdependence" and "transnational mobility"—in a word, globalization—were fostering a rootless, sprawling "landscape of the temporary," with no connection to place or community, Leach wrote. Such concerns over the consequences of economic globalization—in which western states like California, Washington, and Texas were major players—surely lay behind the broader assumption that the West had arrived at a postregional era. In *Re-Imagining the Modern American West* (1996), historian Richard Etulain marked its beginning as far back as the economic and demographic transformations of World War II, which had boosted these states profoundly. But other scholars insisted on defining postregional or postwestern less as a consequence of economic than of cultural and intellectual change, "post-" as in "abandoning that which is obsolete or objectionable." Kerwin Klein put forward postwestern history as a corrective to the essentialist, exclusionary, if not racist taint of "West-as-region," by which western historians had self-marginalized from the national mainstream of their profession. Robert Johnston expressed the belief that "regional identities are becoming increasingly attenuated" and heralded the advent of a whole body of recent work set in western states that made little or no reference to the West-as-region, foretelling a "postwestern future."[23]

Certainly there remained in academia those who still found some "Uses of Region in a Postregional World," as Audrey Goodman titled the epilogue of her book that had helped disenchant the concept. As long as scholars stayed vigilant about the dangers of reifying and essentializing them, she wrote, "regions and localities have distinct natural and cultural histories that can be more concretely apprehended than abstract formations like nationality or ethnicity." Her study of the Southwest's Anglo literature had convinced Goodman that regionalism still had lessons that were of the moment for contemporary globalized society, such as learning how to "apprehend an unfamiliar culture with all one's senses, to listen to its stories." Tom Lutz, in the course of defending literary regionalism from critics past and present in his 2004 book *Cosmopolitan Vistas*, put it more bluntly: "The feeling of purposeful earth can certainly appear preposterous . . . but so can its opposite, the urban refusal to understand the attachments that people have to the land."[24]

Perhaps one of the strongest arguments against abandoning regionalism appeared in Kerwin Klein's own magisterial *Frontiers of Historical Imagination* (1997), where he highlighted Edward Spicer's countertragic conclusion that the "impulse toward cultural sameness produced cultural difference" in the American Southwest, as Klein put it, or again: "European expansion had brought technological and economic change to wide reaches of the globe. . . . But universal homogenization had not been the result. Instead, the process . . . had created new cultural forms, diversified rather than homogenized the world." Forces seeking homogenization seem to provoke cultural resistance, syncretism, and ultimately differentiation, because the locals are also actors in the process, not just passive clay to be paved over. The continual reemergence of western regionalism during the twentieth century, despite and because of recurrent forewarnings (or celebrations) of lost regional distinctiveness, provided ample evidence. Katherine G. Morrissey, a leading historian of western regionalism, observed that "the West as a whole maintains a protean regional identity." The process of defining the West and its subregions was unfinished and would never be finished. Regions, she concluded, "are as much about the future as the past."[25]

"Academic regionalists remain reluctant to engage in normative discourse," Stephen M. Wheeler wrote with considerable understatement in his 2002 overview of the "new regionalism" in urban planning. Arising out of the fields of "landscape architecture and urban design," the new regionalism in planning was "more overtly normative in its goals," he believed. It was therefore "more interested in actively addressing current regional problems," especially the "ills of the postmodern landscape, with its amorphous, placeless sprawl of suburbs." Between 1990 and 2009, all western states posted population gains (North Dakota lost before rebounding slightly), with most in the double digits, and some in the spectacular range: Texas (46 percent, to nearly 25 million), Idaho (54 percent), Arizona (78 percent), and Nevada (117 percent). Seven of the nation's ten largest cities were located in the West by 2009. During the 1990s, California alone added 1.9 million new housing units, continuing the sprawl that had eaten up one-quarter of the state's farmland since the mid-1960s. Metropolitan Phoenix in the late 1990s was developing desert land on its margins at the rate of one acre per hour; into the mid-2000s, greater Maricopa County, Arizona, was adding an average of 42,000 new residents per year, drawn by the area's 189 golf courses and other amenities watered out of the desert. Growth spread outward from the fringes of giant metropolises like Phoenix and from the smaller towns and cities that were reoriented into exurbs or served as subregional economic hubs. For example, in Greeley, Colorado (population 92,625)—one hour away from Denver—the population grew by 53 percent from 1990 to 2009, and the land area of the city increased from twenty-nine square miles to forty-six square miles.[26] As land-use planners struggled to channel and mitigate this rapid growth, they may have been less tortured by epistemological issues than their regionalist counterparts in the humanities, yet they also could get balled up in their own contradictions, paradoxes, and dilemmas.

A good example of the fearlessly "normative" approach, the very title of which would have raised the hackles of some academic postwesterners, was *True West: Authentic Development Patterns for Small Towns and Rural Areas* (2003), written by two Colorado-based planners, Christopher J. Duerksen and James van Hemert. "Many westerners say they live there for the landscape before career or family," Duerksen and van Hemert noted. Unfortunately, they wrote, "Our technology, ambitions, 'can do' attitude, greed, and love of the land are taking us where we don't want to go: destroying the place that we love and that attracted us here in the beginning." Drawing detailed inspiration from Native American, Spanish colonial, as well as nineteenth-century Mormon communities and frontier railroad towns—the "authentic" West as defined by a century of western regionalists—Duerksen and van Hemert then derived a remarkable template of eighty-three planning principles to guide future land-use, development, and architectural decisions in western towns and small cities, and in outlying countryside liable to erupt at any time in vacation homes and convenience stores. Some of these principles were truisms ("Identify and preserve unique views"), some verged on the utopian ("Encourage the growth of new, self-contained towns in a dispersed manner across the landscape"), and some were unintentionally humorous ("Avoid development in wildfire-prone areas"). But most of the authors' guidelines offered concrete advice for enhancing a communal sense of place through arrangement of physical space—for example, "Create an intimate relationship between buildings and the street by placing buildings close to the public right-of-way. . . . Construct streets in such a manner so as to take advantage of distant views."[27]

One cannot help noticing that many of Duerksen and van Hemert's successful case studies were affluent cities and resorts such as Santa Fe; Park City, Utah; Claremont, California; and Jackson, Wyoming, where private munificence could more readily make up for public shortfalls, and well-organized, well-educated pro-planning constituencies could be mobilized to fight the many battles necessary for the care and cultivation of place. These conditions, to be sure, remained the exception rather than the rule in the turn-of-the-century West, but "new regionalist" planners like Duerksen and van Hemert had some reason to be ambitious. Despite announcements that a postregional world was nigh, a 1999 Brookings Institution survey spotlighted an "important new regional trend": the "increase in dollars committed to parks, trails, resource protection, and open space in the West." Ballot measures on these issues were approved the previous year by voters in localities as diverse as Austin, Texas; Bernalillo County, New Mexico; Park City; and statewide in Arizona. Citizens of several communities in the San Francisco Bay area went further, voting for Portland-like "urban growth boundaries" that put a twenty-year moratorium on the rezoning of farmland without subsequent voter approval.[28]

Additional evidence of rising western interest in regionalism was provided by the Western Regionalism Project (WRP), launched in 2000 by a nonprofit group, the Western Consensus Council. Its first order of business was to develop an inventory of current initiatives in the West dedicated to taking a regional approach to environmental and land-use policy. The WRP tallied seventy-two regional initiatives, plus an additional sixty "councils of government or metropolitan planning organizations," not to mention hundreds more local watershed councils. The initiatives ranged from small, locally focused groups like Montana's Flathead Lakers ("Over 1,000 citizens concerned about . . . clean water, a healthy ecosystem and the preservation of quality of life" in the Flathead River basin) to complex institutional networks like the Grand Canyon Forests Partnership (eighteen local, state, federal, and private entities including the US Forest Service, US Fish and Wildlife Service, the Nature Conservancy, and Northern Arizona University, dedicated to managing the "Flagstaff urban-wildland interface" for ecosystem restoration). A telling discovery in the WRP inventory was that only two recent regional initiatives in the West were actually empowered for "governance"—the Columbia River Gorge Commission and the Lake Tahoe Regional Planning Authority. The rest engaged in "research and education," sought to "stimulate conversation," made efforts to "share resources," provided "input and advice," and undertook "advocacy." According to the WRP, the majority of the initiatives defined success by "procedural indicators—improving communication and collaboration, increasing understanding, and raising public awareness." Success, in other words, was not immediately to be seen in "on-the-ground accomplishments."[29]

Perhaps this was as it should be: the main trunk of western regionalism back to the time of Powell's first plans had stood for noncoercive, decentralized cooperation. But the consequences on the ground from a lack of more comprehensive regional governance were there to be seen in the western landscape. A decade or so after their famous road show, the Poppers looked back on what had been achieved of the Buffalo Commons so far. It seemed "likely to come into being through local, state, tribal, and private-sector activities rather than federal ones," they admitted. "Buffalo populations have increased on both private and public land. Land-preservation organizations such as the Nature Conservancy have bought land in part for raising buffalo." The year 2002, when these words were published, was the first in which the Agricultural Census counted the number of commercially raised bison. The leading state nationally, South Dakota, had over 40,000 bison, sprinkled in among a population of 3.7 million head of cattle. These numbers remained more or less steady through the next census in 2007. That the changeover would be "generations-long," as Frank Popper said during the road show, seemed to be an accurate prediction.[30]

The creation of a publicly accessible bison range also seemed to be rather slow in coming. The most grandiose attempt to realize at least a segment of the Buffalo Commons, the projected 3-million-acre American Prairie Reserve in north-central Montana, was launched by the private American Prairie Foundation (APF) in 2001; by the end of 2009, they were still nearly 2.8 million acres short of their goal. From the outset it was clear that the APF was hoping to come close to the Poppers' original vision of restoring an authentic "pre-white" Plains environment. In his book *Rewilding the West: Restoration in a Prairie Landscape* (2009), journalist Richard Manning gave a sympathetic account of their project, while volunteering that agriculture "has evolved into the most environmentally destructive force on the planet." He conceded that the Montana prairie that APF hoped to restore was "human-formed," peopled by ranchers with "a real attachment to and affection for the landscape they inhabit." But as of 2009, the APF seemed inclined to treat ranching as a removable historical artifact on the lands it had obtained, even if it recognized "agriculture as the dominant industry in the region." A carefully preserved country schoolhouse was to remind "future generations" of the "courage and resilience of their pioneering ancestors." Although the APF, like Manning, in this way evoked the agrarian West that so appealed to tourists, their principal goal remained to "assemble a fully functioning grassland ecosystem able to support a full complement of prairie-based wildlife," including what they touted as a herd of "genetically pure" bison.[31]

Other, more modest efforts suggested some of the difficulties confronting regional "reinhabitation." For example, just a notch to the east of the

98th meridian Plains boundary insisted on by the Poppers, two projects to save remnants of the tallgrass prairie by the Nature Conservancy yielded 10,000 acres in Kansas (Tallgrass Prairie National Preserve) and 40,000 acres in Oklahoma (Tallgrass Prairie Preserve), out of the original 140 million acres of grassland that once spanned the middle of the continent. A small herd of bison was established on the Kansas preserve, and more than 2,500 roamed the one in Oklahoma by 2009. Some of the finest ranchland in either state occupied the Flint Hills subregion, the natural feedlot where the preserves were created in the late 1980s and mid-1990s after a lot of local resistance. The private intercession of the Nature Conservancy was essential to the deals going through because of the locals' great suspicion of the federal government. The Kansas preserve was located in Chase County, where Heat-Moon made his "deep-map" of *PrairyErth*. At the time that the book was published, the locals had fought the idea to a standstill. "I don't say that the prairie park was all that bad an idea," Heat-Moon quotes the reasoning, "I just say I don't want some government telling me what to do." Heat-Moon then commented: "Those words, better than any others I know, situate Chase County in the American West."[32]

When the Nature Conservancy announced their first major ranch purchase in Oklahoma's oil-rich Osage County, they sought to reassure locals that "future federal involvement is absolutely not part of our plan." As their land-use strategy for the area took shape, the Conservancy worked to implement a "bioreserve" approach that would "balance protection of the original prairie . . . with grazing use and oil and gas production."[33] This acknowledgment that entrenched local interests must be accommodated to secure any amount of natural preservation—buyouts failing—was often couched in terms of "open space" or "landscape" preservation, a growing trend among land-use planners by the 1990s. Cultural landscape preservationism involved a recognition that aspects of human use, including industrial, might actually enhance and lend character to a natural setting. Pumpjacks and grazing cattle were a characteristic landscape of the southern Plains, for example, and far preferable as a western-themed "viewshed" to strip malls and other features of the mass-cultural "world without a country." Livestock raisers and mineral royalty owners could potentially be partners (and donors) to conservation rather than automatic opponents.

Farther to the west, former Arizona governor Bruce Babbitt, serving as secretary of the Interior under the Clinton administration, sought a similarly centrist approach with his department's *Rangeland Reform '94* proposals, attempting to balance the demands of 74 million recreational visitors to BLM and national forest rangelands (in 1992 alone) with the needs of 20,000 or so public lands ranchers. Though bowing to the masses might have seemed a no-brainer, the report on *Rangeland Reform '94* cited the importance of ranching to the West's rural communities, emphasizing what a solid citizen the typical rancher was: a 1991 survey in eleven western states found that he was "55 years old and has worked on the same ranch for more than 31 years." Moreover, the "average ranching family had ranched in the same state for 68 years." Babbitt saw his reforms as a way to continue making public lands ranching sustainable over the long term. One aspect of the program would have involved an extremely modest reduction of "authorized forage" of 3 percent in the next twenty years to help restore watersheds and reduce erosion. Ranchers, for their part, looked askance at his proposals to raise grazing permit fees, to require "permittees to more intensively manage their operations," and to replace local grazing boards (run by ranchers) with "multiple resource advisory councils" that would include recreational and other users of the public lands. The "Proposed Action . . . would intensify feelings of mistrust and loss of personal control" on the part of some ranchers, the *Rangeland* report admitted. But it was hoped that the "multiple resource advisory councils would return some of the control back to public land users of all types" and "provide a forum for consensus building."[34]

If preservationists were forced to compromise in the conservative political climate of the 1990s and 2000s, so too commercial interests in the West, especially cattle ranchers, felt an increasing pressure to acquiesce to the cultural revolution of environmentalism and prove their "green" credentials. Consumer demand for more healthy, natural, and ethically raised foods obliged ranchers to rethink some of their traditional ways of doing business; the economics of so-called agritourism also began to carry weight. "We're proud to celebrate the 20th anniversary of Earth Day," ran an advertisement by the National Cattlemen's Association in 1990, "because every day is Earth Day for American Cattlemen." More convincing were magazines like *The Cattleman* of the Texas and Southwestern Cattle Raisers Association, which offered advice on "long-term ranch sustainability" and featured models like White's Ranch on the Texas Gulf coast, founded by James Taylor White in 1819 and still operated by a sixth generation of Whites in the 1990s. Part of the ranch's holdings were leased from the federal government (much in the western vein), but some of its private lands were grazed under a perpetual conservation easement purchased by the US Fish and Wildlife Service, helping preserve open marshland.

This kind of cooperation was heartening to advocates for both conservation and ranching—and there were some, most notably biologist Allan

Savory. Savory's book *Holistic Resource Management* (1988) put forward the provocative idea (adopted from research in his native Zimbabwe) that the "herd effect," or intensive grazing, could actually be beneficial to the land when properly applied, aerating, fertilizing, and encouraging plant growth. A whole subgenre of such ecologically conscious, pro-ranching books emerged, including Dan Dagget and Jay Dusard's *Beyond the Rangeland Conflict: Toward a West That Works* (1995) and Paul F. Starrs's *Let the Cowboy Ride: Cattle Ranching in the American West* (1998).[35]

It remained unclear how far private landowners as well as state and local officials—not to mention Congress—were willing to go on behalf of other, more grandiose regionalist dreams floating around the West in the 1990s and 2000s. Particularly after 2001, in a polarized political climate whipsawed by wars and economic hard times, citizens seemed to be in little mood for bold new public projects. A good example was "rewilding," which became the watchword of planners and conservation biologists who dreamed on a larger scale than the American Prairie Reserve. In what was probably the ultimate expression of the wilderness West regional identity, such a Yellowstone-sized park would merely form the "core wild area" of one of several "regional wildlands networks" within a greater "North American Wildlands Network," as outlined by Dave Foreman in his 2004 book, *Rewilding North America*. A flurry of proposals by biologists Reed Noss, Michael Soulé, and others guided by "wildlands network design" principles sought to achieve ecosystem conservation and biodiversity on a continental scale—a supranational Buffalo Commons for more than just bison, stretching northward into Canada and southward into Mexico. The core wild areas would be connected by wilderness corridors or "wildlife movement linkages," and surrounded and buffered by "compatible-use areas" of public and private land where "sensitive, conservative resource use" could occur. Rewilding advocates like Foreman, Soulé, and Noss required (on paper, at least) that land-use compromises come from the opposite direction. Rather than allowing traditional economic activities to share space in balance with reintroduced wildlife, as at the Nature Conservancy's Tallgrass Prairie Preserve, private landowners would now have to yield access for wildlife—including predators like bears, mountain lions, and wolves, crucial to ecosystem functionality—to roam out of the core areas.[36]

The degree to which these ambitions of the wildlands network designers seemed out of proportion with the turn-of-the-century political climate was shown by the fate of a modest government program called Regional Connections, as reported by Victoria Basolo in her 2003 article, "U.S. Regionalism and Rationality." First proposed in 1999, Regional Connections was intended to encourage states and localities to find "regional solutions to metro-

Figure 9 Western regional wildlands networks showing wildlife movement link-ages. *Pacific and Spine of the Continent MegaLinkages,* from *Rewilding North America,* by Dave Foreman, © 2004. Courtesy of Dave Foreman.

politan problems." An initial $100 million budget was proposed, which Con-gress "failed to move forward in 1999," Basolo noted. The following year, $50 million was "budgeted . . . but not appropriated." In 2001, another budget of $25 million was put forward, and as Basolo observed, "Ironically, federal sup-port for the programme appears to be dwindling even before one dollar has been spent." Today, there seems to be no trace of it. Babbitt's *Rangeland Re-form '94* fared little better. The limited portion of it that was actually imple-mented was soon supplanted by new, more rancher-friendly regulations un-der the George W. Bush administration. It was a classic case of what happens when "reform imposes a cost on a small, well-organized group for the benefit of a large, undifferentiated group," as one postmortem concluded. "It will be almost as though Rangeland Reform '94 never existed."[37]

One might argue that regional governance should not come from on high, imposed from the federal level. But a small western city's struggles with growth revealed some of the challenges facing local and state governments seeking on their own to steer development in more regionally sustaining directions. Greeley, Colorado, which in John Wesley Powell's time had been originally platted along the lines of a one-square-mile New England town, served Duerksen and van Hemert as a model of a well-designed western downtown, where an "enclosed and inviting space" had been constructed to "create a community 'living room' with immediate access to central civic, recreation, entertainment, commerce, and religious functions." The forty-six-square-mile (circa 2008) Greeley was hardly bucolic though, despite its views of the Front Range. It was the hub of a metropolitan statistical area with a population of a quarter of a million, and a component of the greater Denver-Aurora-Boulder Combined Statistical Area (population 3 million).[38] Growth control in Colorado, which first took shape when the Sagebrush Rebellion was heating up, ceded much more leeway to local governments than was the case with the Oregon model. Greeley's own vast metropolitan area—the 4,000 square miles of Weld County—actually encompassed a lot of very empty High Plains landscape where Kathleen Norris or William Least Heat-Moon would feel right at home communing with nature, including the 300 square miles of Pawnee National Grassland. Thus there has been the temptation to continue expanding into the apparent infinity of rural land stretching away from Greeley proper.

The city grew toward its current forty-six square miles by partially succumbing to that temptation after 2000, annexing 10,000 acres of the surrounding countryside but zoning it with a "Holding Agriculture" status that must be rezoned before future development can occur (hardly an impediment, of course). Greeley planners also made no guarantees regarding the intrastate-level Northern Colorado Community Separators Study (1998), which suggested the communal, environmental, and aesthetic importance of maintaining "physical and visual separation" between towns and cities in the region. Most of the Greeley metro's thirty-one incorporated cities and towns were actually concentrated together in the southwestern portion of Weld County, and many of them felt increasing pressure by constituents to save open space. In 2002, the Greeley municipal government commissioned a "parks and trails master plan" that foresaw an additional 20 percent population increase for the city in the decade after 2010 and recommended the construction of sixty-eight miles of new trails. These trails could "link to schools, public parks, recreational facilities and open space areas, to other neighborhoods, or to work and shopping destinations," the consultants wrote, and would be built so as to "minimize habitat fragmentation" for wildlife. The communitarian historic heart of Greeley might thereby radiate through the trail system to make the city as a whole more walkable, bike-friendly, and cohesive. There was just one small problem, the consultants noted in their conclusion: "Currently, there is no dedicated funding source for trail corridor acquisition or trail construction."[39] Greeley residents, yearning for the public amenity of open space, also liked their taxes low.

Lack of funding was far from the only impediment to effective regional governance in the turn-of-the-century West. In a 1997 study, Scott Bollens of the University of California at Irvine looked at the other extreme of the metropolitan (or megalopolitan) scale: Southern California. There he discerned only "fragmented" or "shadow" regionalism—Hugh R. Pomeroy's original 1920s planning vision still unrealized. It was not for lack of effort. Any number of "regional governance alternatives" were at work in Southern California, seeking to navigate and coordinate among 160 cities and many more localities. Bollens concluded that single-issue regional planning agencies, such as transportation authorities, were effective at producing mandated results on the ground, but because they were not empowered with broader jurisdiction over land use along tracks and near stations, for example, the social benefit of new infrastructure was limited. Shiny new stations were built, but within walking distance of only 11 percent of the region's population. Land-use decisions were left to local governments and private entities, and such "compartmentalization" and "institutional insularity" defeated the main purpose of regionalism. Frank Popper had surmised as much in his analysis of American land-use planning a decade earlier: "No principle of administrative rationality, constitutional entitlement, economic efficiency, or even ideological predisposition truly determines the locus of decisions. It is more often a matter of the inevitably uncertain catch-as-catch-can pluralism of democratic power politics."[40]

Not everyone considered this situation to be a bad thing. Particularly since the 1980s, a growing number of urban observers have risen in defense of "postsuburban" places, such as Orange County in greater Los Angeles. Joel Garreau first called national media attention to the idea that a new urban "frontier" was taking shape primarily in (though not limited to) the Sunbelt, coining a term for it with his book title, *Edge City* (1991). Irvine, California, where Bollens resided, was a prime example: clusters of office buildings, shopping malls, educational facilities, and hospitals, all far from any traditional central-city downtown. People had simply voted with their feet and liked working and living in edge cities or, as some analysts preferred to call them, "urban villages." Another group of planning scholars at Irvine refined Garreau's idea in their book, *Postsuburban California: The Transformation of Orange County Since World War II* (1991). The Orange County "postsuburban region" was more than the sum of its parts and far more than an appendage of Los Angeles, or so argued volume editors Rob Kling, Spencer Olin, and Mark Poster. Its $70 billion economic output was larger than that of many individual states. In their view, postsuburban regions like Orange County comprised vast "interactive" and "decentralized" urbanized spaces that were "fundamentally decentered or multicentered . . . complex, incoherent, and dynamic."[41] Orange County's coming-of-age as a place with its own distinctive regional identity seemed to be confirmed in popular culture after 2000, with such television offerings as *The O.C.* (2003–2007), *Laguna Beach: The Real Orange County* (2004–2006), and *The Real Housewives of Orange County* (2006–).

It remains debatable whether the "postsuburban region" concept actually constitutes a new form of city or merely an apologia for sprawl—or, as Bollens suggested, a kind of shadow regionalism. Bollens was among many planning advocates who continued to take up the refrain of "comprehensive metropolitan government," fully able to "integrate environmental, social, and economic policies," and animated by "metropolitan constituencies," as the solution to uncoordinated regional governance.[42] He did not have to mention Portland as the standard of comparison, yet on a larger scale than the metropolitan, Oregonians in this same period were validating Popper's insight, recognizing that a hodgepodge of planning policies—rather than "comprehensive"—might be the most realistic at the statewide level.

After surviving several ballot initiatives in its first years of existence, Senate Bill 100 had been modified by new legislation in 1983 that sought to accommodate the concerns of predominantly rural counties in the southern and eastern parts of Oregon, where opposition to planning was strongest. On the heels of the Reagan recession, local plans were now required to outline how they might foster economic development. "You can't plan our area, Eastern Oregon, the way you plan Portland," a local official remarked. Although officials like this one at least left the door open to planning, such a spirit of compromise faltered in the growing ideological polarization of the late 1990s, with antigovernment animus directed not against Washington bureaucrats but at the state-level Land Conservation and Development Commission (LCDC). A new ballot initiative designed to gut SB 100 was approved by voters in 2000, though it was subsequently ruled unconstitutional. Again, by large margins, opposition was concentrated outside the Willamette Valley. By 2008, the LCDC was touting how it provided "regional solutions for a diverse state," representing a "diversity of planning approaches" that reflected the "unique geographical, economic, social and political setting of each community." Among other "differences by area of the state," what was considered "high-value" farmland, the approval criteria for constructing "non-farm dwellings" on farmland, and the possibility of engaging in "aggregate mining" depended on whether one lived in the Willamette Valley or in the other 85,000 square miles of Oregon. Towns with populations below 2,500 were also "exempt from certain planning requirements."[43]

Were land-use planning proponents bowing to political reality with these kinds of concessions, hoping to preserve the grand Portland experiment from another statewide conservative backlash? Or was this accommodation of local diversity as it should be under regionalism? As Frederick Jackson Turner long ago pointed out, regions were meant to serve as "restraints upon a deadly uniformity" and as "fields for experiment in the growth of different types of society, political institutions, and ideals."[44] This principle seemed to be writ not so small in Oregon's evolving attempt to make regional planning work across its wide range of climate, terrain, and ideology. There still seemed room enough in the West for an American Prairie Reserve, a White's Ranch, a Greeley, a Portland, and an Orange County.

Nothing in the contemporary West laid bare the collision of geography and ideology more starkly than the overriding issue of water. A whole series of histories, analyses, and exposés began appearing in the 1980s and later years, all sharing John Wesley Powell's basic assumption of aridity. "Water defines 'the West,'" the Western Water Policy Review Advisory Commission (WWPRAC) observed in its major report, *Water in the West: Challenge for the Next Century* (1998). Marc Reisner, in his widely read book *Cadillac Desert: The American West and Its Disappearing Water*, took the argument further. "In the West," he wrote, "lack of water is the central fact of existence, and a whole culture and set of values have grown up around it." Most works like Reisner's struck a culturally radical tone similar to the Poppers' Buffalo Commons proposal: western water development was a monumental mistake, fundamentally misguided from the beginning and not sustainable over the long term. The case could be made by localist studies focusing on a single state (California in Norris Hundley Jr.'s *The Great Thirst*, 1992, rev. ed. 2001), a particular river (the Colorado River in Philip L. Fradkin's *A River No More*, 1981, rev. ed. 1996), or a specific project (Lake Powell in James Lawrence Powell's *Dead Pool*, 2008). These localist studies often devoted attention to the more symbiotic and communitarian modes of water use typifying earlier Native American and Hispanic inhabitants, which as Hundley wrote, "contrast sharply with the individualism and monopolistic impulses . . . following the American conquest."[45] Such studies could and did generalize regarding the broader absurdity and failure of modern water management in the greater West. But it was especially books like Reisner's or Donald Worster's *Rivers of Empire: Water, Aridity, and the Growth of the American West* (1985) that sought most deliberately to explode nationalist West myths of progress, freedom, and democracy, and to cast an antiexceptionalist pall over the whole enterprise of settling the arid West.

Reisner took particular aim at the technocratic dimension of water development, focusing on the depletion of groundwater, the siltification of dams, and water salinization ("slow liquid death") to call into question the West as a frontier for American know-how. The great multipurpose dams of the West had once been a chief symbol of technological prowess, Reisner declared, but now they were revealed to be "a vandalization of both our natural heritage and our economic future." The crazed bureaucratic rivalry between the Bureau of Reclamation and the Army Corps of Engineers, both reckless and blinkered, had carved the "credibility gap" into the landscape. A word that Reisner used more than once was "unnatural," as in, "Irrigation is a profoundly unnatural act," and this word resonated with readers in the environmental era, the opposite of "natural" as well as "legitimate." For examples he pointed to the siphons that pumped water uphill to supply Los Angeles and to wild schemes left on paper to divert some of the flow of the Mississippi River westward using nuclear power. The West had been made into a "fool's paradise," Reisner wrote; it was untenably artificial. "One does not really conquer a place like this," he believed, and he began and ended his story with allusions to "desert civilizations throughout history" that had tried—and eventually, "collapsed."[46]

That the West might not embody American exceptionalism but could be likened to ancient empires was Worster's point of departure in *Rivers of Empire*. He summoned Karl Wittfogel's theory of the hydraulic society and did what Wittfogel had been unwilling to do in the Cold War years—apply it to the region around him. "The hydraulic society of the West," Worster wrote, "is increasingly a coercive, monolithic, and hierarchical system, ruled by a power elite based on the ownership of capital and expertise." Worster's standards of freedom, however, were "what Thoreau had in mind for the region," or variously, "the social and environmental ideals of

John Wesley Powell," which were effective contrasts rhetorically, though somewhat questionable as guides for the late twentieth century. Thoreau and Powell would have been relieved to learn that in the view of other analysts, "chaotic management" rather than monolithic control best described the governance of the West's water infrastructure, as Hundley wrote in *The Great Thirst*. Instead of a nascent totalitarianism, Hundley found in California a "total complex of institutions" that was "hobbled and confused" and unable to "provide reasonable supervision and guidance at all." Much like the technological tragedy of errors that Reisner recounted in *Cadillac Desert*, Hundley pointed to the morass of "nine major federal agencies . . . eight major state organizations . . . and nearly a thousand public and private entities at the regional and local levels," all trying to make decisions about California's water supply and distribution.[47]

This was essentially the same conclusion that the WWPRAC reached about the West as a whole: "multiple, and often conflicting, jurisdictions, authorities, and program objectives . . . duplicative or overlapping programs." The commission recommended that "we should organize or integrate water planning, programs, agencies, funding, and decisionmaking around natural systems—the watersheds and river basins"—Powell might yet have something to say to the twenty-first century. This transformation, the authors noted, "may require reorganization of existing offices and agencies to maximize efficiency." Eleven years later, a study by the Army Corps of Engineers for the Western States Water Council (Western Governors' Association) was still recommending essentially the same thing— "organizing our water resources goals, policies, and rules around the concept of 'places' (i.e. basins or watersheds)"—albeit with a "pivotal role" reserved for the states. This 2009 study envisioned the West's watersheds divided among nine hydrologic regions: Pacific Northwest, California, Missouri, Great Basin, Upper Colorado, Lower Colorado, Rio Grande, Texas-Gulf, and Arkansas-White-Red. Each region's watersheds could be divided into "smaller, more manageable regions or focus areas" to "make the work more manageable." But the study's authors cautioned, "Strategies are needed to re-integrate these smaller components back to the watershed scale." They referred to pilot projects like that for the Bear River watershed, which stretches across 7,500 square miles of Idaho, Utah, and Wyoming. Geographic Information Systems (GIS) and other Internet-based "collaborative planning tools," it was envisioned, could coordinate water management among the 143 federal, state, local, and private entities listed on a roster of those involved in the Bear River's governance. With some reason, Wyoming rancher and WWPRAC member Pat O'Toole had dissented from the commission's "amorphous" watershed proposals back in 1998, stating that the commission's recommendation was "devoid of any meaningful explanation of how these proposals would work in the 'maze of agencies and programs' that would . . . apparently remain untouched."[48] Powell's ideas seemed destined to succeed only at the rhetorical level.

Much like the Poppers, Marc Reisner stopped himself at one point in *Cadillac Desert* to ask the question: "So we want to know . . . what it all amounts to that we have done out here in the West. How much was sensible? How much was right? Was it folly to allow places like Los Angeles and Phoenix to grow up? Were we insane or farsighted to build all the dams?" Above all, he wrote, "What are we going to do next?"[49] For the riverine West, the emotional equivalent of the Buffalo Commons, a way to begin reinhabiting western waterways, was dam removal. Hundreds of dams across the West have come under consideration for removal, though far fewer have proceeded to the level of actual planning. In the Pacific Northwest, where the bulk of the West's waters flow, three such removals promised to restore a powerful animal symbol of the region to its former range: the salmon. In his 1992 revised edition, Reisner mentioned one of these restoration projects, involving dams on the Elwha River of the Olympic Peninsula. The other, more ambitious "dam deconstruction" proposals targeted four dams on a segment of the Snake River in southeastern Washington and another four hydroelectric dams on the Klamath River in Oregon and California.

The Elwha removal was finally scheduled to begin in 2011 and would require up to three years to complete. An ecosystem based on the salmon would return to the area for the first time in almost 100 years, it was believed, and sacred sites of local tribes would be revealed again after reservoir waters drained away. As for the Snake River dams, a ninety-eight-page "plan of study" to determine the steps to "prepare a feasibility study" was released by the Army Corps of Engineers in spring 2010. The feasibility study, if it ever occurs, would itself take several years to complete, in the estimation of the Corps, and even then, removal or breaching of one or more of the dams would be considered a "contingency of last resort," requiring an act of Congress. A 2011 review also cast doubt on the $1.4 billion Klamath deconstruction project and whether salmon restoration could be successful there. The dams might be removed, but parts of the river were so polluted that the fish migrating upriver would have to be portaged in trucks to reach their spawning beds. One of the scientists on the project review panel remarked, "It doesn't seem to me like they've thought about the big picture very much."[50]

Hope

This is not exhortation, neither is it prophesy. It is only, since I am from the West and incorrigible, hope.

WALLACE STEGNER, "BORN A SQUARE —
THE WESTERNER'S DILEMMA" (1964)

The solitary square mile of southeastern Wyoming that the writer Annie Proulx purchased for her dream home in 2003 brings to focus many of the enduring themes of modern western regionalism. As described in Proulx's 2011 memoir, *Bird Cloud*, the 640 acres straddling the North Platte River had a past and a present layered in the multiple regional identities of the West. Much of the area of Carbon County, where the property was situated, could still be considered frontier under the old definition of fewer than two people per square mile. But the emptiness was deceptive. The influence of the urban West also reached to the place that Proulx called Bird Cloud, which had once been subdivided for a housing addition because of its spectacular riverside cliffs. Nothing had come of the venture, and the landscape remained in the condition in which Proulx discovered it, overgrazed rangeland. One of her first improvements was to install several miles of fence to keep out the agrarian West in the form of Wyoming's open-range laws. From her vantage point—the wilderness West framed by the picture windows of a brand-new modern custom home—cattle were an invasive species.

Proulx describes herself in *Bird Cloud* as a writer for whom place matters. Certainly she occupies a distinguished position in the long line of artists and intellectuals who have gone west seeking inspiration from its cultures and landscapes. Thanks to the success of her gay Western "Brokeback Mountain" (1997)—including the Oscar-winning film version (2005) coadapted by Larry McMurtry—her credentials as a regionalist cultural radical were impeccable. At Bird Cloud, Proulx seemed especially intent not only on fencing out cow country but on establishing a connectedness with both the natural and Native American history of the place. The cattle that periodically break through her perimeter are treated as vermin, while elk and eagle sightings are recorded with delight, as are the prehistoric fire pits uncovered during home construction. In this light, Bird Cloud could be seen as an expression of bioregionalist "reinhabitation," albeit a privatized one. There was nothing inherently wrong with this, of course. Private visions had long been a crucial part of western regionalism, most especially the agrarian republicanism that extolled the independent homesteader. Yet Proulx's saga of building her high-end home on the range could also be read in an entirely different light—as an instance of certain tendencies identified with the New West, namely, rural gentrification, and ultimately as a document of the Great Recession as surely as books like *American Exodus* or *Factories in the Field* embodied the Great Depression.

During the 1990s, a growing number of social observers began to note the spread of affluent property buyers into remote rural areas and small towns of the West. Deep-pocketed interlopers had been a fixture of the scenic West throughout the twentieth century, but the scope of contemporary gentrification increased in sync with the turn-of-the-century population surge of the Mountain states and desert Southwest. It was aided and abetted by technology. The basic infrastructure of rural sprawl had been around for some time, and one of the several unacknowledged ironies of *Bird Cloud* was the extent to which Proulx's dream home shared these rudiments—septic system, private well, propane tank—with the low-end blight of trailer houses. Newer technologies allowed moneyed people not merely to vacation but to live and work from far-flung locations previously off the grid—private planes, fax machines, cell phones, satellite dishes, the Internet. Most of these were installed at Bird Cloud along with the stained concrete, exotic solar windows, Japanese soak tub, granite counters, and heart pine floors. For someone as ecologically attuned as Proulx, she seemed oblivious to the audacity (if not hubris) of plunking her "poem of landscape, architecture and fine craftsmanship" onto a location where seventy-mile-an-hour winds were known to occur, and where blizzards routinely cut off the outside world.[1] One is not at all surprised to read of Proulx's disappointment that her dream home is only habitable in the warmer months, because frontier Carbon County cannot afford to plow all of its roads.

Unlike Thoreau in *Walden*, Proulx never gives a full accounting of the costs of building her poem in southeastern Wyoming. Instead, she emerges in *Bird Cloud* as a type of the affluent New West settler, who like her may escape the travails of custom home construction with trips to Germany,

Ireland, and Capri, wintering in Santa Fe. Highly mobile and powerfully connected, these are individuals who can afford to live well anywhere in the world that they choose. Thus, from one perspective, what Proulx and others have come to typify is globalization, the elimination of space and borders by the ready flow of capital, goods, communications, and technology. What also seems to attend globalization, at least at this stage in the United States, is growing inequality, as a small percentage—including the creative class that counts Proulx as a member—reaps the benefits, while increasing numbers lose their middle-class wage scales when industries are outsourced overseas. In the West, extractive industries like mining have played out in many areas or cannot compete with cheap foreign labor, and the only alternative has been to shift to a service-oriented tourist economy, with its comparatively poor pay. Hence the spread of exurban trailer houses and ramshackle apartments that don't offer rooms with a view, occupied by locals who can no longer afford to live in the town where they work, or by immigrant laborers with no ties to place. This trend has come to be known as "aspenization," after the jet-set ski resort where it has been manifested so gaudily. What has seemed new and disturbing is that the trend has not remained confined to resorts but has spread into remoter areas of the West like Carbon County, where there is a paucity of opportunity and a surplus of scenery. While celebrities like Proulx or outright land barons like Ted Turner have been the most visible exemplars of the trend, the cheapening of the technological means of rural gentrification has put it in range of larger numbers of urban professionals as a potential lifestyle change.[2]

If *Bird Cloud* stands, then, as an expression of globalization, should it be counted as a "postregional" or "postwestern" text, one of those new postmodern forms heralded by critics of regionalism during the 1990s? *Bird Cloud* undercuts the "postwestern" concept with the range of its references to western regional identities; these things clearly still have meaning and resonance for Proulx and her audience. Even the exasperating cattle on her property allow Proulx to conjure a misadventure of the ranching life, familiar to anyone who has sung "Git Along Little Dogies." Although she may wish to have no truck with the agrarian West, the wilderness West remains compelling for Proulx, particularly the solitude and freedom it seems to offer. She embraces the West as a field for grand personal, if not utopian, schemes; this notion, too, has proven remarkably resilient over the decades.

Rather than postregional, Proulx's scheme at Bird Cloud, in fact, may be seen as regionalist in the deepest sense—much like the Buffalo Commons, to allow native species to recuperate and regain the ancient ground from which they had been marginalized by the monoculture of the cattle industry. To be "postwestern" in this case would require that one accept a monocultural definition of the West, identifying it solely with the agrarian West of the cowboy. But as has been seen throughout the story of modern western regionalism, no identity for the region has ever had such a clear field, though the cowboy's West came closest to hegemony thanks to the Old West culture industry. There have always been competing and conflicting ways of defining the West, and there is little reason to doubt that this condition will change. Many recent clashes in the localist West stem from the gentrifiers' injection of greater environmental awareness into the debate. Looking to protect their serenity, viewsheds, and water supplies, they object to economic activities like logging and mining that might bring only short-term benefit to local merchants and working people, but long-term scarification of the landscape.[3]

Yet what of the other connotations of "post-" regional and postwestern, that is, "no longer having the qualities of"? If the gentrification and globalization represented by Proulx at Bird Cloud are structural changes in how people may live in the West and what they may (or may not) aspire to there, the West might arguably be transfigured into someplace unrecognizable to the terms of its earlier regions, subregions, and regional identities. From this perspective, the nationalist West at first glance seems likeliest to fade off the map. The long-standing beacon of the nationalist West, California, together with other western precincts of Sunbelt prosperity like Nevada and Arizona, were particularly hard hit by the Great Recession. Since 2008, the urban West identity of these three states has been rebranded as the "foreclosure belt."[4] Proulx's expectations for Bird Cloud were as high as any driving this bubble, and after it burst, *Bird Cloud* the book became an artifact of another time.

The aftermath found John B. Judis wondering in a prominent 2009 *New Republic* article whether "California's days as a politico-cultural vanguard and economic bellwether" might be ending.[5] But such perceptions could just as readily be interpreted as products of the historical moment, with the nationalist West once again serving as the projection screen for American anxieties over exceptionalism, just as it did in the 1930s. There seems little probability in the foreseeable future that America will permanently turn its back on places like Hollywood and Silicon Valley as no longer relevant. Their penumbra of trendiness and innovation, coupled with a whole series of energy booms across the West since 2000—wind, natural gas, coal, and most recently, shale oil—suggests that the nationalist West may resume beckoning in short order.

The Native American West, out of all of the West's regional identities, has taken perhaps the most drastic turn over the past decade or so, landing out beyond its previous terms. For many Americans under the age of eighteen, Native Americans are now known as the people who own gambling casinos. Whether this is a good thing or bad, it is a definite break with the past. At the same time, the economic well-being that gaming represents has been the incentive that resurrected many tribal groups out of disintegration and obscurity. The Indian gaming phenomenon has occurred nationally since the passing of the Indian Gaming Regulatory Act (1988), but its impact has been widespread out in the more extensive western subregions of Indian country. As of 2009, California and Oklahoma ranked first and second nationally in Indian gaming revenues, accounting for almost 38 percent of the $26 billion national industry; overall, Indian gaming within western states generated nearly 60 percent of total national revenues. Gaming advocates argue that the tribal operations have an economic multiplier effect in the states where they reside; opponents just see new pockets of exploitation and sprawl. Though such consequences would seem to contradict traditional Native American values of simplicity and symbiosis, many tribes and nations have used their gaming profits to construct cultural centers and launch educational programs, including some sophisticated multimedia campaigns like that undertaken by the Chickasaw Nation, Chickasaw.tv.[6] So the ultimate effect of Indian gaming may be to revivify and enhance Native cultures and further strengthen the sovereignty of Indian country, along with the regional decentralization it represents. It may well be the most recent confirmation of Edward Spicer's insight that cultural homogenization — in this case, the hypercommercialism of gaming — begets cultural differentiation.

The empowering of Indian country in all its diversity has been one of the ironic side effects of modern conservative political activism. Indian gaming arose in part out of the fiscal stalemate that has tormented state legislatures and Congress over the past twenty years. Tax-averse states found it difficult to deny casinos to tribes after they themselves resorted to lotteries to raise revenue, and most states also gladly took a piece of the casinos' action. Social conservatives acquiesced in this legalization of "vice" because, like fiscal conservatives, they had come to view taxation to fund the welfare state as a greater evil. Similarly, the two wings of modern conservatism have found common cause on the issue of illegal immigration, with officials in Arizona leading a state-level crusade to "control the border" through two harsh laws passed in 2010. Demographic growth will ultimately doom such efforts to reassert Anglo supremacy in the borderlands, and it may well win the day in another subregion where the Hispanic West has recently gained a surprising but tentative foothold: the Great Plains. It seems that in the last ten years, Hispanics have been refilling the Plains neo-frontier heralded by the Poppers; in seven Plains states (including Iowa and Minnesota), the rural Hispanic population has increased by 54 percent. In many areas, the influx has more than offset white Anglo out-migration, reversing the decline of small towns and rural communities.[7] Whether this transformation will be seen as a miracle or a plague may well depend on legislators who will have to choose if enforcing cultural and racial homogeneity is more important than preserving small-town life on the Plains.

While antitaxation dogma underlay the political context for expanded Indian sovereignty, and nativism roiled the old and new states of the Hispanic West, antiregulatory fervor has led to a redoubled push to roll back western land-use planning. The conservative-inspired strategy centered on planning laws construed as legislative "takings," that is, depriving private property owners of the use or value of their property by government regulation. This effort, with roots in the "wise use" movement of the 1990s, seemed to have scored a major victory against regional planning in the West with the 2004 passage of Measure 37 in Oregon, which required compensation to property owners affected by state-mandated land-use planning. "That an Owner May Do with His Property as He Likes" was one of the precepts of western individualism that the Depression-era Great Plains Committee thought needed reform, but many in the West still held to it in the twenty-first century. Even Annie Proulx was swept up in the liberating spirit of sovereign property rights, her conservation easement notwithstanding. Oregon's voters had second thoughts about Measure 37 and passed another referendum in 2007 limiting some of its more extreme consequences—which might have cost the state and local governments hundreds of millions of dollars in compensation—while explicitly protecting high-quality farmland and forestland.[8] Future rounds between planning advocates and property rights activists are a certainty, yet the curbing of Measure 37 involved the recognition by many but the most libertarian that property values are not inherent but relative to the development of the larger community, much of which hinges on publicly funded infrastructure—something that Henry George long ago pointed out. Proulx seems to have learned it the hard way; she could not have the full use and enjoyment of her private property because public resources were limited. Just as her characters discover in "Brokeback Mountain," absolute freedom in the West is illusory.

Piecing together the few clues that Proulx provides about the exact location of Bird Cloud, you may zoom down on her rooftop using the satellite view of Google Maps (luckily for her, not in real time). Literary scholar Neil Campbell has observed that in this and myriad other ways, the larger world "leaks into" the West. We may today call this process globalization, but it has always been there in some form. And surely one of the most foreboding ways the world is presently breaking in on the West is through climate change. Proulx took note of some of the effects in *Bird Cloud*, such as the pine beetle infestation that has turned millions of acres of trees in the Mountain states into vast stands of kindling. In the year when these words are being written (2011), a drought worse than the Dust Bowl is gripping the southern Plains and elsewhere in the West has dropped lakes like Powell and Mead to historically low levels. Oklahoma has witnessed the hottest individual month (July) ever recorded by any state. Texas, New Mexico, and Arizona have each experienced their largest wildfires on record, consuming millions of acres. Record snowpacks have piled up in the Rockies and Sierras, threatening to unleash disastrous floods if they melt too fast. The extremes are becoming more extreme, as climate scientists have predicted, and no place can be a haven. In my own locality, the past four years have seen the deepest single-day snowfall, the heaviest single-day rainstorm, and the wettest annual rainfall total on record. In 2008, Hurricane Ike—one of a record six storms to strike the United States that year—roared onto the Gulf coast of Texas, bringing with it a massive seventeen-foot storm surge that swept onto the 189-year-old White's Ranch mentioned in chapter 4. Dead cows were found hanging from tree limbs twenty feet in the air, and a salty crust covered pastures long after the ocean water receded. As many as 10,000 cattle were killed on the White's and nearby ranches, and there were doubts whether some of the operations could remain viable.[9]

The same might be said about the future of the cowboy as an icon of the West. Compared to previous generations, when the cowboy character played relentlessly through the media, today the figure is scarcely to be seen. The Old West culture industry flickers weakly at best. "Woody" from the animated *Toy Story* franchise (1995–2010), alluding nostalgically to the industry in its heyday, is among the very few cowboys familiar to children. Two of the half dozen or so western films to find a degree of recent box office success (or at least break even) in the past decade, *3:10 to Yuma* (2007) and *True Grit* (2010), were remakes of previous movies. *No Country for Old Men* (2007), the Oscar-winning adaptation of a Cormac McCarthy novel set in the present-day borderlands, was essentially a film about a serial killer, that modern cinematic anti-hero who has done a much better job than the cowboy in sating the American appetite for violence. *Brokeback Mountain* also did the conventional Western film and the cowboy archetype no favors. It imploded the sexual boundaries of the masculine code of the West, and it called widespread attention to the unromantic social reality that many so-called cowboys and ranchhands are poorly paid, seasonal wage laborers. Both the film and Proulx's original story—along with the real-world homophobic murder of Matthew Shepard—went further still to subvert the notion of the West as the land of the free, where diverse people may coexist under the old-fashioned ethic of live and let live. Certainly, regardless of the regional image projected in the media, the cattle industry will continue into the foreseeable future in the West. And perhaps, as Kevin Landis suggests in his book, *The Cowboy Steward* (2006), we may consider that anywhere there is a cow, there must be "somebody tending that cow" whom we should call "cowboy," which presumably would include employees of feedlots where cattle are packed in 50,000 at a time, waiting for processing. "There was some open space between what he knew and what he tried to believe," Proulx writes at the conclusion of "Brokeback Mountain."[10]

Landis has served as the pastor of the Trail to Heaven Cowboy Church, located in Celina, Texas. The Cowboy Church Network of North America is currently one of the fastest growing niches of American Protestantism, especially strong in Texas and Oklahoma but with congregations nationwide, including places like Pennsylvania that haven't been called "the West" in a very long time. Members often dress in cowboy clothing and listen to sermons that relate the cowboy way of life to Christian teachings. They participate in church-sponsored roping and riding contests. To close the open space between the West that we know and the West we would like to believe in, whether it be the West of cowboys, or Indians, or wilderness, might not require us to form a cult from a subculture. But Wallace Stegner, after a lifetime of contemplating the West, thought that westerners could also do better than Proulx's counsel at the end of "Brokeback"— the stoic acceptance of some hard and ugly truths. Proulx herself did not heed it, as *Bird Cloud* testified. Looking back late in his life, Stegner recalled his own catchphrase from the "Wilderness Letter"—the "geography of hope"—and he admitted that the West had not lived up to its promise. "Nothing would gratify me more than to see it, in all its subregions and subcultures, both prosperous and environmentally healthy, with a civilization to match its scenery."[11] He did not see that future yet, but he still had his hopes.

Notes

Preface

1. On the adversary tradition, see Thomas, *Alternative America*, esp. 354–66.
2. US Western Water Policy Review Advisory Commission, *Water in the West*, 2-1.

Introduction

1. Darrah, *Powell*, 100–101. See also Stegner, *Beyond the Hundredth Meridian*, 25–30; Hartemann and Hauptman, *Mountain Encyclopedia*, 126–27, 257–59. Barometers were employed to measure altitude by calculating the change in air pressure relative to sea level using a formula. See R. S. Williamson, *On the Use of the Barometer*.

2. For examples of this viewpoint, see Boime, *Magisterial Gaze*; Pratt, *Imperial Eyes*, esp. 78; Stout, *Picturing a Different West*, 11; Dilworth, *Imagining Indians*, 103–4; Green, "Tribe Called Wannabee," 31; Rosaldo, "Imperialist Nostalgia," 107–8.

3. McMurtry, *Lonesome Dove*, 939. See also Debo, *And Still the Waters Run*; Limerick, *Legacy of Conquest*; Hough, *North of 36*; see also by Hough, "Slaughter of the Trees," 579–92; Sandoz, *Old Jules*.

4. On both Long and Gilpin, see Lewis, "William Gilpin and the Concept of the Great Plains Region," 35–36, 43–44. On Native American maps, see Warhus, *Another America*.

5. Powell, *Report*, 1, 3, 5–6; on the assumptions underlying Powell's land classification, see Kirsch, "John Wesley Powell," 548–72.

6. Powell, "Non-Irrigable Lands," 922; Powell, *Report*, 23–24, 29; Powell, *Three Methods*, 51–52.

7. Powell, *Report*, 22.

8. Royce, *Basic Writings*, 1:34. See also Hine, *Josiah Royce*.

9. Royce, *Basic Writings*, 2:1154, 1:45–46.

10. Royce, *Race Questions*, 61.

11. On civil or civic religion, see the classic essay by Bellah, "Civil Religion in America." For the southern variety, see Wilson, *Baptized in Blood*.

12. Royce, *Race Questions*, 98, 74, 81, 97.

13. National Park Service, "Rocky Mountain National Park: History & Culture"; National Park Service, "Rocky Mountain National Park: Time Line of Historic Events." A fourteener is mountaineering jargon for a mountain at least 14,000 feet in elevation.

14. Semple, *American History*, 231. On the nationalist West, see also Cronon, Miles, and Gitlin, "Becoming West," 22–25; and Campbell, *Rhizomatic West*, esp. 2, 20. On Semple's work, see Schulten, *Geographical Imagination*, 81–84. The phrase "culture industry" is credited to Theodor W. Adorno, who applied it more generally to mass culture. See Adorno, *Culture Industry*.

15. Turner, *Frontier and Section*, 39, 32, 55, 38. On American exceptionalism, see Noble, *End of American History*, and Wrobel, *End of American Exceptionalism*.

16. Turner, *Frontier and Section*, 43, 63; Turner, *Frederick Jackson Turner's Legacy*, 61.

17. Turner, *Frederick Jackson Turner's Legacy*, 48; Turner, *Frontier and Section*, 93; Turner, *Significance of Sections*, 297.

18. Brigham, *Geographic Influences*, 142, 321; Turner, *Significance of Sections*, 289, 311.

19. The scholarship of nationalism is vast; see two works by Smith, *Myths and Memories of the Nation* and *Antiquity of Nations*. For a comparison to Ireland and a discussion of cultural nationalism, see Hutchinson, *Dynamics of Cultural Nationalism*.

20. Turner, *Significance of Sections*, 313–14, 338.

Chapter 1

1. Powell, "Major Powell's Address," 410–12; Rölvaag, *Giants in the Earth*, 323; Gates, *History*, 466; the total of homesteads includes those in Minnesota.

2. Pisani, *To Reclaim a Divided West*, 141; Folklore Project, "Autobiographical Sketch"; Gates, in *History* (p. 433) points out that 200,000 homesteads were "proved up" during the 1880s, but this figure may precede the worst of the drought in some areas and may not reflect longer tenure.

3. Garland, *Son of the Middle Border*, 458. For an excellent recent biography of Garland, see Newlin, *Hamlin Garland*.

4. Garland, *Son of the Middle Border*, 435, 438.

5. Ibid., 460, 437, 461, 463.

6. Ibid., 461; quoted in Newlin, *Hamlin Garland*, 103.

7. Garland, *Crumbling Idols*, 24, 35, 3, 6, 8, 14.

8. Ibid., 17, 25. On local color, see Brodhead, *Cultures of Letters*.

9. Powell, "Institutions for the Arid Lands," 113–14. On the fight over the Irrigation Survey, see Pisani, *To Reclaim a Divided West*, 143–65.

10. Smythe, *Conquest of Arid America*, v–vi, 84, 260; Powell, *Report*, 11; Bureau of Reclamation, *Story of Boulder Dam*, 18; Worster, *River Running West*, 477–79.

11. Mead, *Helping Men Own Farms*, 52, 141, 2. On Mead's accomplishments, see Pisani, *To Reclaim a Divided West*, 61–64; and Kluger, *Turning on Water with a Shovel*.

12. Garland, *Crumbling Idols*, 33, 36.

13. Ibid., 64; Garland, *Daughter of the Middle Border*, 31. See also by Garland, *Main-Travelled Roads* and *Rose of Dutcher's Coolly*.

14. Roosevelt, *Autobiography*, 103; Roosevelt, *Hunting Trips*, 1:23.

15. Wister, "Evolution of the Cow-Puncher," 617; Hough, "The West, and Certain Literary Discoveries," 508.

16. Hough, *Story of the Cowboy*, viii; Roosevelt, "An Appreciation," 395; Maxwell, "Frederic Remington," 399.

17. Roosevelt to Thomas Collier Platt, Albany, 8 May 1899, in *Letters and Speeches*, 170; Wister, "Evolution of the Cow-Puncher," 603–4. See also Wister, *Virginian*.

18. Hough, *Passing of the Frontier*, 3, 91, 172–73, 29; Wister, *Virginian*, 357.

19. See Hough, *Covered Wagon* and *North of 36*. On the film version of *The Covered Wagon*, see McCaffrey and Jacobs, *Guide to the Silent Years*, 92–93.

20. Gruber, *Zane Grey*, 4, 243; H. G. Merriam to Victor Shaw, 30 November 1928. H. G. Merriam Papers, Box 25, University of Montana Archives, Missoula, MT.

21. On tourism and western regional identity in this period, see Rothman, *Devil's Bargains*, 29–142; Dilworth, *Imagining Indians*, 17–124.

22. Semple and Jones, *American History*, 232, 486–99.

23. MacKaye, *New Exploration*, 71; H. G. Merriam to Carey McWilliams, 28 September 1930 and Merriam to Norman Macleod, 5 May 1929, H. G. Merriam Papers, Box 22; Merriam to H. L. Davis, 11 June 1930, H. G. Merriam Papers, Box 19.

24. Davis, *Collected Essays*, 359, 365.

25. Quoted in Fite, *Mount Rushmore*, 6, 28. On Native American occupations, see Taliaferro, *Great White Fathers*, 348–64.

26. Quoted in Boime, "Patriarchy Fixed in Stone," 143, 150; quoted in Fite, *Rushmore*, 45, 47.

27. Henry's review is reproduced in Hutchinson, *Bar Cross Man*, esp. 193, 198.

28. Quoted in Furman, *Walter Prescott Webb*, 100; Henry, *Conquering*, 374.

29. Henry, *Conquering*, 366, 376; Norris, *Responsibilities of the Novelist*, 61, 65.

30. Webb, *Great Plains*, iii.

31. Ibid., ii, 8, 141, 507. On Ratzel's influence through Semple, see Dickinson, *Regional Concept*, 262–64.

32. Webb to Louis Pelzer, 18 August 1944. Walter Prescott Webb Papers, Box 2M264, Briscoe Center for American History, University of Texas, Austin, Texas; Webb, *Great Plains*, 227, 246, 497, 3–8.

33. Webb, *Great Plains*, 141, 509; Webb to Abe Melton, 10 October 1943. Walter Prescott Webb Papers, Box 2M263.

34. Cather, *Early Novels and Stories*, 866.

35. Ibid., 900.

36. Ibid., 178; Cather, *Collected Stories*, 261. On Cather's conception of home and landscape, see Fryer, *Felicitous Space*.

37. Wilder, *Little House*, 237.

38. Sandoz, *Old Jules*, 19, viii. The standard biography of Sandoz is Stauffer, *Mari Sandoz*.

39. Sandoz, *Old Jules*, 53, 33.

Chapter 2

1. Lummis, *Tramp Across the Continent*, 2. For biographical background on Lummis, see Thompson, *American Character*.

2. Lummis, *Tramp Across the Continent*, 244.

3. Ibid., 190, 74–75.

4. Ibid., 93–94.

5. See Rothman, *Devil's Bargains*, 50–80; Dilworth, *Imagining Indians*, 21–124; and Hutchinson, *Indian Craze*, 1–50.

6. Roosevelt, *Presidential Addresses*, 1:327–28, 1:325.

7. Roosevelt, *Theodore Roosevelt's America*, 293; Pinchot, *Fight for Conservation*, 128, 133; Hough, *Let Us Go Afield*, 145; Hough, "Slaughter of the Trees," 586–87, 592.

8. Hough, *Passing of the Frontier*, 91, 82.

9. On the conservation legacy of Pinchot and Roosevelt, see Strong, *Dreamers and Defenders*, 61–84; see also Morris, *Theodore Rex*, 447–48, 485–87, 519.

10. Muir, *Mountains of California*; Muir, *Our National Parks*; Wister, *Virginian*, 56. On Muir's contribution, see Cohen, *Pathless Way*.

11. On the role of dispossession in creating national parks and forests in the West, see Spence, *Dispossessing the Wilderness*, and deBuys, *Enchantment and Exploitation*.

12. Leopold, *Aldo Leopold's Southwest*, 148, 150, 163.

13. On western urbanization in this period, see Abbott, *How Cities Won the West*, esp. 31–34; Weber, *From Max Weber*, 363; Weber letter from Indian Territory excerpted in Marianne Weber, *Max Weber*, 291–94.

14. Howard, "Motorizing the Frontier," 596, 475, 588, 592; on rural adoption of the automobile, see Flink, *Automobile Age*, 131–32, 150; on metropolitanization, see President's Research Committee on Social Trends, *Recent Social Trends*, 1:443, 451.

15. *Recent Social Trends*, 1:456; on urban subregional promotion, see Wrobel, *Promised Lands*, esp. 57–65.

16. Elkins, "Beauty in Garden Pools," 764, 766. For an exhaustive treatment of the California dream, see Starr, *Americans and the California Dream*, esp. 46.

17. Royce, *Race Questions*, 208, 209, 205.

18. Bertha H. Smith, "California's First Cubist House," 372, 374; Croly, "California Country House," 55–56; see Steinbeck, *Grapes of Wrath*, esp. 124.

19. Croly, "California Country House," 56; Target Science, "Population Growth by Single Year"; Scott, *American City Planning*, 208, 193; Wannop, *Regional Imperative*, 274–77; Pomeroy, "Regional Planning in Practice," 111; Whitnall, "City and Regional Planning," 106–7.

20. Pomeroy, "Regional Planning," 111–13, 123, 120.

21. Ibid., 113–14; Scott, *American City Planning*, 206–8; Whitnall, "City and Regional Planning," 107.

22. Whitnall, "City and Regional Planning," 109–10, 106.

23. On Morgan's theories, see Bieder, *Science Encounters the Indian*, 194–246.

24. Quoted in Cole, *Franz Boas*, 79; Boas, *Franz Boas Reader*, 280. See also Kuper, *Reinvention of Primitive Society*, 120–32.

25. Powell, *Philosophic Bearings*, 12.

26. Quoted in Bingham, *Charles F. Lummis*, 13.

27. Bancroft, *California Pastoral*, 292–93, 437, 620, 308, 750.

28. Lummis, *Spanish Pioneers*, 11, 20, 77, 91–92, 23–24.

29. Ibid., 65; Austin, *Land of Little Rain*, 265.

30. Jackson, *Ramona*, 16.

31. For an excellent account of the Spanish colonial revival in California, see Kropp, *California Vieja*.

32. Espinosa, *Studies in New Mexican Spanish*, 7. See also Wilson, *Myth of Santa Fe*.

33. Cather, *Death Comes for the Archbishop*; Gibson, *Santa Fe and Taos Colonies*, esp. 163–75, 211–12.

34. Bolton, *Bolton and the Spanish Borderlands*, 25, 189; Bolton, "Material for Southwestern History," 516; Bolton, *Spanish Borderlands*, viii, x.

35. Bolton, "Epic of Greater America," 463, 473.

36. Ibid., 473, 454.

37. Quoted in Woodress, *Willa Cather*, 335. On the modernist cultural crisis, see Singal, "Towards a Definition," 7–26; and May, *End of American Innocence*.

38. Quoted in Stineman, *Mary Austin*, 31.

39. Austin, *Lost Borders*, 2, 25, 3, 198, 209. On Austin's western regionalism, see Goodman and Dawson, *Mary Austin*; and Schaefer, *Mary Austin's Regionalism*.

40. Austin, *Lost Borders*, 202; Austin, *Land of Little Rain*, 3.

41. Austin, *Land of Little Rain*, 128, 131, 266, 279–80.

42. Austin, *American Rhythm*, 18–19; Austin, *Land of Little Rain*, 168.

43. Zitkala-Ša, *American Indian Stories*; Zitkala-Ša, *Dreams and Thunder*. On DeCora, see Hutchinson, *Indian Craze*, 171–220; Hutchinson's book offers multiple case studies of the phenomenon of transculturation, as does Pratt in *Imperial Eyes*. See also Hallowell, "American Indians," esp. 523–24, 529; Trigo, "On Transculturation."

44. Cole, *Franz Boas*, 205; Jones, *Fox Texts*; Neihardt, *Black Elk Speaks*.

45. Boas, *Franz Boas Reader*, 186.

46. Wissler, *American Indian*, 242–43; Wissler, *North American Indians*; Woods, "Criticism of Wissler's North American Culture Areas," 520; Kroeber, *Cultural and Natural Areas*, 2, map 6.

47. Benedict, *Patterns*; Curtis, *North American Indian*, 1: xxi; W. B. Bizzell, untitled essay on Grant Foreman's books (1935), University of Oklahoma Press Collection, Box 10, Western History Collections, University of Oklahoma Libraries, Norman, OK. On Curtis's project, see Gidley, *Edward S. Curtis*.

48. Joseph Brandt to W. B. Bizzell, 13 November 1928, University of Oklahoma Press Collection, Box 1; B. A. Botkin, *Folk-Say* (1930) advertising flyer, University of Oklahoma Press Collection. B. A. Botkin to Henry Nash Smith, 11 January 1931 and 20 December 1930, B. A. Botkin folder, Southern Methodist University Archives, DeGolyer Library, Southern Methodist University, Dallas, TX.

49. Benedict, *Patterns*, 21–22.

50. Hewett, "Southwest: Yesterday and Tomorrow," 5; Hewett, *Ancient Life*, 53.

51. Collier, "Red Atlantis," 16.

52. Quoted in Rudnick, *Mabel Dodge Luhan*, 142.

53. Mabel Dodge Luhan to Mary Austin, December 1922, T. M. Pearce Collection, Box 5, Folder 20 (photocopy of original in Mary Hunter Austin Papers, Huntington Library, San Marino, CA), University of New Mexico Special Collections, University of New Mexico Libraries; quoted in Rudnick, *Mabel Dodge Luhan*, 179.

54. Quoted in Rudnick, *Mabel Dodge Luhan*, 179; Collier, "Red Atlantis," 66.
55. See Lisle, *Portrait of an Artist*, esp. 77, 245–46.

Chapter 3

1. Henderson, *Letters*, 140.
2. Ibid., 144–45.
3. Lane, *Free Land*, iii; Great Plains Committee, *Future of the Great Plains*, 41; Webb, *Divided*, 171.
4. The best overview of this period remains Lowitt, *New Deal and the West*.
5. Sauer, "Land Resource," 252, 207, 254; Sauer, *Land and Life*, 343, 349.
6. Great Plains Committee, *Future of the Great Plains*, 63–65.
7. Sauer et al., "Preliminary Recommendations," 155.
8. Lane, *Let the Hurricane Roar*, 86, 129; Lane, *Discovery of Freedom*. On the collaboration between Lane and Wilder and their political leanings, see Fellman, *Little House*, esp. 39–67.
9. Henderson, *Letters*, 145; Webb, *Divided*, 142.
10. Webb, *Divided*, 11, 158, 110, 118–19; Twelve Southerners, *I'll Take My Stand*; DeVoto, "The West: A Plundered Province," 355–64.
11. Clements and Chaney, *Environment and Life*, 39, 35; Sauer, "Land Resource," 207, 253, 217–18; Sears, *Deserts on the March*, 141–42.
12. Taylor and Lange, *Exodus*, 107, 148–49, 135.
13. Ibid., 144, 85, 133, 68.
14. McWilliams, *Factories*, 3, 103, 21, 58.
15. Ibid., 77, 79, 112, 103, 117, 134, 230.
16. McWilliams, *Ill Fares the Land*, 109; Sanchez, *Forgotten People*, 13, 27, 38–39.
17. Douglas and d'Harnoncourt, *Indian Art*, 14–15, 9; Mathews, *Sundown*, 274.
18. McNickle, *Surrounded*, 286; Mathews, *Sundown*, 90; Debo, *Waters*, 14, 31, 373.
19. Quoted in Beito and Beito, "Isabel Paterson," 566; McWilliams, *Prejudice*.
20. See Sandoz, *Slogum House*, esp. 32, 331, 336; Sandoz, *Capital City*, 72–73, 343.
21. Clark, *Ox-Bow Incident*, 79, 224.
22. See Dorman, *Revolt*, esp. 249–306. See Steiner, "Regionalism in the Great Depression," 430–46.
23. On Woody Guthrie and the BPA, see Klein, *Woody Guthrie*, 194–95, 200–201. Federal Writers' Project, *Idaho Lore*; Federal Writers' Project, *Idaho Encyclopedia*. On Native American artists and the New Deal, see McLerran, *New Deal for Native Art*.
24. Collier, "Red Atlantis," 18, 16; Douglas and d'Harnoncourt, *Indian Art*, 12.
25. Douglas and d'Harnoncourt, *Indian Art*, 16.
26. See Kelly, "United States Indian Policies," 73.
27. See Taylor, *New Deal*, esp. 33, 47. On the Navajo, see Forrest, *Preservation*, 131–32.
28. Sanchez, *Forgotten People*, 53–54; see also Forrest, *Preservation*, 103, 157, 161, 174–79.
29. Gray et al., "Utilization of Our Lands," 504–6.
30. On New Dealers' agricultural fundamentalism, see Worster, *Dust Bowl*, esp. 145.

31. Meriam, *Relief and Social Security*, 279. See also Cannon, *Remaking the Agrarian Dream*.

32. Peffer, *Closing of the Public Domain*, 167, 225; Bureau of Land Management, "The Taylor Grazing Act."

33. On capture, see Foss, *Politics and Grass*, 194–204.

34. Covert, *Return to Dust*, 9, 74–75, 193, 278–79.

35. The complete text of the sign (in the author's private collection) states, "Keep Soil and Water on the Farm . . . Cooperator with the Soil Erosion Service." On the creation of the national grasslands, see Moul, *National Grasslands*, 11–54.

36. Pritchett, "Transplantability," 328.

37. See Billington and Jackson, *Big Dams*, 102–51.

38. See Pritchett, "Transplantability," 333; National Resources Committee, *Regional Factors*, 130; Bessey, "Pacific Northwest," 152, 157.

39. Pritchett, "Transplantability," 328; Springer, *Power and the Pacific Northwest*, 31, 41.

40. See McKinley, *Uncle Sam*, 180–81, 190–91, 193.

41. Lawson, *Dammed Indians Revisited*, 21, 23; Terral, *Missouri Valley*, 194.

42. Terral, *Missouri Valley*, 213.

43. Lilienthal, *TVA*, 53, 151; Pritchett, "Transplantability," 335; Ickes quoted in "Transplantability," 327. On the naturalizing of river basin regions, see also Vogel, "Defining One Pacific Northwest," 32–33, 39–40.

Chapter 4

1. Haystead, *If the Prospect Pleases*, 14.

2. See Nash, *Federal Landscape*, 51; Nash, *American West Transformed*, 38, 59; Hurt, *Great Plains*, 453n28.

3. Nash, *West Transformed*, 19, 59; Hurt, *Great Plains*, 43–44, 59, 33.

4. Mezerik, *Revolt*, xi; Berge, *Economic Freedom*, xi.

5. Haystead, *If the Prospect Pleases*, 81, 85, 178–79, 137–39, 150, 143, 286, 79–80.

6. Mezerik, *Revolt*, 187, 197.

7. Berge, *Economic Freedom*, 95–96, 72.

8. Morgan, *Westward Tilt*, 34–35, 6; Stegner, "West Coast," 41.

9. Chittick, "Editorial Foreword," xiv, xvi; Pollard, "Pacific Northwest: A National Epitome," 33; Haycox, "Is There a Northwest?" 49; Merriam, "Does the Northwest Believe in Itself?" 159.

10. Stegner, "West Coast," 16; Morgan, *Westward Tilt*, 11, 143–44, 137, 9; Mumford, *Highway*, 245. On California growth, see Johnson and Lovelady, "Migration," 8.

11. Haystead, *If the Prospect Pleases*, 205–6; Chittick, "Editorial Foreword," xiv; Harrison, "Regionalism," 154.

12. Malin, "Grassland," 363.

13. Smith, *Virgin Land*, 195, 200, 254, 258.

14. Webb, *Great Frontier*; Potter, *People of Plenty*, 160–61, 165; Potter, *History and American Society*, 86, 70.

15. Smith, *Virgin Land*, 260; Pomeroy, "Toward a Reorientation," 581–82, 579, 590, 598, 596.

16. Malin, *Winter Wheat*, 250–51; Malin, "Space and History," 73.

17. Malin, "Grassland," 353–56, 358.

18. Meade, *Missouri River*, 36; Peterson, *Big Dam*, 102.

19. Quoted in Billington and Jackson, *Big Dams*, 191; Odum, "Promise of Regionalism," 413 ; Selznick, *TVA and the Grass Roots*. See also Pritchett, "Transplantability," 335–36, 338.

20. DeVoto, "The West: A Plundered Province," 358, 360.

21. DeVoto, *Easy Chair*, 245, 242, 244, 249, 252, 254–55.

22. Ibid., 329, 345. On DeVoto's environmental activism in this period, see Thomas, *Country in the Mind*, 129–62.

23. Sandoz, "I Do Not Apologize," 107; quoted in Rosier, "'They Are Ancestral Homelands,'" 1309; Wittfogel, *Oriental Despotism*, 27, 68, 166, 234; Castile, *To Show Heart*, xxvi.

24. Rosier, "Ancestral Homelands," 1307, 1320n; Burt, "Termination and Relocation," 22–24; Castile, *To Show Heart*, xxvi; Sandoz, "I Do Not Apologize," 105; Fixico, *Termination*, 185; Lawson, *Dammed Indians Revisited*, 25, 286.

25. Momaday, *House*, 158.

26. Ibid., 1.

27. Quoted in Rosier, "Ancestral Homelands," 1315; Castile, *To Show Heart*, 178–79.

28. Sandoz, "I Do Not Apologize," 120; Momaday, *Way to Rainy Mountain*; Steward, *Theory of Culture Change*; on Steward's western research, see Clemmer, *Julian Steward*.

29. Spicer, *Cycles*, 16, 8, 567, 575.

30. McWilliams, *Southern California*; Garnsey, *America's New Frontier*; Kraenzel, *Great Plains*; Winther, *Great Northwest*.

31. Howard, *Montana*, 2–3, 321; Johansen and Gates, *Empire*, 666.

32. Pomeroy, *Pacific Slope*, 372–73, 375, 392, 385.

33. Vance, "Regional Concept," 119; Pollard, "Pacific Northwest," 205–6; Caughey, "Spanish Southwest," 183–84.

34. Vogt, *Modern Homesteaders*, vii, 181.

35. Spicer, *Cycles*, 2; Vogt, *Homesteaders*, 181; Vogt and Albert, "Comparative Study," 25–26.

36. Pauker, "Political Structure," 220; Vogt, "Ecology and Economy," 190.

37. For a guide to Western films, see Varner, *Historical Dictionary*; McMurtry, *Horseman, Pass By*.

38. Billington, *Westward Expansion*. On Billington and the founding of the Western History Association, see Lamar, "Much to Celebrate," 399–402. On television westerns, see Brode, *Shooting Stars*.

39. See Schiesl, "Designing the Model Community," 63 ; Findlay, *Magic Lands*, 274–75.

40. For a description of the program, see Scott, *American City Planning*, 404–6; Public Administration Service, *Action for Cities*, iv, 65, 6, 29.

41. Morgan, *Westward Tilt*, 89–90.

42. Tunnard and Pushkarev, *Man-Made America*, 38; Abbott, *How Cities Won*, 155.

43. Jackson, *Landscape in Sight*, 237, 40, 364.

44. Stegner, *Beyond the Hundredth Meridian*, 96.

45. Stegner, "Wilderness Letter." Stegner, *This Is Dinosaur*.

46. Morgan, *Westward Tilt*, 97; "Riverboat Runs through . . . Dinosaur National Monument," 22, 25. For an account of the efforts to save Dinosaur and pass the Wilderness Act, see Nash, *Wilderness and the American Mind*, 200–238.
47. On intraregional colonialism, see Gómez, *Quest*, esp. 31–70.
48. PNM, "Four Corners Power Plant"; quoted in Fradkin, *Wallace Stegner*, 191; Fradkin's biography offers an excellent overview of the scope of Stegner's environmental activism in the postwar years.
49. Udall, *Quiet Crisis*, 179, 195–96.
50. Morgan, *Westward Tilt*, 99.
51. Jackson, *Landscape in Sight*, 27.
52. Stegner, "Wilderness Letter."
53. Stegner, *Beyond the Hundredth Meridian*, 367; Wittfogel, "Hydraulic Civilizations," 153, 155.

Chapter 5

1. Gastil, *Cultural Regions*, 297, 299, 305; Matusow, *Unraveling*.
2. Garreau, *Nine Nations*, xvi–xvii; Elazar, *American Federalism*, 122.
3. Yoder, "Folklife Studies," 3.
4. Smith, *Geography of Social Well-Being*, 140–41; Gastil, *Cultural Regions*, 297, 305 (includes quotation of Elazar); Garreau, *Nine Nations*, xvi–xvii.
5. Gordon, *Assimilation*, 50–51; Meinig, *Imperial Texas*, 123–24.
6. Cole and King, *Quantitative Geography*, 631; Yoder, "Folklife Studies," 3; Gastil, *Cultural Regions*, 301; Lasch, *Culture of Narcissism*.
7. Gastil, *Cultural Regions*, 301.
8. Glenn and Simmons, "Are Regional Cultural Differences Diminishing?" 180, 190–91.
9. Sharkansky, *Regionalism*, 76, 144, 158, 174, 103.
10. Phillips, *Emerging Republican Majority*.
11. Mohl, "Preface," xv; Brownell, "Introduction," 3; the authors of a more recent volume, Nickerson and Dochuk, eds., *Sunbelt Rising*, are seeking to revive the Sunbelt concept, as the title implies.
12. Garreau, *Nine Nations*, xii, 204–5 (maps).
13. Elazar, *American Federalism*, 140, 125; Bensel, *Sectionalism*, 417, 37.
14. Meinig, *Southwest*, viii; Meinig, "Mormon Culture Region," 195, 213, 215–16; Meinig, *Imperial Texas*, 117; Meinig, *Great Columbia Plain*, xv, xxi.
15. Meinig, "American Wests," 160–62; Meinig, "Continuous Shaping," 1202–3, 1198.
16. Quoted in Clark, *History, Theory, Text*, 128; Jordan, "Perceptual Regions," 293.
17. Zelinsky, *Cultural Geography*, 112; Zelinsky, "North America's Vernacular Regions," 14.
18. Hale, "A Map of Vernacular Regions in America"; Zelinsky, "Vernacular Regions," 4; Mather, "American Great Plains," 238; Meinig, *Great Columbia Plain*, 3, 466–67.
19. Meinig, "Continuous Shaping," 1202.
20. Mankiller and Wallis, *Mankiller*, xx.

21. Deloria, *Custer Died*, 243–44. Proclamation reproduced in Intertribal Friendship House, *Urban Voices*, 80; quoted in Smith and Warrior, *Like a Hurricane*, 24; Mankiller and Wallis, *Mankiller*, xxi.

22. Quoted in Taliaferro, *Great White Fathers*, 351.

23. Dewing, *Wounded Knee*, 164–65; Castile, *To Show Heart*, 176–78.

24. Berg, *Envisioning Sustainability*, 53; quoted in Aberley, "Interpreting Bioregionalism," 17; Aberley provides a very helpful account of the emergence of bioregionalism; Snyder, *Practice of the Wild*, 46.

25. Berg, *Envisioning Sustainability*, 87, 163; Sale, *Dwellers*.

26. Flores, "Place," 47; Bailey, *Description of the Ecoregions*, 1; Omernik, "Map Supplement," 119.

27. On closing the frontier, see Cannon, *Reopening the Frontier*, 176, 183; Bosselman and Callies, *Quiet Revolution*, 3, 315, 7–8; for an analysis of the "quiet revolution," see Popper, "Understanding American Land Use," 291–301.

28. US Public Land Law Review Commission, *One Third*, 1, 6; Bureau of Land Management, "The Federal Land Policy and Management Act of 1976"; Lamm and McCarthy, *Angry West*, 229.

29. Donahue, *Western Range*, 247; Cawley, *Federal Land*, 43–44.

30. Public Land Law Review Commission, *One Third*, 6.

31. Ehrlich, *Solace*, 5; Smith and Martin, "Socioeconomic Behavior," 220. On 1970s and 1980s film and TV Westerns, see Varner, *Historical Dictionary*, and Brode, *Shooting Stars*.

32. See Donahue, *Western Range*, 51, 252; Cawley, *Federal Land*, 138–39.

33. Hardin, "Tragedy of the Commons," 1243–48; Zaslowsky and the Wilderness Society, *These American Lands*, 138–39; Abbey, "Even the Bad Guys," 52–53; Jacobs, *Waste*, 1, 547, 437.

34. Zaslowsky and the Wilderness Society, *These American Lands*, 204.

35. Bureau of Land Management, *Nevada Contiguous Lands*, 3–4, 6, 8, 10; Zaslowsky and the Wilderness Society, *These American Lands*, 147.

36. Elazar, *American Federalism*, 141. See also Cawley, *Federal Land*, 76–78.

37. Lamm and McCarthy, *Angry West*, 123–24, 244–45.

38. Ibid., 238, 261, 239, 17–18.

39. Ibid., 189; King and Taliaferro, "War for the West," 18.

40. Smith and Martin, "Socioeconomic Behavior," 218; Libecap, *Locking Up the Range*, 66, 39, 68–69, 101.

41. Quoted in Lamm and McCarthy, *Angry West*, 124; Pendley, "Whither the West.

42. Lamm and McCarthy, *Angry West*, 244, 276–77; Cawley, *Federal Land*, ix, 1.

43. Lamm and McCarthy, *Angry West*, 312, 322–23.

44. Popper, "Ambiguous End," 124.

45. Quoted in Resnick, *Politics of Resentment*, 17; quoted in Rawlyk, Bowles, and Hodgins, *Regionalism in Canada*, 2.

46. Abbey, *Desert Solitaire*, 4, xii.

47. Ibid., 51–52, 145.

48. Ibid., 59–60.

49. Quoted in Foreman, *Confessions*, 22; Abbey, *Desert Solitaire*, 149–50; Abbey, *Monkey Wrench Gang*.

50. Popper, "Understanding," 293, 298.

51. Robbins, *Landscapes*, 290, 286.

52. Knaap and Nelson, *Regulated*, 132; quoted in Robbins, *Landscapes*, 291.

53. Robbins, *Landscapes*, 291; Knaap and Nelson, *Regulated*, 22.

54. Abbott, "Portland Region," 26; Leo, "Regional Growth," 372.

55. Venturi, Brown, and Izenour, *Learning from Las Vegas*, 6, 53, 119, 82.

56. Ibid., 155.

Chapter 6

1. Popper and Popper, "Great Plains," 12–18; Wallach, "Evolution," 17; Roebuck, "Great Plains," 16.

2. Matthews, *Where the Buffalo Roam*, 98, 54.

3. Popper and Popper, "Great Plains," 12, 18; Matthews, *Where the Buffalo Roam*, 13–14, 17.

4. Popper and Popper, "Great Plains," 18; Popper and Popper, "Buffalo Commons," 499, 495.

5. Quoted in Matthews, *Where the Buffalo Roam*, 177, 53.

6. Ibid., 151.

7. Quoted in Matthews, *Where the Buffalo Roam*, 83; Popper, "Ambiguous End," 127.

8. Frazier, *Great Plains*, 12; Norris, *Dakota*, 169, 178; Heat-Moon, *PrairyErth*, 82.

9. Reisner, *Cadillac Desert*, 517; see Fradkin, *Wallace Stegner*, 277–78.

10. Limerick, "What on Earth," 87.

11. Said, *Orientalism*; Brown, *Bury My Heart*; Slotkin, *Regeneration*.

12. Slotkin, *Fatal Environment*; Erdrich, *Love Medicine*; Connell, *Son of the Morning Star*; McCarthy, *Blood Meridian*; Wallach, "*Blood Meridian* (1985)."

13. Worster, *Rivers of Empire*; Faragher, *Women and Men*; Cronon, *Nature's Metropolis*; White, "*It's Your Misfortune*"; Kolodny, "Letting Go Our Grand Obsessions," 1–18.

14. See especially by Doig, *This House of Sky*; Radio Reader, "1964–Present Chronological List"; Maslin, "Screen: 'Silverado.'" On Western series and films, see Brode, *Shooting Stars*, and Varner, *Westerns in Cinema*. On Houser, see Allan Houser, Inc., "A Tribute: Honors."

15. Truettner, "Text Panels"; Truettner, *West as America*, 38–39.

16. Smithsonian Museum of American Art, "Showdown," 4, 6–7; McCarthy, *All the Pretty Horses*.

17. Limerick, *Legacy*, 26; Limerick, "What on Earth," 86; White, *Land Use*; White, *Organic Machine*.

18. Klein, "Reclaiming," 208–10; Kolodny, "Letting Go," 3–4, 14.

19. Cronon, Miles, and Gitlin, "Becoming West," 18, 27; Milner, "View from Wisdom," 203–22; Wrobel, "Beyond the Frontier-Region Dichotomy," 409–14; Steiner, "Frederick Jackson Turner," 115–17, 121.

20. Klein, "Reclaiming," 211, 213; Johnston, "Beyond 'The West,'" 261 (Scharff quotation), 251; Lovato, *Santa Fe*, 126–27.

21. Kolodny, "Letting Go," 12–13; Fetterley and Pryse, *Writing Out of Place*, 13, 239, 222.

22. Goodman, *Translating*, xvii; Dilworth, *Imagining Indians*, 209.

23. Leach, *Country of Exiles*, 6; Etulain, *Re-imagining*, 139–40; Klein, "Reclaiming," 211, 213–14; Johnston, "Beyond 'The West,'" 263.

24. Goodman, *Translating*, 165–66; Lutz, *Cosmopolitan Vistas*, 186.

25. Klein, *Frontiers*, 191; Morrissey, *Mental Territories*, 165.

26. Wheeler, "New Regionalism," 274; see 2009 and archived population figures for all states and cities at US Census Bureau, "Population Estimates"; see Press, *Saving Open Space*, 10–11; see Schipper, *Disappearing Desert*, 4, 80, 87. For statistics on Greeley, Colorado, see links at US Census Bureau, "Greeley city, Colorado Quick-Links."

27. Duerksen and van Hemert, *True West*, 2–3, 198, 200–201.

28. Myers, "Livability."

29. McKinney, Fitch, and Harmon, "Regionalism," 104, 137–38, 109–110, 113.

30. Popper and Popper, "Small Can Be Beautiful," 22; see current and archived statistics at National Agricultural Statistics Service, "2002 Census Publications," specifically, "Miscellaneous Livestock and Animal Specialties—Inventory and Number Sold: 2002 and 1997"; quoted in Matthews, *Where the Buffalo Roam*, 83.

31. American Prairie Foundation, "Land Acquisition"; see also links on this page for "Human History Preservation" and "Bison Restoration"; Manning, *Rewilding the West*, 13, 172.

32. National Park Service, "Tallgrass Prairie National Preserve"; Nature Conservancy, "Oklahoma Tallgrass Prairie Preserve"; Heat-Moon, *PrairyErth*, 55.

33. Trammell, "Osage Ranch"; "Nature Conservancy's Goal."

34. Bureau of Land Management, *Rangeland Reform '94*, 23–26, 30–34.

35. Advertisement reproduced in Jacobs, *Waste*, 464; Erramouspe, "Monitoring," 18; Erramouspe, "White's Ranch," 14; Savory, *Holistic Resource Management*, 263–72; Dagget and Dusard, *Beyond the Rangeland Conflict*; Starrs, *Let the Cowboy Ride*.

36. Foreman, *Rewilding North America*, 164–65; on the necessity of regional scale for conservation, see also Soulé and Terborgh, "Policy and Science," 7–9.

37. Basolo, "US Regionalism," 456–57; Nicoll, "Death of Rangeland Reform," 106.

38. Duerksen and van Hemert, *True West*, 201; on Colorado land-use planning, see DeGrove, *Land, Growth & Politics*, 307, 315.

39. Community Development Department, "2060 Comprehensive Plan: Land Use"; EDAW, "Greeley Parks and Trails Master Plan."

40. Bollens, "Fragments," 106, 117, 111; Popper, "Understanding," 299.

41. Garreau, *Edge City*, 197; Kling, Olin, and Poster, "Beyond the Edge," xiv; Kling, Olin, and Poster, "Emergence of Postsuburbia," 9.

42. Bollens, "Fragments," 118–19.

43. Knaap and Nelson, *Regulated*, 32–35; quoted in Robbins, *Landscapes*, 296; Oregon Department of Land Conservation and Development, "Oregon's Land Use Planning Program."

44. Turner, *Significance of Sections*, 338.

45. US Western Water Policy Review Advisory Commission, *Water in the West*, 2-1; Reisner, *Cadillac*, 12; Hundley, *Great Thirst*, 64; Fradkin, *River No More*; Powell, *Dead Pool*.

46. Reisner, *Cadillac*, 12, 7, 485, 458–59, 4, 6.

47. Worster, *Rivers of Empire*, 7, 332; Hundley, *Great Thirst*, 534–35.

48. Western Water Policy Review Advisory Commission, *Water in the West*, 6-4, O'Toole-5; US Army Corps of Engineers, "Western States Watershed Study"; Utah State University, "Bear River Watershed Information System."

49. Reisner, *Cadillac*, 479.

50. National Park Service, "Olympic National Park"; McCullen, "Plan Outlines Snake Dam Removal Steps"; US Army Corps of Engineers, "Lower Snake River Fish Passage"; Boxall, "Scientists find holes."

Conclusion

1. Proulx, *Bird Cloud*, 67.

2. See Johnson, *New Westers*, 351–54; see also Rothman, *Devil's Bargains*, 248, 255, 261, 264–65; Robbins, "In Pursuit of Historical Explanation," esp. 287–91; for a more recent overview of gentrification, see Hines, "Rural Gentrification," 509–25.

3. On gentrification and "postindustrial" values, see Hines, "Rural Gentrification," 509–25.

4. Powers and Lazo, "Leaving North Las Vegas."

5. Judis, "End State," 17.

6. See Mason, *Indian Gaming*, esp. 59–69; Ellis, "State's tribal gambling"; National Indian Gaming Commission, "Gaming Revenue Reports"; Chickasaw Nation, "Chickasaw.tv: United We Thrive."

7. See National Conference of State Legislatures, "Arizona's Immigration Enforcement Laws"; Sulzberger, "Hispanics Reviving Faded Towns."

8. On "takings" and the "wise use" movement, see Echeverria and Eby, *Let the People Judge*, esp. 143–90. On Oregon, see Cook, "Incomprehensible," 245–72; see also Oregon.gov, "DLCD Measure 49."

9. Campbell, *Rhizomatic*, 3, 22; Proulx, *Bird Cloud*, 40–42; Heim and Love-Brotak, "U.S. Drought Monitor"; Brean, "Decade of drought"; National Oceanic and Atmospheric Administration, "NOAA: Heat Wave"; Gamm, "Texas wildfires"; Sharp, "Fire at 114,000 acres"; Pollon, "Arizona wildfire"; Johnson and McKinley, "Record Snowpacks"; Johansen, *Our Evolving Climate Crisis*, 193–209; Dinger, "Four federal emergencies"; National Weather Service Weather Forecast Office, "Record Setting Rainfall"; Rabe, "Things lining up"; Horswell, "Ike's salty floods."

10. On recent Western films and television, see Etulain and Malone, *American West*, 341–43. Landis, *Cowboy Steward*, 1; Proulx, *Close Range*, 283.

11. The author means "cult" in the more benign sense, like Trekkies are to *Star Trek*; see Owen, "Worship at the O.K. Corral," 62–64; Stegner, "Geography of Hope," 218.

Bibliography

Abbey, Edward. *Desert Solitaire*. New York: Ballantine, 1968.

_____. "Even the Bad Guys Wear White Hats: Cowboys, Ranchers, and the Ruin of the West." *Harper's* 272, no. 1628 (January 1986): 51–55.

_____. *The Monkey Wrench Gang*. 1975. Reprint, New York: Harper Perennial Modern Classics, 2006.

Abbott, Carl. *How Cities Won the West: Four Centuries of Urban Change in Western North America*. Albuquerque: University of New Mexico Press, 2008.

_____. "The Portland Region: Where City and Suburbs Talk to Each Other—and Often Agree." *Housing Policy Debate* 8, no. 1 (1997): 11–51.

Aberley, Doug. "Interpreting Bioregionalism: A Story from Many Voices." In *Bioregionalism*, edited by Michael Vincent McGinnis, 13–42. New York: Routledge, 1999.

Adorno, Theodor W. *The Culture Industry: Selected Essays on Mass Culture*. New York: Routledge, 2001.

Allan Houser, Inc. "A Tribute: Honors." http://www.allanhouser.com/honors.php

American Prairie Foundation. "Land Acquisition." http://www.americanprairie.org/projectprogress/land/land-acquisition/

Austin, Mary. *The American Rhythm: Studies and Reexpressions of Amerindian Songs*. 1930 rev. ed. Reprint, New York: Cooper Square, 1970.

_____. *The Land of Little Rain*. Boston: Houghton Mifflin, 1903.

_____. *Lost Borders*. New York: Harper and Brothers, 1909.

Bailey, Robert G. *Description of the Ecoregions of the United States*. Washington, DC: US Department of Agriculture, 1980.

Bancroft, H. H. *California Pastoral, 1769–1848*. San Francisco: History Company, 1888.

Basolo, Victoria. "US Regionalism and Rationality." *Urban Studies* 40, no. 3 (2003): 447–62.

Beito, David T., and Linda Royster Beito. "Isabel Paterson, Rose Wilder Lane, and

Zora Neale Hurston on War, Race, the State, and Liberty." *Independent Review* 12, no. 4 (Spring 2008): 553–73.

Bellah, Robert N. "Civil Religion in America." *Daedalus* 96, no. 1 (Winter 1967): 1–21.

Benedict, Ruth. *Patterns of Culture*. New York: Houghton Mifflin, 1934.

Bensel, Richard Franklin. *Sectionalism and American Political Development: 1880–1980*. Madison: University of Wisconsin Press, 1984.

Berg, Peter. *Envisioning Sustainability*. Billings, MT: Subculture Books, 2009.

Berge, Wendell. *Economic Freedom for the West*. Lincoln: University of Nebraska Press, 1946.

Bessey, R. F. "The Pacific Northwest." In *The American Planning and Civic Annual*, 152–59. Harrisburg, PA: Mount Pleasant Press, 1937.

Bieder, Robert E. *Science Encounters the Indian: The Early Years of American Ethnology*. Norman: University of Oklahoma Press, 1989.

Billington, David P., and Donald C. Jackson. *Big Dams of the New Deal Era: A Confluence of Engineering and Politics*. Norman: University of Oklahoma Press, 2006.

Billington, Ray Allen. *Westward Expansion: A History of the American Frontier*. New York: Macmillan, 1949.

Bingham, Edwin R. *Charles F. Lummis: Editor of the Southwest*. San Marino, CA: Huntington Library Press, 2006.

Boas, Franz. *A Franz Boas Reader: The Shaping of American Anthropology, 1883–1911*, edited by George W. Stocking Jr. Chicago: University of Chicago Press, 1989.

Boime, Albert. *The Magisterial Gaze: Manifest Destiny and American Landscape Painting, c. 1830–1865*. Washington, DC: Smithsonian Institution Press, 1991.

_____. "Patriarchy Fixed in Stone: Gutzon Borglum's 'Mount Rushmore.'" *American Art* 5, no. 1/2 (Winter–Spring 1991): 143–67.

Bollens, Scott A. "Fragments of Regionalism: The Limits of Southern California Governance." *Journal of Urban Affairs* 19, no. 1 (1997): 105–22.

Bolton, Herbert E. *Bolton and the Spanish Borderlands*, edited by John Francis Bannon. Norman: University of Oklahoma Press, 1964.

_____. "The Epic of Greater America." *American Historical Review* 38, no. 3 (April 1933): 448–74.

_____. "Material for Southwestern History in the Central Archives of Mexico." *American Historical Review* 13, no. 3 (April 1908): 510–27.

_____. *The Spanish Borderlands: A Chronicle of Old Florida and the Southwest*. New Haven, CT: Yale University Press, 1921.

Bosselman, Fred, and David Callies. *The Quiet Revolution in Land Use Control*. Washington, DC: Council on Environmental Quality, 1972.

Boxall, Bettina. "Scientists find holes in Klamath River dam removal plan." *Los Angeles Times*, June 25, 2011. http://articles.latimes.com/2011/jun/25/local/la-me-klamath-20110625.

Brean, Henry. "Decade of drought leaves two lakes, Powell and Mead, in same boat." *Las Vegas Review-Journal*, November 29, 2010. http://www.lvrj.com/news/decade-of-drought-leaves-two-lakes-powell-and-mead-in-same-boat-110958814.html

Brigham, Albert Perry. *Geographic Influences in American History*. Boston: Ginn, 1903.

Brode, Douglas. *Shooting Stars of the Small Screen: Encyclopedia of TV Western Actors, 1946–Present.* Austin: University of Texas Press, 2009.

Brodhead, Richard H. *Cultures of Letters: Scenes of Reading and Writing in Nineteenth-Century America.* Chicago: University of Chicago Press, 1993.

Brown, Dee. *Bury My Heart at Wounded Knee: An Indian History of the American West.* New York: Holt, Rinehart, and Winston, 1970.

Bureau of Land Management. "The Federal Land Policy and Management Act of 1976 *As Amended*: Commemorating 25 Years." US Department of the Interior. http://www.blm.gov/flpma/FLPMA.pdf

_____. *Nevada Contiguous Lands: Wilderness Environmental Impact Statement: Draft.* Las Vegas, NV: Bureau of Land Management, Ely, Las Vegas, and Winnemucca Districts, 1988.

_____. *Rangeland Reform '94: Draft Environmental Impact Statement Executive Summary.* Washington, DC: US Department of the Interior, 1994.

_____. "The Taylor Grazing Act." US Department of the Interior. http://www.blm .gov/wy/st/en/field_offices/Casper/range/taylor.1.html

Bureau of Reclamation. *The Story of Boulder Dam.* Washington, DC: Government Printing Office, 1941.

Burt, Larry W. "Termination and Relocation." In *Indians in Contemporary Society*, edited by Garrick A. Bailey, 19–27. Washington, DC: Smithsonian Institution, 2008.

Campbell, Neil. *The Rhizomatic West: Representing the American West in a Transnational, Global, Media Age.* Lincoln: University of Nebraska Press, 2008.

Cannon, Brian Q. *Remaking the Agrarian Dream: New Deal Rural Resettlement in the Mountain West.* Albuquerque: University of New Mexico Press, 1996.

_____. *Reopening the Frontier: Homesteading in the Modern West.* Lawrence: University Press of Kansas, 2009.

Castile, George Pierre. *To Show Heart: Native American Self-Determination and Federal Indian Policy, 1960–1975.* Tucson: University of Arizona Press, 1998.

Cather, Willa. *Collected Stories.* New York: Vintage, 1992.

_____. *Death Comes for the Archbishop.* New York: Knopf, 1927.

_____. *Early Novels and Stories.* New York: Library of America, 1987.

Caughey, John W. "The Spanish Southwest: An Example of Subconscious Regionalism." In *Regionalism in America*, edited by Merrill Jensen, 173–86. Madison: University of Wisconsin Press, 1952.

Cawley, R. McGregor. *Federal Land, Western Anger: The Sagebrush Rebellion and Environmental Politics.* Lawrence: University Press of Kansas, 1993.

Chávez, John R. *The Lost Land: The Chicano Image of the Southwest.* Albuquerque: University of New Mexico Press, 1984.

Chickasaw Nation. "Chickasaw.tv: United We Thrive." http://www.chickasaw.tv/#/home

Chittick, V. L. O., ed. "Editorial Foreword—and Postscript." In *Northwest Harvest: A Regional Stocktaking*, ix–xvi. New York: Macmillan, 1948.

Clark, Elizabeth A. *History, Theory, Text: Historians and the Linguistic Turn.* Cambridge, MA: Harvard University Press, 2004.

Clark, Walter Van Tilburg. *The Ox-Bow Incident.* 1940. Reprint, New York: New American Library, 1960.

Clements, Frederic E., and Ralph W. Chaney. *Environment and Life in the Great Plains*. Washington, DC: Carnegie Institution, 1936.

Clemmer, Richard O. *Julian Steward and the Great Basin: The Making of an Anthropologist*. Salt Lake City: University of Utah Press, 1999.

Cohen, Michael P. *The Pathless Way: John Muir and American Wilderness*. Madison: University of Wisconsin Press, 1984.

Cole, Douglas. *Franz Boas: The Early Years, 1858–1906*. Seattle: University of Washington Press, 1999.

Cole, John P., and Cuchlaine A. M. King. *Quantitative Geography: Techniques and Theories in Geography*. New York: Wiley, 1968.

Collier, John. "The Red Atlantis." *Survey* 49, no. 1 (October 1922): 15–20, 63, 66.

Community Development Department. "2060 Comprehensive Plan: Land Use." City of Greeley, Colorado. http://www.greeleygov.com/CommunityDevelopment/CompPlan2060.aspx

Connell, Evan S. *Son of the Morning Star*. San Francisco: North Point Press, 1984.

Cook, Rebekah R. "Incomprehensible, Uncompensable, Unconstitutional: The Fatal Flaws of Measure 37." *Journal of Environmental Law and Litigation* 20 (2005): 245–72.

Covert, Alice Lent. *Return to Dust*. New York: Kinsey, 1939.

Croly, Herbert D. "The California Country House." *Sunset* 18, no. 1 (November 1906): 50–65.

Cronon, William. *Nature's Metropolis: Chicago and the Great West*. New York: Norton, 1991.

Cronon, William, George Miles, and Jay Gitlin. "Becoming West: Toward a New Meaning for Western History." In *Under an Open Sky: Rethinking America's Western Past*, edited by William Cronon, George Miles, and Jay Gitlin, 3–27. New York: Norton, 1992.

Curtis, Edward S. *The North American Indian*. 20 vols. Seattle, WA: Edward S. Curtis, 1907–30.

Dagget, Dan, and Jay Dusard. *Beyond the Rangeland Conflict: Toward a West That Works*. Layton, UT: Gibbs Smith, 1995.

Darrah, William C. *Powell of the Colorado*. Princeton, NJ: Princeton University Press, 1951.

Davis, H. L. *Collected Essays and Short Stories*. Moscow: University of Idaho Press, 1986.

———. *Honey in the Horn*. Moscow: University of Idaho Press, 1992.

Debo, Angie. *And Still the Waters Run: The Betrayal of the Five Civilized Tribes*. 1940. Reprint, Norman: University of Oklahoma Press, 1984.

deBuys, William. *Enchantment and Exploitation: The Life and Hard Times of a New Mexico Mountain Range*. Albuquerque: University of New Mexico Press, 1985.

DeGrove, John M. *Land, Growth and Politics*. Chicago: American Planning Association, 1984.

Deloria, Vine, Jr. *Custer Died for Your Sins: An American Indian Manifesto*. New York: Avon Books, 1969.

DeVoto, Bernard. *The Easy Chair*. Boston: Houghton Mifflin, 1955.

———. "The West: A Plundered Province." *Harper's Monthly Magazine* 169 (August 1934): 355–64.

Dewing, Rolland. *Wounded Knee: The Meaning and Significance of the Second Incident*. New York: Irvington, 1985.

Dickinson, Robert E. *Regional Concept: The Anglo-American Leaders*. Boston: Routledge and Kegan Paul, 1976.

Dilworth, Leah. *Imagining Indians in the Southwest: Persistent Visions of a Primitive Past*. Washington, DC: Smithsonian Institution Press, 1996.

Dinger, Matt. "Four federal emergencies declared in state in 2009." *Oklahoman*, January 12, 2010.

Doig, Ivan. *This House of Sky: Landscapes of a Western Mind*. San Diego: Harcourt, 1978.

Donahue, Debra L. *The Western Range Revisited: Removing Livestock from Public Lands to Conserve Native Biodiversity*. Norman: University of Oklahoma Press, 1999.

Dorman, Robert L. *Revolt of the Provinces: The Regionalist Movement in America, 1920–1945*. Chapel Hill: University of North Carolina Press, 1993.

Douglas, Frederic H., and René d'Harnoncourt. *Indian Art of the United States*. New York: Museum of Modern Art, 1941.

Duerksen, Christopher J., and James van Hemert. *True West: Authentic Development Patterns for Small Towns and Rural Areas*. Chicago: American Planning Association, 2003.

Echeverria, John D., and Raymond Booth Eby. *Let the People Judge: Wise Use and the Private Property Rights Movement*. Washington, DC: Island Press, 1995.

EDAW. "Greeley Parks and Trails Master Plan." City of Greeley, Colorado. http://www.greeleygov.com/parks/information.aspx

Ehrlich, Gretel. *The Solace of Open Spaces*. New York: Viking, 1985.

Elazar, Daniel J. *American Federalism: A View from the States*, 3rd ed. New York: Harper & Row, 1984.

Elkins, Elizabeth. "Beauty in Garden Pools." *Sunset* 35, no. 4 (October 1915): 764–70.

Ellis, Randy. "State's tribal gambling expansion defies trend." *Oklahoman*, March 3, 2011.

Erdrich, Louise. *Love Medicine: A Novel*. New York: Holt, Rinehart, and Winston, 1984.

Erramouspe, Roxanne. "Monitoring, Managing, Manipulating Rangelands." *Cattleman* 82, no. 11 (April 1996): 18–32.

———. "White's Ranch: Carved from Land and Cattle Along the Texas Coast." *Cattleman* 82, no. 9 (February 1996): 10–20.

Espinosa, Aurelio M. *Studies in New Mexican Spanish: Part 1: Phonology*. Chicago: University of Chicago, 1909.

Etulain, Richard W. *Re-Imagining the Modern American West: A Century of Fiction, History, and Art*. Tucson: University of Arizona Press, 1996.

Etulain, Richard W., and Michael P. Malone. *The American West: A Modern History, 1900 to the Present*, 2nd ed. Lincoln: University of Nebraska, 2007.

Faragher, John Mack. *Women and Men on the Overland Trail*. New Haven, CT: Yale University Press, 1979.

Federal Writers' Project. *The Idaho Encyclopedia*. Caldwell, ID: Caxton Printers, 1938.

———. *Idaho Lore*. Caldwell, ID: Caxton Printers, 1939.

Fellman, Anita Clair. *Little House, Long Shadow: Laura Ingalls Wilder's Impact on American Culture*. Columbia: University of Missouri Press, 2008.

Fetterley, Judith, and Marjorie Pryse. *Writing Out of Place: Regionalism, Women, and American Literary Culture*. Urbana: University of Illinois Press, 2003.

Findlay, John M. *Magic Lands: Western Cityscapes and American Culture After 1940*. Berkeley: University of California Press, 1992.

Fite, Gilbert C. *Mount Rushmore*. Norman: University of Oklahoma Press, 1952.

Fixico, Donald L. *Termination and Relocation: Federal Indian Policy, 1945–1960*. Albuquerque: University of New Mexico Press, 1986.

Flink, James J. *The Automobile Age*. Cambridge, MA: MIT Press, 2001.

Flores, Dan. "Place: Thinking about Bioregional History." In *Bioregionalism*, edited by Michael Vincent McGinnis, 43–60. New York: Routledge, 1999.

Folklore Project. "Autobiographical Sketch of Rose Wilder Lane." Federal Writers' Project. http://lcweb2.loc.gov/wpa/15100107.html.

Foreman, Dave. *Confessions of an Eco-Warrior*. New York: Harmony Books, 1991.

———. *Rewilding North America: A Vision for Conservation in the 21st Century*. Washington, DC: Island Press, 2004.

Forrest, Suzanne. *The Preservation of the Village: New Mexico's Hispanics and the New Deal*. Albuquerque: University of New Mexico Press, 1989.

Foss, Phillip O. *Politics and Grass: The Administration of Grazing on the Public Domain*. Seattle: University of Washington Press, 1960.

Fradkin, Philip L. *A River No More: The Colorado River and the West*, rev. ed. Berkeley: University of California Press, 1996.

———. *Wallace Stegner and the American West*. New York: Knopf, 2008.

Frazier, Ian. *The Great Plains*. 1989. Reprint, New York: Penguin Books, 1990.

Fryer, Judith. *Felicitous Space: The Imaginative Structures of Edith Wharton and Willa Cather*. Chapel Hill: University of North Carolina Press, 1986.

Furman, Necah Stewart. *Walter Prescott Webb: His Life and Impact*. Albuquerque: University of New Mexico Press, 1976.

Gamm, Joe. "Texas wildfires burn 3 million acres." *Amarillo Globe-News*, June 20, 2011. http://amarillo.com/news/latest-news/2011-06-20/texas-wildfires-burn-3-million-acres#.ThECG4LmvfM

Garland, Hamlin. *Crumbling Idols: Twelve Essays on Art Dealing Chiefly Literature, Painting and the Drama*. Chicago: Stone and Kimball, 1894.

———. *A Daughter of the Middle Border*. 1921. Reprint, New York: Grosset and Dunlap, 1926.

———. *Main-Travelled Roads*. 1891. Reprint, New York: Harper, 1956.

———. *Rose of Dutcher's Coolly*. 1895. Reprint, London: Neville Beeman, 1896.

———. *A Son of the Middle Border*. 1917. Reprint, New York: Grosset and Dunlap, 1927.

Garnsey, Morris E. *America's New Frontier: The Mountain West*. New York: Knopf, 1950.

Garreau, Joel. *Edge City: Life on the New Frontier*. New York: Random House, 1991.

———. *The Nine Nations of North America*. Boston: Houghton Mifflin, 1981.

Gastil, Raymond D. *Cultural Regions of the United States*. Seattle: University of Washington Press, 1975.

Gates, Paul W. *History of Public Land Law Development*. Washington, DC: Government Printing Office, 1968.

Gibson, Arrell Morgan. *The Santa Fe and Taos Colonies: Age of the Muses, 1900–1942*. Norman: University of Oklahoma Press, 1983.

Gidley, Mick. *Edward S. Curtis and the North American Indian, Incorporated.* Cambridge: Cambridge University Press, 1998.

Glenn, Norval D., and J. L. Simmons. "Are Regional Cultural Differences Diminishing?" *Public Opinion Quarterly* 31, no. 2 (Summer 1967): 176–93.

Gómez, Arthur R. *Quest for the Golden Circle: The Four Corners and the Metropolitan West, 1945–1970.* Albuquerque: University of New Mexico Press, 1994.

Goodman, Audrey. *Translating Southwestern Landscapes: The Making of an Anglo Literary Region.* Tucson: University of Arizona Press, 2002.

Goodman, Susan, and Carl Dawson, *Mary Austin and the American West.* Berkeley: University of California Press, 2008.

Gordon, Milton M. *Assimilation in American Life.* New York: Oxford University Press, 1964.

Gray, L. C., O. E. Baker, F. J. Marschner, B. O. Weitz, W. R. Chapline, Ward Shepard, and Raphael Zon. "The Utilization of Our Lands for Crops, Pasture, and Forests." In *Agriculture Yearbook: 1923*, edited by O. E. Baker, 415–506. Washington, DC: Government Printing Office, 1924.

Great Plains Committee. *The Future of the Great Plains.* Washington, DC: Government Printing Office, 1936.

Green, Rayna. "The Tribe Called Wannabee: Playing Indian in America and Europe." *Folklore* 99, no. 1 (1988): 30–55.

Gruber, Frank. *Zane Grey: A Biography.* Roslyn, NY: Walter J. Black, 1969.

Hale, Ruth F. "A Map of Vernacular Regions in America." PhD diss., University of Minnesota, 1971.

Hallowell, A. Irving. "American Indians, White and Black: The Phenomenon of Transculturalization." *Current Anthropology* 4, no. 5 (December 1963): 519–31.

Hardin, Garrett. "The Tragedy of the Commons." *Science* 162, no. 3859 (December 13, 1968): 1243–48.

Harrison, Joseph B. "Regionalism Is Not Enough." In *Northwest Harvest: A Regional Stocktaking*, edited by V. L. O. Chittick, 146–55. New York: Macmillan, 1948.

Hartemann, Frederic V., and Robert Hauptman. *The Mountain Encyclopedia.* Lanham, MD: Taylor Trade, 2005.

Haycox, Ernest. "Is There a Northwest?" In *Northwest Harvest: A Regional Stocktaking*, edited by V. L. O. Chittick, 39–51. New York: Macmillan, 1948.

Haystead, Ladd. *If the Prospect Pleases: The West the Guidebooks Never Mention.* Norman: University of Oklahoma Press, 1945.

Heat-Moon, William Least. *PrairyErth: (a deep map).* Boston: Houghton Mifflin, 1991.

Heim, Richard, and Liz Love-Brotak. "U.S. Drought Monitor," June 28, 2011. http://droughtmonitor.unl.edu/archive.html

Henderson, Caroline. *Letters from the Dust Bowl.* Edited by Alvin O. Turner. Norman: University of Oklahoma Press, 2003.

Henry, Stuart. *Conquering Our Great American Plains: A Historical Development.* New York: Dutton, 1930.

Hewett, Edgar L. *Ancient Life in the American Southwest.* Indianapolis, IN: Bobbs-Merrill, 1930.

———. "The Southwest: Yesterday and Tomorrow," *Papers of the School of American Research*, new series no. 2 (1921): 3–8.

Hine, Robert V. *Josiah Royce: From Grass Valley to Harvard.* Norman: University of Oklahoma Press, 1992.

Hines, J. Dwight. "Rural Gentrification as Permanent Tourism: The Creation of the 'New' West Archipelago as Postindustrial Cultural Space." *Environment and Planning D: Society and Space* 28, no. 3 (June 2010): 509–25.

Horswell, Cindy. "Ike's salty floods leach ranches of life." *Houston Chronicle*, March 8, 2009. http://www.chron.com/news/hurricanes/article/Ike-s-salty-floods-leach-ranches-of-life-1588682.php

Hough, Emerson. *The Covered Wagon*. 1922. Reprint, New York: Barnes and Noble, 2009.

_____. *Let Us Go Afield*. New York: Appleton, 1916.

_____. *North of 36*. New York: Appleton, 1923.

_____. *The Passing of the Frontier: A Chronicle of the Old West*. New Haven, CT: Yale University Press, 1918.

_____. "The Slaughter of the Trees." *Everybody's Magazine* 18, no. 5 (May 1908): 579–92.

_____. *The Story of the Cowboy*. New York: Appleton, 1897.

_____. *The Way to the West*. Indianapolis, IN: Bobbs-Merrill, 1903.

_____. "The West, and Certain Literary Discoveries; or, How Fiction May be Stranger than Truth." *Century Magazine* 59, no. 4 (February 1900): 506–11.

Howard, Joseph Kinsey. *Montana: High, Wide, and Handsome*. New Haven, CT: Yale University Press, 1943.

Howard, Randall R. "Motorizing the Frontier." *Sunset* 35, no. 3 (September 1915): 588–96.

Hundley, Norris Jr. *The Great Thirst: Californians and Water: A History*, rev. ed. Berkeley: University of California Press, 2001.

Hurt, R. Douglas. *The Great Plains during World War II*. Lincoln: University of Nebraska Press, 2008.

Hutchinson, Elizabeth. *The Indian Craze: Primitivism, Modernism, and Transculturation in American Art, 1890–1915*. Durham, NC: Duke University Press, 2009.

Hutchinson, John. *The Dynamics of Cultural Nationalism: The Gaelic Revival and the Creation of the Irish Nation State*. Boston: Allen and Unwin, 1987.

Hutchinson, W. H. *A Bar Cross Man: The Life and Personal Writings of Eugene Manlove Rhodes*. Norman: University of Oklahoma Press, 1956.

Intertribal Friendship House. *Urban Voices: The Bay Area American Indian Community*. Tucson: University of Arizona Press, 2002.

Jackson, Helen Hunt. *Ramona: A Story*. 1884. Reprint, Boston: Roberts Brothers, 1885.

Jackson, John Brinckerhoff. *Landscape in Sight: Looking at America*, edited by Helen Lefkowitz Horowitz. New Haven, CT: Yale University Press, 1997.

Jacobs, Lynn. *Waste of the West: Public Lands Ranching*. Tucson, AZ: Jacobs, 1991.

Johansen, Bruce E. *Our Evolving Climate Crisis*. Westport, CT: Praeger, 2006.

Johansen, Dorothy O., and Charles M. Gates. *Empire of the Columbia: A History of the Pacific Northwest*. New York: Harper and Row, 1957.

Johnson, Hans P., and Richard Lovelady. "Migration Between California and Other States, 1985–1994." California Department of Finance, 1995. http://www.dof.ca.gov/research/demographic/reports/immigration-migration/migration_1985-1994/documents/DOMMIG.PDF

Johnson, Kirk, and Jesse McKinley. "Record Snowpacks Could Threaten Western

States." *New York Times*, May 21, 2011. http://www.nytimes.com/2011/05/22/us/22snow.html

Johnson, Michael L. *New Westers: The West in Contemporary American Culture*. Lawrence: University Press of Kansas, 1996.

Johnston, Robert D. "Beyond 'The West': Regionalism, Liberalism, and the Evasion of Politics in the New Western History." *Rethinking History* 2, no. 2 (1998): 239–77.

Jones, William. *Fox Texts*. Leiden: Brill, 1907.

Jordan, Terry G. "Perceptual Regions in Texas." *Geographical Review* 68, no. 3 (July 1978): 293–307.

Judis, John B. "End State: Is California Finished?" *New Republic* 240, no. 20 (November 4, 2009): 16–22.

Kelly, Lawrence C. "United States Indian Policies, 1900–1980." In *History of Indian-White Relations*, edited by Wilcomb E. Washburn, 66–80. Washington, DC: Smithsonian Institution, 1988.

King, P., and J. Taliaferro. "The War for the West." *Newsweek* 118, no. 14 (September 30, 1991): 18.

Kirsch, Scott. "John Wesley Powell and the Mapping of the Colorado Plateau: Survey Science, Geographical Solutions, and the Economy of Environmental Values." *Annals of the Association of American Geographers* 92, no. 3 (September 2002): 548–72.

Klein, Joe. *Woody Guthrie: A Life*. New York: Ballantine, 1980.

Klein, Kerwin Lee. *Frontiers of Historical Imagination: Narrating the European Conquest of Native America, 1890–1990*. Berkeley: University of California Press, 1997.

———. "Reclaiming the 'F' Word, or Being and Becoming Postwestern." *Pacific Historical Review* 65, no. 2 (May 1996): 179–215.

Kling, Rob, Spencer Olin, and Mark Poster, eds. "Beyond the Edge: The Dynamism of Postsuburban Regions." In *Postsuburban California: The Transformation of Orange County Since World War II*, vii–xx. Berkeley: University of California Press, 1995.

———. "The Emergence of Postsuburbia: An Introduction." In *Postsuburban California: The Transformation of Orange County Since World War II*, 1–30. Berkeley: University of California Press, 1995.

Kluger, James R. *Turning on Water with a Shovel: The Career of Elwood Mead*. Albuquerque: University of New Mexico Press, 1992.

Knaap, Gerrit, and Arthur C. Nelson. *The Regulated Landscape: Lessons on State Land Use Planning from Oregon*. Cambridge, MA: Lincoln Institute of Land Policy, 1992.

Kolodny, Annette. "Letting Go Our Grand Obsessions: Notes toward a New Literary History of the American Frontiers." *American Literature* 64, no. 1 (March 1992): 1–18.

Kraenzel, Carl Frederick. *The Great Plains in Transition*. Norman: University of Oklahoma Press, 1955.

Kroeber, A. L. *Cultural and Natural Areas of Native North America*. Berkeley: University of California Press, 1939.

Kropp, Phoebe S. *California Vieja: Culture and Memory in a Modern American Place*. Berkeley: University of California Press, 2006.

Kuper, Adam. *The Reinvention of Primitive Society: Transformations of Myth*. New York: Routledge, 2005.

Lamar, Howard R. "Much to Celebrate: The Western History Association's Twenty-Fifth Birthday." *Western Historical Quarterly* 17, no. 4 (October 1986): 399–416.

Lamm, Richard D., and Michael McCarthy. *The Angry West: A Vulnerable Land and Its Future*. Boston: Houghton Mifflin, 1982.

Landis, Kevin. *The Cowboy Steward: The Cowboy Way to the Christian Life*. New York: iUniverse, 2006.

Lane, Rose Wilder. *The Discovery of Freedom: Man's Struggle Against Authority*. New York: John Day, 1943.

_____. *Free Land*. New York: Longmans, Green, 1938.

_____. *Let the Hurricane Roar*. New York: Longmans, Green, 1933.

Lasch, Christopher. *The Culture of Narcissism: American Life in an Age of Diminishing Expectations*. New York: Norton, 1978.

Lawson, Michael L. *Dammed Indians Revisited: The Continuing History of the Pick-Sloan Plan and the Missouri River Sioux*. Pierre: South Dakota State Historical Society Press, 2009.

Leach, William. *Country of Exiles: The Destruction of Place in American Life*. New York: Pantheon, 1999.

Leo, Christopher. "Regional Growth Management Regime: The Case of Portland, Oregon." *Journal of Urban Affairs* 20, no. 4 (1998): 363–94.

Leopold, Aldo. *Aldo Leopold's Southwest*, edited by David E. Brown and Neil B. Carmony. Albuquerque: University of New Mexico Press, 1995.

Lewis, G. Malcolm. "William Gilpin and the Concept of the Great Plains Region." *Annals of the Association of American Geographers* 56, no. 1 (March 1966): 33–51.

Libecap, Gary D. *Locking Up the Range: Federal Land Controls and Grazing* Cambridge, MA: Ballinger, 1981.

Lilienthal, David E. *TVA: Democracy on the March*. 1944. Reprint, New York: Harper, 1953.

Limerick, Patricia Nelson. *The Legacy of Conquest: The Unbroken Past of the American West*. New York: Norton, 1987.

_____. "What on Earth Is the New Western History?" In *Trails: Toward a New Western History*, edited by Patricia Nelson Limerick, Clyde A. Milner II, and Charles E. Rankin, 81–88. Lawrence: University Press of Kansas, 1991.

Lisle, Laurie. *Portrait of an Artist: A Biography of Georgia O'Keeffe*. New York: Seaview Books, 1980.

Lovato, Andrew Leo. *Santa Fe Hispanic Culture: Preserving Identity in a Tourist Town*. Albuquerque: University of New Mexico Press, 2004.

Lowitt, Richard. *The New Deal and the West*. Norman: University of Oklahoma Press, 1993.

Lummis, Charles F. *The Land of Poco Tiempo*. 1893. Reprint, New York: Scribner's, 1897.

_____. *The Spanish Pioneers*. 1893. Reprint, Chicago: McClurg, 1899.

_____. *A Tramp across the Continent*. 1892. Reprint, New York: Scribner's, 1917.

Lutz, Tom. *Cosmopolitan Vistas: American Regionalism and Literary Value*. Ithaca: Cornell University Press, 2004.

MacKaye, Benton. *The New Exploration: A Philosophy of Regional Planning.* 1928. Reprint, Urbana: University of Illinois Press, 1990.

Malin, James C. "The Grassland of North America: Its Occupance and the Challenge of Continuous Reappraisals." In *Man's Role in Changing the Face of the Earth*, edited by William L. Thomas Jr., 350–66. Chicago: University of Chicago Press, 1956.

_____ . "Space and History: Reflections on the Closed-Space Doctrines of Turner and Mackinder and the Challenge of Those Ideas by the Air Age: Part 1." *Agricultural History* 18, no. 2 (April 1944): 65–74.

_____ . *Winter Wheat in the Golden Belt of Kansas.* Lawrence: University of Kansas Press, 1944.

Mankiller, Wilma, and Michael Wallis. *Mankiller: A Chief and Her People.* New York: St. Martin's, 1993.

Manning, Richard. *Rewilding the West: Restoration in a Prairie Landscape* Berkeley: University of California Press, 2009.

Maslin, Janet. "Screen: 'Silverado,' a Western." *New York Times*, July 10, 1985.

Mason, W. Dale. *Indian Gaming: Tribal Sovereignty and American Politics.* Norman: University of Oklahoma Press, 2000.

Mather, E. Cotton. "The American Great Plains." *Annals of the Association of American Geographers* 62, no. 2 (June 1972): 237–57.

Mathews, John Joseph. *Sundown.* 1934. Reprint, Norman: University of Oklahoma Press, 1988.

Matthews, Anne. *Where the Buffalo Roam: The Storm over the Revolutionary Plan to Restore America's Great Plains.* New York: Grove Weidenfeld, 1992.

Matusow, Allen J. *The Unraveling of America: A History of Liberalism in the 1960s.* New York: Harper and Row, 1984.

Maxwell, Perriton. "Frederic Remington: Most Typical of American Artists." *Pearson's Magazine* 18, no. 4 (October 1907): 395–407.

May, Henry F. *The End of American Innocence, 1912–1917: A Study of the First Years of Our Time.* New York: Columbia University Press, 1992.

McCaffrey, Donald W., and Christopher P. Jacobs. *Guide to the Silent Years of American Cinema.* Westport, CT: Greenwood Press, 1999.

McCarthy, Cormac. *All the Pretty Horses.* New York: Knopf, 1992.

_____ . *Blood Meridian, or, The Evening Redness in the West.* New York: Random House, 1985.

McCullen, Kevin. "Plan Outlines Snake Dam Removal Steps." *Tri-City Herald*, April 1, 2010. http://www.tri-cityherald.com/2010/04/01/960129/plan-outlines-dam-removal-steps.html

McKinley, Charles. *Uncle Sam in the Pacific Northwest: Federal Management of Natural Resources in the Columbia River Valley.* Berkeley: University of California Press, 1952.

McKinney, Matthew, Craig Fitch, and Will Harmon. "Regionalism in the West: An Inventory and Assessment." *Public Land and Resources Law Review* 23 (2002): 101–90.

McLerran, Jennifer. *A New Deal for Native Art: Indian Arts and Federal Policy, 1933–1943.* Tucson: University of Arizona Press, 2009.

McMurtry, Larry. *Horseman, Pass By*. 1961. Reprint, New York: Simon and Schuster, 2002.

———. *Lonesome Dove*. 1985. Reprint, New York: Pocket Books, 1986.

McNickle, D'Arcy. *The Surrounded*. 1936. Reprint, Albuquerque: University of New Mexico Press, 1978.

McWilliams, Carey. *Factories in the Field*. 1939. Reprint, Berkeley: University of California Press, 2000.

———. *Ill Fares the Land: Migrants and Migratory Labor in the United States*. Boston: Little, Brown, 1942.

———. *Prejudice: Japanese-Americans, Symbol of Racial Intolerance*. Boston: Little, Brown, 1944.

———. *Southern California Country: An Island on the Land*. New York: Duell, Sloan and Pearce, 1946.

Mead, Elwood. *Helping Men Own Farms: A Practical Discussion of Government Aid in Land Settlement*. New York: Macmillan, 1920.

Meade, Marvin. *The Missouri River Basin Proposals for Development*. Lawrence: University of Kansas Bureau of Government Research, 1952.

Meinig, D. W. "American Wests: Preface to a Geographical Interpretation." *Annals of the Association of American Geographers* 62 (June 1972): 159–84.

———. "The Continuous Shaping of America: A Prospectus for Geographers and Historians." *American Historical Review* 83, no. 5 (December 1978): 1186–1205.

———. *The Great Columbia Plain: A Historical Geography, 1805–1910*. 1968. Reprint, Seattle: University of Washington Press, 1995.

———. *Imperial Texas: An Interpretive Essay in Cultural Geography*. Austin: University of Texas Press, 1969.

———. "The Mormon Culture Region: Strategies and Patterns in the Geography of the American West, 1847–1964," *Annals of the Association of American Geographers* 55, no. 2 (June 1965): 191–220.

———. *Southwest: Three Peoples in Geographical Change, 1600–1970*. New York: Oxford University Press, 1971.

Meriam, Lewis. *Relief and Social Security*. Washington, DC: Brookings Institution, 1946.

Merriam. Harold G. "Does the Northwest Believe in Itself?" In *Northwest Harvest: A Regional Stocktaking*, edited by V. L. O. Chittick, 156–73. New York: Macmillan, 1948.

Mezerik, A. G. *The Revolt of the South and West*. New York: Duell, Sloan and Pearce, 1946.

Milner, Clyde A. II. "The View from Wisdom: Four Layers of History and Regional Identity." In *Under an Open Sky: Rethinking America's Western Past*, edited by William Cronon, George Miles, and Jay Gitlin, 203–22. New York: Norton, 1992.

Mohl, Raymond A. ed. *Searching for the Sunbelt: Historical Perspectives on a Region*. Knoxville: University of Tennessee Press, 1990.

Momaday, N. Scott. *House Made of Dawn*. 1968. Reprint, New York: HarperPerennial, 1999.

———. *The Way to Rainy Mountain*. 1969. Reprint, Albuquerque: University of New Mexico Press, 1976.

Morgan, Neil. *Westward Tilt: The American West Today.* New York: Random House, 1963.

Morris, Edmund. *Theodore Rex.* New York: Modern Library, 2002.

Morrissey, Katherine G. *Mental Territories: Mapping the Inland Empire.* Ithaca, NY: Cornell University Press, 1997.

Moul, Francis. *The National Grasslands: A Guide to America's Undiscovered Treasures.* Lincoln: University of Nebraska Press, 2006.

Muir, John. *The Mountains of California.* New York: Century, 1894.

_____ . *Our National Parks.* Boston: Houghton Mifflin, 1901.

Mumford, Lewis. *The Highway and the City.* New York: Harcourt, Brace and World, 1963.

Myers, Phyllis. "Livability at the Ballot Box: State and Local Referenda on Parks, Conservation, and Smarter Growth, Election Day 1998." Brookings Institution, 1999. http://www.brookings.edu/reports/1999/01metropolitanpolicy_myers.aspx

Nash, Gerald. *The American West Transformed: The Impact of the Second World War.* Lincoln: University of Nebraska Press, 1990.

_____ . *The Federal Landscape: An Economic History of the Twentieth-Century West.* Tucson: University of Arizona Press, 1999.

Nash, Roderick. *Wilderness and the American Mind,* 4th ed. New Haven, CT: Yale University Press, 2001.

National Agricultural Statistics Service. "2002 Census Publications: Volume 1 Chapter 2: State Level Data." US Department of Agriculture. http://www.agcensus.usda .gov/Publications/2002/Volume_1,_Chapter_2_US_State_Level

National Conference of State Legislatures. "Arizona's Immigration Enforcement Laws." http://www.ncsl.org/?tabid=20263

National Indian Gaming Commission. "Gaming Revenue Reports: Gaming Revenue by Region 2008 and 2009." http://www.nigc.gov/Gaming_Revenue_Reports.aspx

National Oceanic and Atmospheric Administration. "NOAA: Heat wave leads to fourth warmest July on record for the U.S." US Department of Commerce. http://www .noaanews.noaa.gov/stories2011/20110808_julystats.html

National Park Service. "Olympic National Park: Elwha River Restoration," US Department of the Interior. http://www.nps.gov/olym/naturescience/elwha-ecosystem-restoration.htm

_____ . "Rocky Mountain National Park: History & Culture." US Department of the Interior. http://www.nps.gov/romo/historyculture/index.htm

_____ . "Rocky Mountain National Park: Time Line of Historic Events." US Department of the Interior. http://www.nps.gov/romo/historyculture/time_line_of_historic _events.htm

_____ . "Tallgrass Prairie National Preserve." US Department of the Interior. http:// www.nps.gov/tapr/index.htm

National Resources Committee. *Regional Factors in National Planning and Development.* Washington, DC: Government Printing Office, 1935.

National Weather Service Weather Forecast Office. "Record Setting Rainfall and Significant Flooding over Oklahoma." June 15, 2010. http://www.srh.noaa.gov/oun/ ?n=events-20100614

Nature Conservancy. "Oklahoma Tallgrass Prairie Preserve." http://www.nature.org/

ourinitiatives/regions/northamerica/unitedstates/oklahoma/placesweprotect/tall grass-prairie-preserve.xml

"Nature Conservancy's Goal: To Preserve State's Heritage." *Daily Oklahoman.* June 20, 1993.

Neihardt, John G. *Black Elk Speaks.* New York: Morrow, 1932.

Newlin, Keith. *Hamlin Garland: A Life.* Lincoln: University of Nebraska Press, 2008.

Nickerson, Michelle, and Darren Dochuk, eds. *Sunbelt Rising: The Politics of Place, Space, and Region.* Philadelphia: University of Pennsylvania Press, 2011.

Nicoll, Scott. "The Death of Rangeland Reform." *Journal of Environmental Law and Litigation* 21, no. 47 (2006): 54–111.

Noble, David W. *The End of American History: Democracy, Capitalism, and the Metaphor of Two Worlds in Anglo-American Historical Writing, 1880–1980.* Minneapolis: University of Minnesota Press, 1985.

Norris, Frank. *The Responsibilities of the Novelist and Other Literary Essays.* New York: Doubleday, Page, 1903.

Norris, Kathleen. *Dakota: A Spiritual Geography.* New York: Ticknor and Fields, 1993.

Odum, Howard W. "The Promise of Regionalism." In *Regionalism in America,* edited by Merrill Jensen, 395–425. Madison: University of Wisconsin Press, 1952.

Omernik, James M. "Map Supplement: Ecoregions of the Conterminous United States." *Annals of the Association of American Geographers* 77, no. 1 (March 1987): 118–25.

Oregon Department of Land Conservation and Development. "Oregon's Land Use Planning Program: Providing Regional Solutions for a Diverse State." http://www .oregon.gov/LCD/docs/publications/regdiff.pdf

Oregon.gov. "DLCD Measure 49." http://www.oregon.gov/LCD/MEASURE49/index .shtml.

Owen, Linda. "Worship at the O.K. Corral." *Christianity Today* 47, no. 9 (September 2003): 62–64.

Pauker, Guy J. "Political Structure." In *People of Rimrock: A Study of Values in Five Cultures,* edited by Evon Z. Vogt and Ethel M. Albert, 191–226. Cambridge, MA: Harvard University Press, 1966.

Peffer, E. Louise. *The Closing of the Public Domain: Disposal and Reservation Policies 1900–50.* Stanford, CA: Stanford University Press, 1951.

Pendley, William Perry. "Whither the West: A Call to Action." Lecture, Heritage Foundation, Washington, DC, June 17, 1992. http://www.policyarchive.org/handle/ 10207/bitstreams/12775.pdf

Peterson, Elmer T. *Big Dam Foolishness: The Problem of Modern Flood Control and Water Storage.* New York: Devin-Adair, 1954.

Phillips, Kevin P. *The Emerging Republican Majority.* New Rochelle, NY: Arlington House, 1969.

Pinchot, Gifford. *The Fight for Conservation.* New York: Doubleday, Page, 1910.

Pisani, Donald J. *To Reclaim a Divided West: Water, Law, and Public Policy, 1848–1902.* Albuquerque: University of New Mexico Press, 1992.

PNM. "Four Corners Power Plant." PNM Resources. http://www.pnm.com/systems/4c .htm

Pollard, Lancaster. "The Pacific Northwest." In *Regionalism in America,* edited by Merrill Jensen, 187–212. Madison: University of Wisconsin Press, 1952.

_____. "The Pacific Northwest: A National Epitome." In *Northwest Harvest: A Regional Stock-Taking*, edited by V. L. O. Chittick, 25–38. New York: Macmillan, 1948.

Pollon, Zelie. "Arizona wildfire sets new record at 469,000 acres." Reuters, June 14, 2011. http://www.reuters.com/article/2011/06/14/us-wildfire-arizona-idUSTRE754 2JD20110614

Pomeroy, Earl. *The Pacific Slope: A History of California, Oregon, Washington, Idaho, Utah, and Nevada*. New York: Knopf, 1965.

_____. "Toward a Reorientation of Western History: Continuity and Environment." *Mississippi Valley Historical Review* 41, no. 4 (March 1955): 579–600.

Pomeroy, Hugh R. "Regional Planning in Practice." In *Proceedings of the Sixteenth National Conference on City Planning*, 111–28. Baltimore, MD: Norman Remington, 1924.

Popper, Deborah Epstein, and Frank J. Popper. "The Buffalo Commons: Metaphor as Method." *Geographical Review* 89, no. 4 (October 1999): 491–510.

_____. "The Great Plains: From Dust to Dust." *Planning* 53 (December 1987): 12–18.

_____. "Small Can Be Beautiful." *Planning* 68, no. 7 (July 2002): 20–23.

Popper, Frank J. "The Ambiguous End of the Sagebrush Rebellion." In *Land Reform, American Style*, edited by Charles C. Geisler and Frank J. Popper, 117–28. Totowa, NJ: Rowman and Allanheld, 1984.

_____. "Understanding American Land Use Regulation since 1970: A Revisionist Interpretation." *Journal of the American Planning Association* (Summer 1988): 291–301.

Potter, David M. *History and American Society: Essays of David M. Potter*, edited by Don E. Fehrenbacher. New York: Oxford University Press, 1973.

_____. *People of Plenty: Economic Abundance and the American Character*. Chicago: University of Chicago Press, 1954.

Powell, James Lawrence. *Dead Pool: Lake Powell, Global Warming, and the Future of Water in the West*. Berkeley: University of California Press, 2008.

Powell, John Wesley. *Canyons of the Colorado*. Meadville, PA: Flood & Vincent, 1895.

_____. "Institutions for the Arid Lands." *Century Magazine* 40, no. 1 (May 1890): 111–16.

_____. "Major Powell's Address." In *Official Report of the Proceedings and Debates of the First Constitutional Convention of North Dakota*. Bismarck, ND: Tribune, State Printers and Binders, 1889.

_____. "The Non-Irrigable Lands of the Arid Region." *Century Magazine* 39, no. 6 (April 1890): 915–22.

_____. *The Philosophic Bearings of Darwinism*. Washington, DC: Judd and Detweiler, 1882.

_____. *Physiographic Regions of the United States*. New York: American Book Company, 1895.

_____. *Report on the Lands of the Arid Region of the United States, with a More Detailed Account of the Lands of Utah*, 2nd ed. Washington, DC: Government Printing Office, 1879.

_____. *The Three Methods of Evolution*. Washington, DC: Judd and Detweiler, 1883.

Powers, Ashley, and Alejandro Lazo. "Leaving North Las Vegas no option for many 'underwater' homeowners." *Los Angeles Times*, May 31, 2011. http://articles.latimes .com/2011/may/31/nation/la-na-underwater-homeowners-20110531.

Pratt, Mary Louise. *Imperial Eyes: Travel Writing and Transculturation*. New York: Routledge, 1992.

President's Research Committee on Social Trends. *Recent Social Trends in the United States*. 2 vols. New York: McGraw-Hill, 1933.

Press, Daniel. *Saving Open Space: The Politics of Local Preservation in California*. Berkeley: University of California Press, 2002.

Pritchett, C. Herman. "The Transplantability of the TVA." *Iowa Law Review* 32 (1946–47): 327–38.

Proulx, Annie. *Bird Cloud: A Memoir*. New York: Scribner, 2011.

_____. *Close Range: Wyoming Stories*. New York: Scribner, 1999.

Public Administration Service. *Action for Cities: A Guide for Community Planning*. Chicago: Public Administration Service, 1943.

Rabe, Josh. "Things lining up for rain record." *Oklahoman*, October 16, 2007.

Radio Reader. "1964–Present Chronological List of Books Read on Radio Reader." National Public Radio. http://radioreader.net/files/Chronological_List.pdf.

Rawlyk, G. A., R. P. Bowles, and B. W. Hodgins. *Regionalism in Canada: Flexible Federalism or Fractured Nation?* Scarborough, ON: Prentice Hall of Canada, 1979.

Reisner, Marc. *Cadillac Desert: The American West and Its Disappearing Water*, rev. ed. New York: Penguin Books, 1993.

Resnick, Phillip. *The Politics of Resentment: British Columbia Regionalism and Canadian Unity*. Vancouver: University of British Columbia Press, 2000.

"Riverboat Runs through . . . Dinosaur National Monument." *Sunset* 112, no. 3 (March 1954): 22, 25.

Robbins, William G. "In Pursuit of Historical Explanation: Capitalism as a Conceptual Tool for Knowing the American West." *Western Historical Quarterly* 30, no. 3 (Autumn 1999): 277–93.

_____. *Landscapes in Conflict: The Oregon Story, 1940–2000*. Seattle: University of Washington Press, 2004.

Roebuck, Paul. "The Great Plains: From Bust to Bust." *Focus* 43, no. 4 (1993): 16.

Rölvaag, O. E. *Giants in the Earth*. 1927. Reprint, New York: HarperPerennial, 1999.

Roosevelt, Theodore. "An Appreciation of the Art of Frederic Remington." *Pearson's Magazine* 18, no. 4 (October 1907): 395.

_____. *Autobiography*. New York: Macmillan, 1913.

_____. *Hunting Trips of a Ranchman*, 2 vols. New York: Putnam's, 1885.

_____. *Letters and Speeches*, edited by Louis Auchincloss. New York: Library of America, 2004.

_____. *Presidential Addresses and State Papers, February 19, 1902, to May 13, 1903*, 2 vols. 1904. Reprint, New York: Review of Reviews, 1910.

_____. *Theodore Roosevelt's America: Selections from the Writings of the Oyster Bay Naturalist*, edited by Farida A. Wiley. Garden City, NY: Anchor Books, 1962.

Rosaldo, Renato. "Imperialist Nostalgia." *Representations*, no. 26 (Spring 1989): 107–22.

Rosier, Paul C. "'They Are Ancestral Homelands': Race, Place, and Politics in Cold War Native America, 1945–1961." *Journal of American History* 92, no. 4 (March 2006): 1300–1326.

Rothman, Hal K. *Devil's Bargains: Tourism in the Twentieth-Century American West*. Lawrence: University Press of Kansas, 1998.

Royce, Josiah. *The Basic Writings of Josiah Royce*, 2 vols, edited by John J. McDermott. Chicago: University of Chicago Press, 1969.

_____. *Race Questions, Provincialism, and Other American Problems*. New York: Macmillan, 1908.

Rudnick, Lois Palken. *Mabel Dodge Luhan, New Woman, New Worlds*. Albuquerque: University of New Mexico Press, 1984.

Said, Edward. *Orientalism*. New York: Pantheon Books, 1978.

Sale, Kirkpatrick. *Dwellers in the Land: The Bioregional Vision*. 1985. Reprint, Athens: University of Georgia Press, 2000.

Sanchez, George I. *Forgotten People: A Study of New Mexicans*. Albuquerque: University of New Mexico Press, 1940.

Sandoz, Mari. *Capital City*. 1939. Reprint, Lincoln: University of Nebraska Press, 1982.

_____. *"I Do Not Apologize for the Length of This Letter": The Mari Sandoz Letters on Native American Rights, 1940–1965*, edited by Kimberli A. Lee. Lubbock: Texas Tech University Press, 2009.

_____. *Old Jules*. 1935. Reprint, Lincoln: University of Nebraska Press, 1985.

_____. *Slogum House*. 1937. Reprint, Lincoln: University of Nebraska Press, 1981.

Sauer, Carl O. *Land and Life: A Selection from the Writings of Carl Ortwin Sauer*, edited by John Leighly. Berkeley: University of California Press, 1963.

_____. "Land Resource and Land Use in Relation to Public Policy." In *Report of the Science Advisory Board, July 31, 1933 to September 1, 1934*, 165–260. Washington, DC: Government Printing Office, 1934.

Sauer, Carl O., et al. "Preliminary Recommendations Relating to Soil Erosion and Critical Land Margins." In *Report of the Science Advisory Board, July 31, 1933 to September 1, 1934*, 137–61. Washington, DC: Government Printing Office, 1934.

Savory, Allan. *Holistic Resource Management*. Washington, DC: Island Press, 1988.

Schaefer, Heike. *Mary Austin's Regionalism: Reflections on Gender, Genre, and Geography*. Charlottesville: University of Virginia Press, 2004.

Schiesl, Martin J. "Designing the Model Community: The Irvine Company and Suburban Development, 1950-88." In *Postsuburban California: The Transformation of Orange County Since World War II*, edited by Rob Kling, Spencer Olin, and Mark Poster, 55–91. Berkeley: University of California Press, 1995.

Schipper, Janine. *Disappearing Desert: The Growth of Phoenix and the Culture of Sprawl*. Norman: University of Oklahoma Press, 2008.

Schulten, Susan. *The Geographical Imagination in America, 1880–1950*. Chicago: University of Chicago Press, 2002.

Scott, Mel. *American City Planning since 1890*. Berkeley: University of California Press, 1971.

Sears, Paul. *Deserts on the March*. Norman: University of Oklahoma Press, 1935.

Selznick, Philip O. *TVA and the Grass Roots: A Study in the Sociology of Formal Organization*. Berkeley: University of California Press, 1949.

Semple, Ellen Churchill. *American History and Its Geographic Conditions*. Boston: Houghton Mifflin, 1903.

Semple, Ellen Churchill, and Clarence Fielden Jones. *American History and Its Geographic Conditions*, rev. ed. Boston: Houghton Mifflin, 1933.

Sharkansky, Ira. *Regionalism in American Politics*. Indianapolis, IN: Bobbs-Merrill, 1970.

Sharpe, Tom. "Fire at 114,000 acres; Los Alamos prepares for reopening." *Santa Fe New Mexican*, July 2, 2011. http://www.santafenewmexican.com/Local%20News/Los-Alamos-prepares-for-reopening

Singal, Daniel Joseph. "Towards a Definition of American Modernism." *American Quarterly* 39, no. 1 (Spring 1987): 7–26.

Slotkin, Richard. *The Fatal Environment: The Myth of the Frontier in the Age of Industrialization, 1800–1890*. New York: Atheneum, 1985.

———. *Regeneration through Violence: The Mythology of the American Frontier, 1600–1860*. Middletown, CT: Wesleyan University Press, 1973.

Smith, Anthony D. *The Antiquity of Nations*. Malden, MA: Polity, 2004.

———. *Myths and Memories of the Nation*. New York: Oxford University Press, 1999.

Smith, Arthur H., and William E. Martin. "Socioeconomic Behavior of Cattle Ranchers, with Implications for Rural Community Development in the West." *American Journal of Agricultural Economics* 54, no. 2 (May 1972): 217–25.

Smith, Bertha H. "California's First Cubist House." *Sunset* 35, no. 2 (August 1915): 368–75.

Smith, David M. *The Geography of Social Well-Being in the United States: An Introduction to Territorial Social Indicators*. New York: McGraw-Hill, 1973.

Smith, Henry Nash. *Virgin Land: The American West as Symbol and Myth*. 1950. Reprint, Cambridge, MA: Harvard University Press, 1971.

Smith, Paul Chaat, and Robert Allen Warrior. *Like a Hurricane: The American Indian Movement from Alcatraz to Wounded Knee*. New York: New Press, 1997.

Smithsonian Museum of American Art. "Showdown at the 'West as America' Exhibition." *American Art* 5, no. 3 (Summer 1991): 2–11.

Smythe, William E. *The Conquest of Arid America*. New York: Harper and Brothers, 1900.

Snyder, Gary. *The Practice of the Wild: Essays*. San Francisco: North Point Press, 1990.

Soulé, Michael E., and John Terborgh, eds. "The Policy and Science of Regional Conservation." In *Continental Conservation: Scientific Foundations of Regional Reserve Networks*, 1–17. Washington, DC: Island Press, 1999.

Spence, Mark David. *Dispossessing the Wilderness: Indian Removal and the Making of the National Parks*. New York: Oxford University Press, 1999.

Spicer, Edward H. *Cycles of Conquest: The Impact of Spain, Mexico, and the United States on the Indians of the Southwest, 1533–1960*. 1962. Reprint, Tucson: University of Arizona Press, 1967.

Springer, Vera. *Power and the Pacific Northwest: A History of the Bonneville Power Administration*. Washington, DC: Bonneville Power Administration, 1976.

Starr, Kevin. *Americans and the California Dream, 1850–1915*. New York: Oxford University Press, 1986.

Starrs, Paul F. *Let the Cowboy Ride: Cattle Ranching in the American West*. Baltimore, MD: Johns Hopkins University Press, 1998.

Stauffer, Helen Winter. *Mari Sandoz: Story Catcher of the Plains*. Lincoln: University of Nebraska Press, 1982.

Stegner, Wallace. *Beyond the Hundredth Meridian: John Wesley Powell and the Second*

Opening of the American West. 1954. Reprint, Lincoln: University of Nebraska Press, 1982.

———. "A Geography of Hope." In *A Society to Match the Scenery: Personal Visions of the Future of the American West*, edited by Gary Holthaus et al., 218–29. Boulder: University Press of Colorado, 1991.

———. "The West Coast: Region with a View." *Saturday Review* 42 (May 2, 1959): 15–17, 41.

———. "Wilderness Letter." Wilderness Society. 1960. http://wilderness.org/content/wilderness-letter.

Stegner, Wallace, ed. *This Is Dinosaur: Echo Park Country and Its Magic Rivers*. New York: Knopf, 1955.

Steinbeck, John. *The Grapes of Wrath*. New York: Modern Library, 1939.

Steiner, Michael. "Frederick Jackson Turner and Western Regionalism." In *Writing Western History: Essays on Major Western Historians*, edited by Richard Etulain, 103–35. 1991. Reprint, Reno: University of Nevada Press, 2002.

———. "Regionalism in the Great Depression." *Geographical Review* 73, no. 4 (October 1983): 430–46.

Steward, Julian. *Theory of Culture Change: The Methodology of Multilinear Evolution*. 1955. Reprint, Urbana: University of Illinois Press, 1990.

Stineman, Esther Lanigan. *Mary Austin: Song of a Maverick*. New Haven, CT: Yale University Press, 1989.

Stout, Janis P. *Picturing a Different West: Vision, Illustration, and the Tradition of Austin and Cather*. Lubbock: Texas Tech University Press, 2007.

Strong, Douglas H. *Dreamers and Defenders: American Conservationists*. Lincoln: University of Nebraska Press, 1981.

Sulzberger, A. G. "Hispanics Reviving Faded Towns on the Plains." *New York Times*, November 13, 2011.

Taliaferro, John. *Great White Fathers: The Story of the Obsessive Quest to Create Mount Rushmore*. New York: PublicAffairs, 2002.

Target Science. "Population Growth by Single Year, Los Angeles County, 1850–1998." Los Angeles Education Partnership. http://www.laep.org/target/science/population/table.html

Taylor, Graham D. *The New Deal and American Indian Tribalism: The Administration of the Indian Reorganization Act, 1934–45*. Lincoln: University of Nebraska Press, 1980.

Taylor, Paul Schuster, and Dorothea Lange. *An American Exodus: A Record of Human Erosion*. 1939. Reprint, New York: Arno Press, 1975.

Terral, Rufus. *The Missouri Valley: Land of Drouth, Flood, and Promise*. New Haven, CT: Yale University Press, 1947.

Thomas, John L. *Alternative America: Henry George, Edward Bellamy, Henry Demerest Lloyd and the Adversary Tradition*. Cambridge, MA: Harvard University Press, 1983.

———. *A Country in the Mind: Wallace Stegner, Bernard DeVoto, History, and the American Land*. New York: Routledge, 2000.

Thompson, Mark. *American Character: The Curious Life of Charles Fletcher Lummis and the Rediscovery of the Southwest*. New York: Arcade, 2001.

Trammell, Bobby. "Osage Ranch Becomes Focus for Prairie Preservation Project." *Daily Oklahoman*, November 9, 1989.

Trigo, Abril. "On Transculturation: Toward a Political Economy of Culture in the Periphery." *Studies in Latin American Popular Culture* 15 (January 1996): 99–118.

Truettner, William H. "Text Panels for *West as America*, Section 1, Prelude to Expansion: Repainting the West, Seeing Is Not Believing." National Museum of American Art. http://people.virginia.edu/~mmw3v/west/home.htm.

Truettner, William H., ed. *The West as America: Reinterpreting Images of the Frontier, 1820–1920*. Washington, DC: Smithsonian Institution Press, 1991.

Tunnard, Christopher, and Boris Pushkarev. *Man-Made America: Chaos or Control?* New Haven, CT: Yale University Press, 1963.

Turner, Frederick Jackson. *Frederick Jackson Turner's Legacy: Unpublished Writings in American History*, edited by Wilbur R. Jacobs. San Marino, CA: Huntington Library, 1965.

_____. *Frontier and Section: Selected Essays of Frederick Jackson Turner*. Englewood Cliffs, NJ: Prentice Hall, 1961.

_____. *The Significance of Sections in American History*. 1932. Reprint, New York: Peter Smith, 1950.

Twelve Southerners. *I'll Take My Stand: The South and the Agrarian Tradition*. 1930. Reprint, Baton Rouge: Louisiana State University Press, 2006.

Udall, Stewart. *The Quiet Crisis*. New York: Avon Books, 1963.

US Army Corps of Engineers. "Lower Snake River Fish Passage Improvement Plan: Dam Breaching Plan of Study." Federal Columbia River Power System. http://www.nww.usace.army.mil/amip/lsrfip/default.asp

_____. "Western States Watershed Study." Western States Water Council. http://www.westgov.org/wswc/wsws%20report.html

US Census Bureau. "Greeley city, Colorado QuickLinks." US Department of Commerce. http://quickfacts.census.gov/qfd/states/08/0832155lk.html.

_____. "Population Estimates." US Department of Commerce. http://www.census.gov/popest/cities/cities.html

US Public Land Law Review Commission. *One Third of the Nation's Land*. Washington, DC: Government Printing Office, 1970.

US Western Water Policy Review Advisory Commission. *Water in the West: Challenge for the Next Century*. Arlington, VA: Western Water Policy Review Advisory Commission, 1998.

Utah State University. "Bear River Watershed Information System." http://www.bearriverinfo.org/guide/organizations

Vance, Rupert B. "The Regional Concept as a Tool for Social Research." In *Regionalism in America*, edited by Merrill Jensen, 119–40. Madison: University of Wisconsin Press, 1952.

Varner, Paul. *Historical Dictionary of Westerns in Cinema*. Lanham, MD: Scarecrow Press, 2008.

Venturi, Robert, Denise Scott Brown, and Steven Izenour. *Learning from Las Vegas*, rev. ed. Cambridge, MA: MIT Press, 1977.

Vogel, Eve. "Defining One Pacific Northwest among Many Possibilities: The Political Construction of a Region and Its River during the New Deal." *Western Historical Quarterly* 42, no. 1 (Spring 2011): 28–53.

Vogt, Evon Z. "Ecology and Economy." In *People of Rimrock: A Study of Values in Five*

Cultures, edited by Evon Z. Vogt and Ethel M. Albert, 160–90. Cambridge, MA: Harvard University Press, 1966.

———. *Modern Homesteaders: The Life of a Twentieth-Century Frontier Community*. Cambridge, MA: Harvard University Press, 1955.

Vogt, Evon Z., and Ethel M. Albert, eds. "The 'Comparative Study of Values in Five Cultures' Project." In *People of Rimrock: A Study of Values in Five Cultures*, 1–33. Cambridge, MA: Harvard University Press, 1966.

Wallach, Bret. "The Evolution of an Idea." *Focus* 43, no. 4 (1993): 17.

Wallach, Rick. "*Blood Meridian* (1985)." Cormac McCarthy Society. http://www.cor macmccarthy.com/works/bloodmeridian.htm.

Wannop, Urlan A. *The Regional Imperative: Regional Planning and Governance in Britain, Europe and the United States*. New York: Routledge, 1995.

Warhus, Mark. *Another America: Native American Maps and the History of Our Land*. New York: St. Martin's, 1997.

Webb, Walter Prescott. *Divided We Stand: The Crisis of a Frontierless Democracy*. New York: Farrar and Rinehart, 1937.

———. *The Great Frontier*. Boston: Houghton Mifflin, 1952.

———. *The Great Plains*. 1931. Reprint, Lincoln: University of Nebraska Press, 1981.

Weber, Marianne. *Max Weber: A Biography*. New York: Wiley, 1975.

Weber, Max. *From Max Weber: Essays in Sociology*. Edited by H. H. Gerth and C. Wright Mills. New York: Oxford University Press, 1958.

Wheeler, Stephen M. "The New Regionalism: Key Characteristics of an Emerging Movement." *Journal of the American Planning Association* 68, no. 3 (Summer 2002): 267–78.

White, Richard. *"It's Your Misfortune and None of My Own": A New History of the American West*. Norman: University of Oklahoma Press, 1991.

———. *Land Use, Environment, and Social Change : The Shaping of Island County, Washington*. Seattle: University of Washington Press, 1980.

———. *The Organic Machine: The Remaking of the Columbia River*. New York: Hill and Wang, 1996.

Whitnall, G. Gordon. "City and Regional Planning in Los Angeles." In *Proceedings of the Sixteenth National Conference on City Planning*, 105–10. Baltimore, MD: Norman Remington, 1924.

Wilder, Laura Ingalls. *Little House on the Prairie*. 1935. Reprint, New York: Harper, 1953.

Williamson, R. S. *On the Use of the Barometer on Surveys and Reconnaissances*. New York: Van Nostrand, 1868.

Wilson, Charles Reagan. *Baptized in Blood: The Religion of the Lost Cause, 1865–1920*, 2nd ed. Athens: University of Georgia Press, 2009.

Wilson, Chris. *The Myth of Santa Fe: Creating a Modern Regional Tradition*. Albuquerque: University of New Mexico Press, 1997.

Winther, Oscar Osburn. *The Great Northwest*. New York: Knopf, 1947.

Wissler, Clark. *The American Indian: An Introduction to the Anthropology of the New World*. New York: McMurtrie, 1917.

———. *North American Indians of the Plains*. New York: American Museum of Natural History, 1912.

Wister, Owen. "The Evolution of the Cow-Puncher." *Harper's New Monthly Magazine* 91, no. 544 (September 1895): 602–17.

_____ . *The Virginian: A Horseman of the Plains*. 1902. Reprint, Tucson, AZ: Fireship Press, 2009.

Wittfogel, Karl. "The Hydraulic Civilizations." In *Man's Role in Changing the Face of the Earth*, edited by William L. Thomas Jr., 152–64. Chicago: University of Chicago Press, 1956.

_____ . *Oriental Despotism: A Comparative Study of Total Power*. New Haven, CT: Yale University Press, 1957.

Woodress, James. *Willa Cather: A Literary Life*. Lincoln: University of Nebraska Press, 1989.

Woods, Carter A. "A Criticism of Wissler's North American Culture Areas." *American Anthropologist* 36, no. 4 (Oct.–Dec., 1934): 517–23.

Worster, Donald. *Dust Bowl: The Southern Plains in the 1930s*. New York: Oxford University Press, 1979.

_____ . *A River Running West: The Life of John Wesley Powell*. New York: Oxford University Press, 2001.

_____ . *Rivers of Empire: Water, Aridity, and the Growth of the American West*. New York: Pantheon Books, 1985.

Wrobel, David M. "Beyond the Frontier-Region Dichotomy." *Pacific Historical Review* 65, no. 3 (August 1996): 401–29.

_____ . *The End of American Exceptionalism: Frontier Anxiety from the Old West to the New Deal*. Lawrence: University Press of Kansas, 1993.

_____ . *Promised Lands: Promotion, Memory, and the Creation of the American West*. Lawrence: University Press of Kansas, 2002.

Yoder, Don, ed. "Folklife Studies in American Scholarship." In *American Folklife*, 3–18. Austin: University of Texas Press, 1976.

Zaslowsky, Dyan, and the Wilderness Society. *These American Lands: Parks, Wilderness, and the Public Lands*. New York: Henry Holt, 1986.

Zelinsky, Wilbur. *The Cultural Geography of the United States*. Englewood Cliffs, NJ: Prentice Hall, 1973.

_____ . "North America's Vernacular Regions," *Annals of the Association of American Geographers* 70, no. 1 (March 1980): 1–16.

Zitkala-Ša. *American Indian Stories*. Washington, DC: Hayworth, 1921.

_____ . *Dreams and Thunder: Stories, Poems, and The Sun Dance Opera*, edited by P. Jane Hafen. Lincoln: University of Nebraska Press, 2001.

Index

Page numbers in italics refer to figures.

About the Author

Robert L. Dorman holds a Ph.D. in history from Brown University. He is the author of *Revolt of the Provinces: The Regionalist Movement in America, 1920–1945* and *A Word for Nature: Four Pioneering Environmental Advocates, 1845–1913*, both published by the University of North Carolina Press. He is currently Associate Professor of Library Science at Oklahoma City University.